Women in Engineering and Science

Series Editor

Jill S. Tietjen, Greenwood Village, CO, USA

MyCopy

AF865921

Dear MyCopy Customer,

This Springer Nature book is a high quality monochrome, digitally printed version of the eBook, which is accessible to you on SpringerLink. As a result of your library investing in licensing at least one Springer Nature eBook subject collection, this copy is provided to you at a highly discounted price from the usual softcover edition.

MyCopy books are only offered to patrons of a library with access to at least one Springer Nature eBook subject collection and are strictly for individual use only. Personal resale or library shelving of the MyCopy book is in breach of this agreement.

You may cite this book by referencing the bibliographic data and/or the DOI (Digital Object Identifier) found in the front-matter. This book is an exact but monochrome copy of the print version of the eBook on SpringerLink.
www.springernature.com/mycopy

The Springer Women in Engineering and Science series highlights women's accomplishments in these critical fields. The foundational volume in the series provides a broad overview of women's multi-faceted contributions to engineering over the last century. Each subsequent volume is dedicated to illuminating women's research and achievements in key, targeted areas of contemporary engineering and science endeavors.The goal for the series is to raise awareness of the pivotal work women are undertaking in areas of keen importance to our global community.

Dipti Singh • Vanita Garg • Kusum Deep
Editors

Design and Applications of Nature Inspired Optimization

Contribution of Women Leaders in the Field

Springer

Editors
Dipti Singh
Department of Applied Mathematics
Gautam Buddha University
Greater Noida, India

Vanita Garg
School of Basic and Applied Sciences, Galgotias University
Greater Noida, India

Kusum Deep
Department of Mathematics
Indian Institute of Technology Roorkee
Roorkee, India

ISSN 2509-6427 ISSN 2509-6435 (electronic)
Women in Engineering and Science

https://doi.org/10.1007/978-3-031-17929-7

© The Editor(s) (if applicable) and The Author(s), under exclusive license to Springer Nature Switzerland AG 2022
This work is subject to copyright. All rights are solely and exclusively licensed by the Publisher, whether the whole or part of the material is concerned, specifically the rights of translation, reprinting, reuse of illustrations, recitation, broadcasting, reproduction on microfilms or in any other physical way, and transmission or information storage and retrieval, electronic adaptation, computer software, or by similar or dissimilar methodology now known or hereafter developed.
The use of general descriptive names, registered names, trademarks, service marks, etc. in this publication does not imply, even in the absence of a specific statement, that such names are exempt from the relevant protective laws and regulations and therefore free for general use.
The publisher, the authors, and the editors are safe to assume that the advice and information in this book are believed to be true and accurate at the date of publication. Neither the publisher nor the authors or the editors give a warranty, expressed or implied, with respect to the material contained herein or for any errors or omissions that may have been made. The publisher remains neutral with regard to jurisdictional claims in published maps and institutional affiliations.

This Springer imprint is published by the registered company Springer Nature Switzerland AG
The registered company address is: Gewerbestrasse 11, 6330 Cham, Switzerland

Preface

Nature-inspired optimization techniques are not only useful but also needed for solving open-ended problems. Understanding nature-inspired techniques and their importance for solving real life problems can open many directions for researchers and academicians.

The main objective of this book is to include the related work about nature-inspired optimization techniques and their applications.

This book is an attempt to promote women in the field of science and engineering. Women contributing to the field of technology play a vital role in the overall sustained society.

This book also includes a survey of the nature-inspired techniques. Besides the survey, it gives the recent advances in the field of nature-inspired algorithms for solving real-life problems in various fields related to manufacturing, artificial intelligence, finance, etc. In Chap. 1, an overview of swarm intelligence-based algorithms is presented so that readers can understand the basics of nature-inspired optimization algorithms. Chapter 2 gives an illustration of one of these swarm algorithms in manufacturing industry problem. To prove the versatility of the nature-inspired algorithms, the role of machine learning in bioprocess engineering is given in Chap. 3. Chapter 4 gives the details about how a simple modification in one of the operators of a nature-inspired algorithm can enhance the working of the algorithm. Application of one of the nature-inspired algorithms in profit optimization is presented in Chap. 5. Chapter 6 provides the empirical results for portfolio-optimization problem using a recent sine cosine algorithm. Grey wolf optimizer is another well-known stochastic technique which is used in Chap. 7 for detecting group shilling profiles in recommender systems. Chapter 8 gives the application in single image reflection removal. Chapter 9 attempts to use machine learning techniques for social media analysis.

This book will be helpful to aquire the knowledge of nature-inspired optimization techniques in various field of real life applications.

The vision of this book is highly achieved on the expectations of the editors, given the quality of the contributions from the authors.

The editors would like to express their sincere gratitude to all authors, reviewers, and Springer, without whose support the quality and standards of the book could not have been maintained.

Greater Noida, India — Dipti Singh
Greater Noida, India — Vanita Garg
Roorkee, India — Kusum Deep

Contents

Contributors

Sumaiya Ahmed Department of Mathematics, Lady Shri Ram College for Women, University of Delhi, New Delhi, India

Niyati Baliyan Department of Information Technology, Indira Gandhi Delhi Technical University for Women, Delhi, India

Mousumi Banerjee Division of Mathematics, SBAS, School of Basic & Applied Sciences, Galgotias University, Greater Noida, Uttar Pradesh, India

Saumya Bansal Department of Information Technology, Indira Gandhi Delhi Technical University for Women, Delhi, India

Shashi Barak Jaypee Institute of Information Technology, Noida, India

Pinkey Chauhan Jaypee Institute of Information Technology, Noida, India

Kusum Deep Division of Mathematics, SBAS, School of Basic & Applied Sciences, Galgotias University, Greater Noida, Uttar Pradesh, India

Divesh Garg J.C. Bose University of Science and Technology, YMCA, Faridabad, India

Reena Garg J.C. Bose University of Science and Technology, YMCA, Faridabad, India

Vanita Garg Division of Mathematics, SBAS, School of Basic & Applied Sciences, Galgotias University, Greater Noida, Uttar Pradesh, India

Sachin Goel Department of IT, ABES Engineering College, Ghaziabad, India

Parita Jain Department of CSE, KIET Group of Institution, Ghaziabad, India

Peeyush Joshi Department of Computer Science & Engineering, National Institute of Technology Warangal, Hanamkonda, Telangana, India

Osheen Khare Department of Mathematics, Lady Shri Ram College for Women, University of Delhi, New Delhi, India

Harshita Khurana Department of CSE (Data Science), ABES Engineering College, Ghaziabad, India

Pravesh Kumar Rajkiya Engineering College Bijnor (AKTU Lucknow), Lucknow, Uttar Pradesh, India

Sushil Kumar Department of Computer Science & Engineering, National Institute of Technology Warangal, Hanamkonda, Telangana, India

Monica Department of IT, ABES Engineering College, Ghaziabad, India

Ashutosh Singh School of Biotechnology, Gautam Buddha University, Greater Noida, Uttar Pradesh, India

Yograj Singh Department of Mathematics, Lady Shri Ram College for Women, University of Delhi, New Delhi, India

Barkha Singhal School of Biotechnology, Gautam Buddha University, Greater Noida, Uttar Pradesh, India

Hira Zaheer School of Basic and Applied Sciences, Galgotias University, Greater Noida, Uttar Pradesh, India

Chapter 1
An Overview of Swarm Intelligence-Based Algorithms

Osheen Khare, Sumaiya Ahmed, and Yograj Singh

1 Introduction

In the past years, mathematicians, computer scientists, and research scholars have been increasingly engaged in researching the possibilities of emulating various natural systems to conceptualize and develop algorithms for the purpose of optimization. Owing to this trend, a prominent class of optimization techniques, known as nature-inspired algorithms, has emerged. The framework of such algorithms is designed to imitate the biological processes observed in nature, such as evolution, mutation, and societal behavior of insects, to arrive at the optimal solution. One of the emerging fields within nature-inspired algorithms has been the swarm intelligence (SI)-based algorithms. The term, swarm intelligence, introduced by G. Beni and J. Wang in 1989 [1] has been used to refer to the branch of optimization algorithms that models the collective behavior of animal colonies and the interactions (with the environment and other members of the swarm) of the members present in such a colony.

While the algorithms have gained widespread popularity today, they have been in work since the late 1980s. Ant colony optimization (ACO) was the first SI algorithm introduced by M. Dorigo and colleagues in the year 1991 to solve hard combinatorial optimization problems [10]. After that, J. Kennedy et al. [12, 20, 24] introduced particle swarm optimization (PSO) simulating the behavior of flocks of birds in 1995. Years later, in 2005, D. Karabago proposed the artificial bee colony algorithm (ABC) [17] in the family of SI algorithms. Over the years, research has increased the scope of swarm intelligence by observing and studying different groups of animals and algorithms, such as cuckoo search (CS), firefly algorithm (FA), dragonfly algorithm (DA) [30], and grey wolf optimizer (GWO), have emerged. The grey

O. Khare · S. Ahmed (✉) · Y. Singh
Department of Mathematics, Lady Shri Ram College for Women, University of Delhi, New Delhi, India

© The Author(s), under exclusive license to Springer Nature Switzerland AG 2022

D. Singh et al. (eds.), *Design and Applications of Nature Inspired Optimization*, Women in Engineering and Science, https://doi.org/10.1007/978-3-031-17929-7_1

wolf optimizer is one of the algorithms which emulates the hierarchical system of an animal group. In each pack of grey wolves, there is an alpha that dominates the pack and a beta wolf who leads the pack in the absence of the alpha wolf. The delta and omega wolves follow the alpha and beta wolves. The algorithm draws inspiration from the hunting approach of a pack of grey wolves. These wolves hunt in an efficient manner by following a routine of steps: chasing, encircling, harassing, and attacking. This enables them to hunt bigger prey. GWO has found applications in medical and bioinformatics, machine learning, environmental applications, and networking applications. The developing SI-based algorithms such as the wolf pack algorithm are gaining wide popularity due to their global convergence and computational robustness.

The rapidly advancing swarm intelligence techniques can be applied to the optimization of telecommunication systems and business, military operations, engineering design problems, transportation systems, data mining, image segmentation, electric machines, and so on [31, 32]. Swarm robotics is a newly emerging field that draws inspiration from swarm intelligence. The field studies the design and interactions of simple robots with each other and their environment. The goal is to develop a collective behavior resulting from the coordination of multiple robots as a system. Such an approach can be applied to various scenarios, such as search and rescue, mapping, and demining.

Though there are ample instances of SI-based optimization techniques being used to solve real-world problems in the available literature, a little amount of work has been done with respect to conducting theoretical analysis of the algorithms to explain how they operate. Besides mathematical analysis, research also needs to be done in parameter tuning and parameter control to enhance the functioning of the algorithms.

The chapter aims to conduct an elaborate survey of SI-based algorithms and is divided into six sections. The first section gives the readers a brief introduction to SI-based optimization methods. The second section elaborates upon the key features and characteristics of SI-based algorithms, highlighting their advantages and limitations. The third section lays out the steps for implementing PSO and demonstrates the process by minimizing the Rosenbrock function. The fourth section details the stages involved in the execution of ABC and presents how the computational technique can be employed to minimize the Schwefel's function. The fifth subsection illustrates how the algorithms can be compared using the fixed iteration test. The last section summarizes the paper and presents the concluding remarks along with the further scope of the study.

2 Characteristics of SI-Based Algorithms

The swarm individuals show relatively simple intellectual abilities, but they are able to survive by using social interactions and certain behavioral patterns. These social interactions can either take place directly or indirectly. Direct interactions are through audio or visual signals, such as the communication between birds of a flock. High-quality vision enables them to search for a food source and pass information related to it to the rest of the swarm. Indirect interactions are known as stigmergy, meaning communication through the environment, such as the pheromone trails of ants. Such a phenomenon occurs when a member of the colony reacts to the changes in the environment introduced by the other member.

Two of the notable characteristics of SI-based algorithms are division of labor and self-organization. To ensure proper division of labor, the entire colony is split into various groups, and each group is assigned a specialized task. Such a strategy results in a more structured and intensive exploration and exploitation of the search space. Self-organization indicates that the interactions among the members of the swarm take place on the basis of purely local information, fluctuations, and positive and negative feedback.

Over the years, SI algorithms have undergone continuous development, and hence, there has been a boom in the research exhibiting the rapid evolution of SI-based algorithms and successful implementation of SI algorithms to real-world optimization problems. Besides operations research [25], vast and diverse domains, such as machine learning [24], bioinformatics, medical informatics [8], business, and finance, have also started using computational modelling of swarms. SI algorithms are widely applied in problems of function optimization, optimal route and scheduling problems, engineering and structural optimization problems, data, and image analysis [13, 23]. Thus, they are considered to be one of the most promising optimization techniques owing to their following characteristics:

1. Scalability: SI algorithms are scalable in the sense that they can be applied to groups with a sufficient number of individuals to thousands of individuals. In other words, SI algorithms are independent of swarm size, as long as the size of the swarm isn't very small [3].
2. Adaptability: Owing to their inherent auto-configuration and self-organization abilities, SI algorithms are able to facilitate the swift adaptation of an individual to the variations in the environment on run-time.
3. Collective robustness: A single minor failure in a system can cause the failure of the entire system. In SI algorithms, such a risk is reduced as there is no single individual which is essential to the functioning of the colony. This makes SI algorithms highly robust with high fault tolerance [11].
4. Individual simplicity: SI algorithms comprises individuals who have rather simple and limited abilities of their own. However, change in the behavior of an individual level is sufficient to bring change in collective organized group behavior.

While SI algorithms can solve optimization problems with large data, compared to the other classes of nature-inspired optimization, they are still at an early stage of research. SI algorithms have certain demerits, such as:

1. Time-critical applications: SI algorithms are useful when it comes to solving non-time-critical problems with numerous repetitions of the same activity. Since SI

algorithms do have predefined and preprogrammed pathways to solutions, they are not suitable for time-critical applications, such as nuclear reactor temperature controllers.

2. Parameter tuning: This is one of the biggest drawbacks of SI algorithms. Most of the parameters involved in SI algorithms are dependent upon the problem; hence, they are either empirically selected using the trial and error method or adaptively adjusted on run-time [5].
3. Stagnation: SI algorithms exhibit a lack of central coordination; hence, they often suffer from stagnation or premature convergence to local optimum. However, the limitation can be overcome with better parameter tuning.

3 Particle Swarm Optimization Algorithm

PSO is a nature-inspired metaheuristic optimization algorithm that imitates the social behavior of a flock of birds. This population-based technique makes use of a set of flying particles that are birds with velocities. When a flock of birds moves in search of food, each bird adjusts its position according to its own historical performance as well as the flock's historical performance, which makes the flock move toward the most promising areas in the search space. Similarly, the particles in PSO dynamically adjust their position in order to reach the optimal solution efficiently [26, 33].

This experience sharing ability of a swarm makes PSO a rather efficient and successful algorithm for optimization. The algorithm begins with initializing n random particles with a certain position and velocity in the search space. At each iteration, in order to calculate the fitness of each of these particles, the objective function value is evaluated at their current position, and the personal best (*pbest*) and the global best (*gbest*) are identified. Then, the particle updates its velocity to imitate the *gbest* and *pbest* particles by moving closer to them. The formula for updating the velocity and position is, respectively, given by:

$$v_{n+1} = (w * v_n) + \left(c_1 * r_1 * \left(x_{pbest} - x_n\right)\right) + \left(c_2 * r_2 * \left(x_{gbest} - x_n\right)\right)$$

$$x_{n+1} = v_{n+1} + x_n$$

where

- v_{n+1} denotes the velocity of the successive particle.
- x_{n+1} denotes the position of the successive particle.
- x_n denotes the particle's current position.
- x_{pbest} denotes the historically personal best position of the particle.
- x_{gbest} denotes the position of the global best particle of the swarm.
- w denotes the given *inertia factor*, which controls the exploration capabilities of the algorithm. It strikes a balance between the global and local search.
- $r_1$and r_2 are random numbers uniformly generated within the range [0,1].

- c_1*and* c_2 are positive parameters called the *cognitive* and *social parameters* respectively. These parameters control the movement of the particle relative to its personal experience and the experience of the swarm [9]. The value of c_1 and c_2 can greatly affect the algorithm by biassing the particle's position towards *pbest* or *gbest*:
  - If $c_1 > c_2$, then the search behavior is biased toward the *pbest.*
  - If $c_1 < c_2$, then the search behavior is biased toward the *gbest.*
  - When high values of c_1 and c_2 are selected, then the particle's new positions are generated in distant regions of the search space, leading to a better global exploration, but it might lead to divergence of the particles.
  - When small values of c_1 and c_2 are selected, then the particle's new positions are generated close by as a result of limited movement, leading to a refined local search.

Before an iteration ends, the index of the swarm's *gbest* particle is updated in case the position of any particle in the swarm turns out to be better than the current position of the swarm's *gbest* particle. This iterative process is terminated when the stopping criterion is met, i.e., the maximum number of iterations is completed or a good enough fitness value is attained, or the algorithm has been giving the same result for a number of consecutive iterations. The fitness value of the *gbest* particle at the end of the process is taken as the optimized function value.

Pseudocode of PSO

1. Initialize the swarm of n random particles with arbitrary positions and velocity in the search space.
2. Define the bounds *(lb, ub)*, inertia factor (w), cognitive and social parameters (c_1, c_2), and maximum number of iterations to be executed.
3. Calculate the objective function value for each particle at their current position.
4. Update the particle's best position (x_{pbest}).
5. Identify the swarm's global best particle and update its position as x_{gbest}.
6. Update the velocity and position of the particle accordingly.
7. Repeat steps 3–6 until the particles converge to an optimal solution or the stopping criteria is met.

Minimizing Rosenbrock Function Using PSO

The implementation of PSO can be exhibited on a number of test functions. One such test function is Rosenbrock function, also known as the banana function. The function has a global minimum in a narrow parabolic valley at (1,1) with $f(x) = 0$.

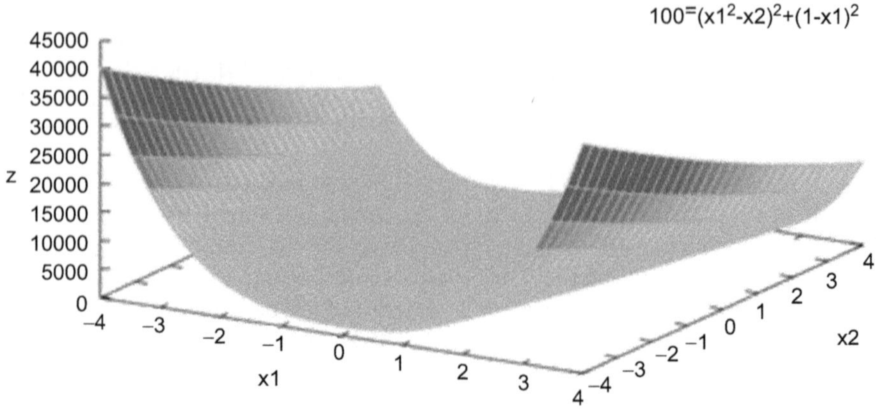

Fig. 1.1 Plotting Rosenbrock function using Maxima

Table 1.1 Optimal values obtained for variables by PSO

Variables	Optimal values
x_1	1
x_2	1
$f(x_1, x_2)$	0

Table 1.2 Values observed for different parameters during the execution of PSO

Parameters	Values
Best value	0
Worst value	4.8625
Mean	0.09602
Standard deviation	0.1635896857

While obtaining this global optimum is easy, the algorithms often get stuck to the local optimum; hence, it is used to assess the efficiency of optimization algorithms.

The general Rosenbrock function is given as:

$$f(x) = \sum_{i=1}^{d-1} \left[100\left(x_{i+1} - x_i^2\right)^2 + \left(x_i - 1\right)^2\right]$$

Here, we will implement PSO on a two-dimensional Rosenbrock function given as:

$$F = 100\left(x_1^2 - x_2\right)^2 + \left(1 - x_1\right)^2 \text{ where } -2.048 \le x_1,\ x_2 \le 2.048.$$

The plot of the function can be observed in Fig. 1.1.

The algorithm was executed for 10 runs with 200 iterations. The number of iterations were fixed after observing the behavior and convergence rate of PSO. The results obtained while minimizing the Rosenbrock function using PSO can be summarized by Tables 1.1 and 1.2, and Fig. 1.2:

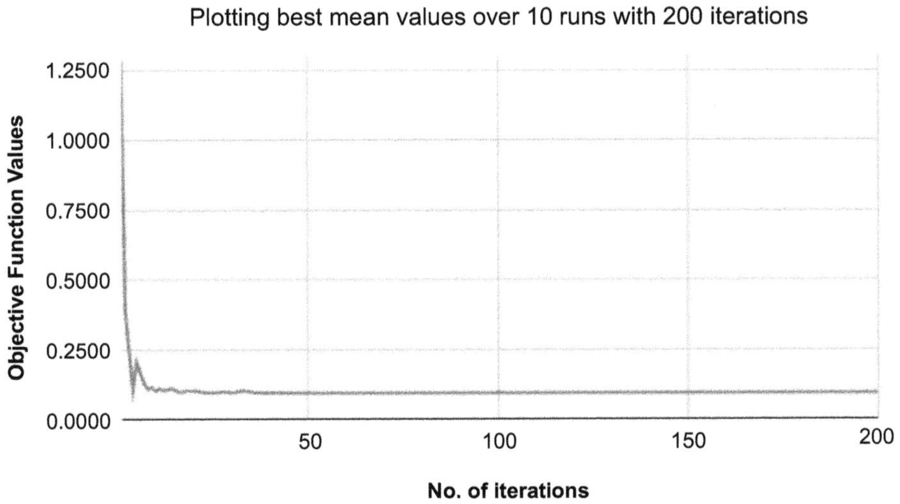

Fig. 1.2 Evolution of best mean results by PSO over 10 runs with 200 iterations

It can be observed that PSO has attained 0 as the best value. Thus, the algorithm has been successful in minimizing the function to the lowest value that can be achieved. The worst value and statistical measures, such as mean and standard deviation, are taken into account while assessing the performance of the algorithm as they indicate the stability and convergence of the solutions. If an algorithm attains a mean closer to the optimal value, a lower value for the worst objective function value and standard deviation, it indicates that the method was efficient and suitable as it was able to generate appropriately lower values (in case of a minimization problem) on sufficiently large numbers of iterations.

Figure 1.3 displays code snippets for executing PSO algorithm in MATLAB.

4 Artificial Bee Colony Algorithm

ABC is one of the most widely used SI-based optimization methods, which has been successfully applied to solve diverse complex numerical problems. The framework of the algorithm designed to emulate the foraging behavior of honeybees was first proposed by Karaboga in 2005 [15].

In ABC, the colony of bees is composed of three categories, i.e., employed, onlooker bees, and scout bees [18]. Employed bees find and exploit a particular food source. Here, the food source represents a feasible solution within the search space. Every employed bee produces a modification and assesses the nectar amount of a specific food source, i.e., fitness of the solution. After evaluating the quality of the food source, they pass this information to other bees in the hive. Onlooker bees, on receiving information related to the position, directions, and the quality of the food

Phase 3: Initialize Population

```
for i=1:N
    for j=1:D
        pos(i,j)=lb(j)+rand.*(ub(j)-lb(j));
    end
end
vel=0.1*pos;
```

Phase 4: Determine pbest, gbest

```
for iter=1:max_iter

for i=1:N
     out(i,1)=fun(pos(i,:));
end
pbestval=out;
pbest=pos;

[fminval,index]=min(out);
gbest=pbest(index,:)

X=pos;

    gbest=pbest(ind1,:);
end
```

Phase 5: Evaluate velocity and new particle position

```
    for i=1:N
        for j=1:D
    vel(i,j)=(w*vel(i,j))+(c1*rand().*(pbest(i,j)-pos(i,j)))+(c2*rand().*(gbest(1,j)-pos(i,j)));
    pos(i,j)=vel(i,j)+pos(i,j);

    if pos(i,j)<lb(j)
        pos(i,j)=lb(j);
    elseif pos(i,j)>ub(j)
        pos(i,j)=ub(j);

    end


        end
    end
end
```

Fig. 1.3 Implementing PSO using MATLAB

sources, select a food source based on a probability proportional to its fitness value. After a food source has been completely exhausted, it is abandoned, and the employed bee associated with that particular food source becomes a scout bee, which randomly chooses a new food source to exploit. Thus, it can be concluded that, while onlooker and employed bees perform the job of exploitation, scout bees ensure that the entire global region is intensively searched for an optimal solution.

To understand the method in-depth, we would now have a closer look at the three stages of the algorithm:

1. Employed Bees Phase: The process is initialized by generating random food source positions or feasible solutions within the search space. The parameters of the algorithms such as the swarm size, number of food sources, and limit are also defined. Each employed bee is assigned a particular food source to exploit. To examine the quality of the food source, the objective value function corresponding to the source/solution is calculated. The fitness values (fit_i) of the food sources are then derived using the following formula with the help of the objective function values (f_i) [16]:

$$\text{if } f_i \geq 0, \text{then } fit_i = \frac{1}{1 + f_i}$$

$$\text{if } f_i < 0, \text{ then } \ fit_i = 1 + |f_i|$$

The employed bees alter the positions of the food sources to produce new solutions (X_{new}) by arbitrarily selecting a partner solution (X_p) and modifying a random variable (j^{th} variable) of the initial solution (X) with the help of the given formula:

$$X^j_{new} = X^j + rand(-1, 1) * \left(X^j - X^j_p\right)$$

The bees then implement greedy selection to discard the less suitable solutions. After retaining the richer food sources, the employed bees disseminate information concerning the quality of the food sources among the onlooker bees.

2. Onlooker Bees Phase: The onlooker bees, on the basis of the information received from the employed bees about the fitness of the solutions ($\forall n = 1, 2, \ldots, SN$), select a particular food source according to the probability (p_i) value assigned to it with the help of the given formula:

$$p_i = \frac{fit_i}{\sum_{n=1}^{SN} fit_n}$$

This ensures selection of better food sources. After choosing a food source to exploit, onlooker bees produce a modification in the food position, similar to the one carried by the employed bees. To determine which food sources to retain and which to abandon, the onlooker bees execute the greedy selection. At the end of the stage, the best solution obtained in the ongoing iteration is stored.

3. Scout Bees Phase: If the position of a particular food source hasn't been modified or if a solution hasn't been improved for a predetermined number of iterations/cycles (represented by the limit parameter), the food source is abandoned. The employed bee associated with the food source becomes a scout bee, which undertakes the random generation of new solutions to be exploited in the next iteration.

The same iterative process is continued till the loop is terminated and the stopping criterion is met, i.e., when the desired accuracy is attained, or a number of iterations get completed.

Minimizing Schwefel's Function Using Artificial Bee Colony Algorithm

*a*To examine the efficiency and utility of ABC, the algorithm has been implemented to minimize the rotated hyper-ellipsoid function, which is popularly known as the

Schwefel's function. The benchmark function is continuous, convex, and unimodal in nature and produces rotated hyper-ellipsoids when plotted. The function has been defined as:

$$f(x) = \sum_{i=1}^{n} \sum_{j=1}^{n} X_j^2$$

The search area is usually restricted to $-65.536 \leq x_i \leq 65.536$ for $i = 1, \ldots, n$. The function attains its global minima, $f(x) = 0$, at $x_i = 0$ for $i = 1, \ldots, n$.

The algorithm has been executed to minimize the function in a two-dimensional space, where it takes the form of $f(x) = (x_1)^2 + ((x_1)^2 + (x_2)^2)$.

The plot of the function can be observed in Fig. 1.4.

Tables 1.3 and 1.4, and Fig. 1.5 summarize the observations and results attained while minimizing Schwefel's function using ABC over 10 runs with 200 iterations:

It can be observed that the best value obtained by ABC while minimizing the function is 0. Thus, the algorithm has been successful in minimizing the function to the lowest value that can be achieved.

Figure 1.6 provides a glimpse into how MATLAB can be programmed to implement ABC.

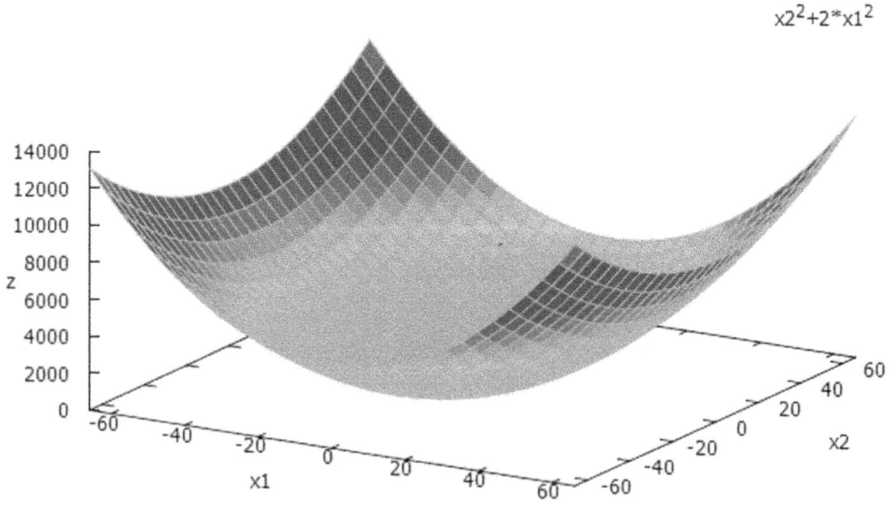

Fig. 1.4 Plotting Schwefel's function using Maxima

Table 1.3 Optimal values obtained for variables by ABC

Variables	Optimal values
x_1	0
x_2	0
$f(x_1, x_2)$	0

Table 1.4 Values observed for different parameters during the execution of ABC

Parameters	Values
Best value	0
Worst value	2.22184299
Mean	0.007044136895
Standard deviation	0.08366737868

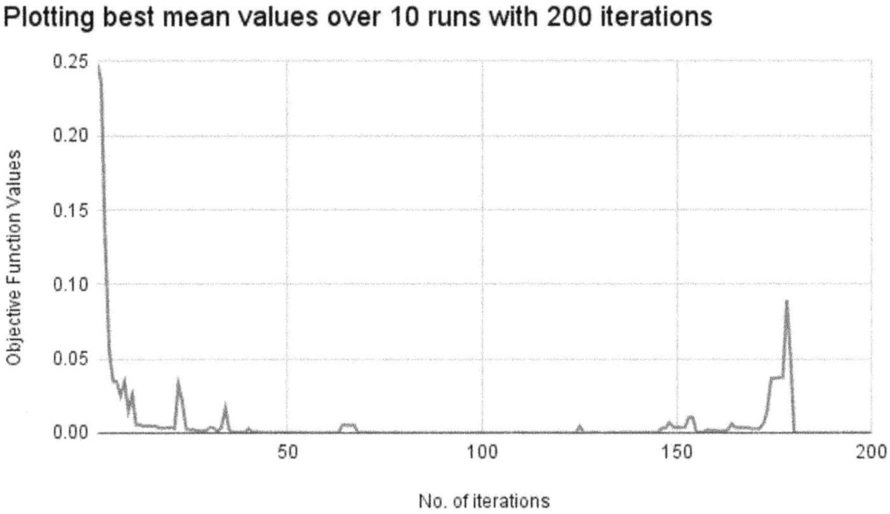

Fig. 1.5 Evolution of best mean results by ABC over 10 runs with 200 iterations

5 Comparative Analysis Using Fixed Iteration Test

The section lays out the framework to compare the performances of the algorithm using the fixed iteration test, wherein the results obtained over a specified no. of iterations and runs are analyzed to determine which algorithm performs better than its counterpart.

To establish a comparison between PSO and ABC algorithms, a fixed iteration test was conducted, wherein both SI-based computational methods were executed to minimize the axis parallel hyper-ellipsoid function. It is a continuous, convex, and unimodal function with a global minimum and no other local minima.

The general formulation of the function is given by:

```
            Xnew(j)=lb(j);
        end
    end

     %%Greedy Selection

     fnew=Bealefunction(Xnew);

     |
    if fnew<fx(i,:)
                pos(i,:)=Xnew;
                fx(i,:)=fnew;
                trial(i)=0;
            else
                trial(i)=trial(i)+1;
            end
    end

```

Onlooker Bee Phase

```
     prob=(fx./sum(fx));


    for i=1:N
        if (rand<prob(i))
            Xnew = pos(i,:);
        p2c = ceil(rand*D);
        partner = ceil(rand*N);
```

Employed Bee Phase

```
%%Selecting partner

for i=1:N
    Xnew = pos(i,:);
    p2c = ceil(rand*D);
    partner = ceil(rand*N);

    while (partner==1)
        partner = ceil(rand*N);

    end

%%Generating new position

X=pos(i,p2c);
Xp=pos(partner,p2c);
Xnew(p2c)=X+(rand-0.5).*2.*(X-Xp);

%%Bounds

for j=1:D
    if Xnew(j)>ub(j)
        Xnew(j)=ub(j);
    elseif Xnew(j)<lb(j)
        Xnew(j)=lb(j);
    end
end
```

Fig. 1.6 Implementing ABC using MATLAB

$$f(x) = \sum_{i=1}^{d} ix_i^2$$

Here, we will be implementing the two algorithms on a two-dimensional sum squares function given by:

$$f(x) = x_1^2 + 2x_2^2$$

The function attains the minimum value of 0 at (0,0). Figure 1.7 shows the plot of the function.

The performances of the algorithm were evaluated and compared on the basis of the best and worst objective function value achieved and statistical parameters such as mean and standard deviation. With respect to optimization problems involving minimization of the given objective function value, the algorithm attaining a lower best objective function value and a higher worst objective function value is considered better. While mean reflects the average value achieved in an iteration, standard deviation measures the variability and dispersion of the dataset around the mean. These statistical parameters give an insight into the efficiency of the search processes employed in the algorithm. A mean closer to the optimal value with a lower standard deviation value indicates that the algorithm has higher convergence rates as it has been successful in producing lower objective functions close to the optimal value on a greater number of iterations.

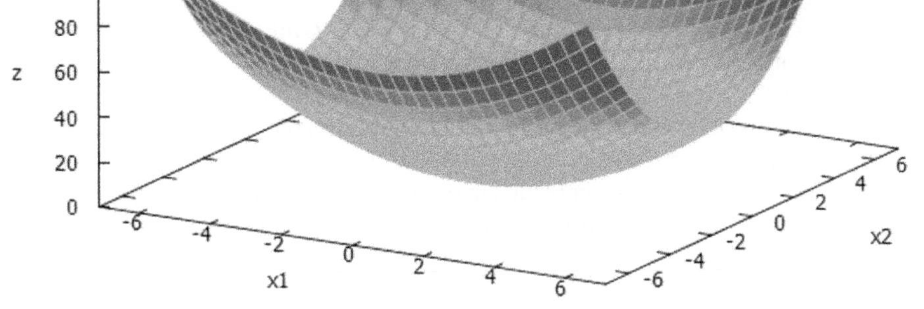

Fig. 1.7 Plotting axis parallel hyper-ellipsoid function using Maxima

Table 1.5 Comparison between performances of ABC and PSO

Parameters of comparison	PSO	ABC
Best value	0	0
Worst value	0.02119116	0.6271
Mean	0.000229697115	0.0015
Standard deviation	0.001051627142	0.01923517001

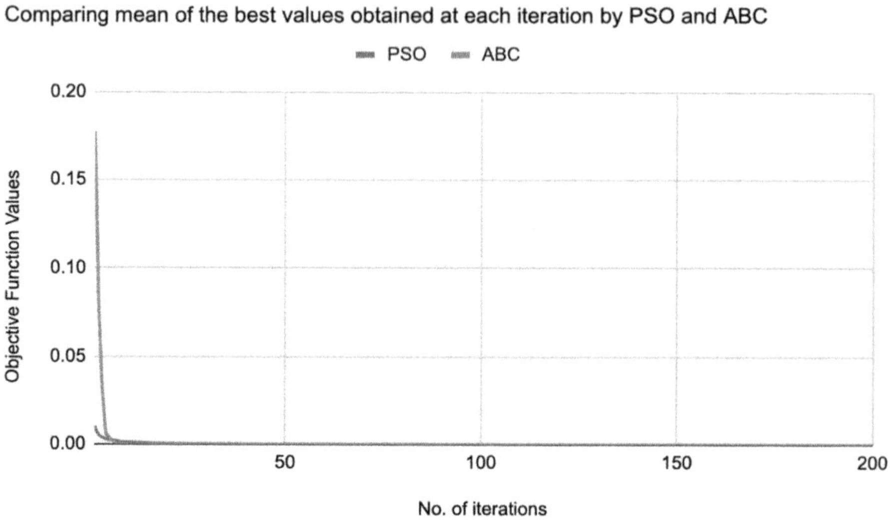

Fig. 1.8 Comparing best objective function values attained over 30 runs with 200 iterations

From Table 1.5 and Fig. 1.8, it can be concluded that PSO performs better than ABC while optimizing, and the given function as a higher worst value is achieved in case of ABC when compared to PSO. The mean calculated in the case of PSO is closer to the optimal value than ABC, which also obtains a greater value for standard deviation.

To further assess the suitability of the systems with respect to solving the minimization problem, the best variable values computed at each iteration were also compared.

By analyzing the results obtained for individual variables with respect to the predetermined parameters from Tables 1.6 and 1.7, Figs. 1.9 and 1.10, it can be deduced that PSO obtains better results in comparison to ABC. Thus, PSO is a more robust and efficient optimization tool than ABC for minimizing the sum squares function.

Table 1.6 Comparison between performances of ABC and PSO for x_1

Parameters of comparison	PSO	ABC
Best value	0	0
Worst value	0.1258	0.4663
Mean	0.000613	0.000642
Standard deviation	0.01077988038	0.01921224285

Table 1.7 Comparison between performances of ABC and PSO for x_2

Parameters of comparison	PSO	ABC
Best value	0	0
Worst value	−0.0986	0.5517
Mean	−0.0001	0.0003
Standard deviation	0.007526091968	0.02382160177

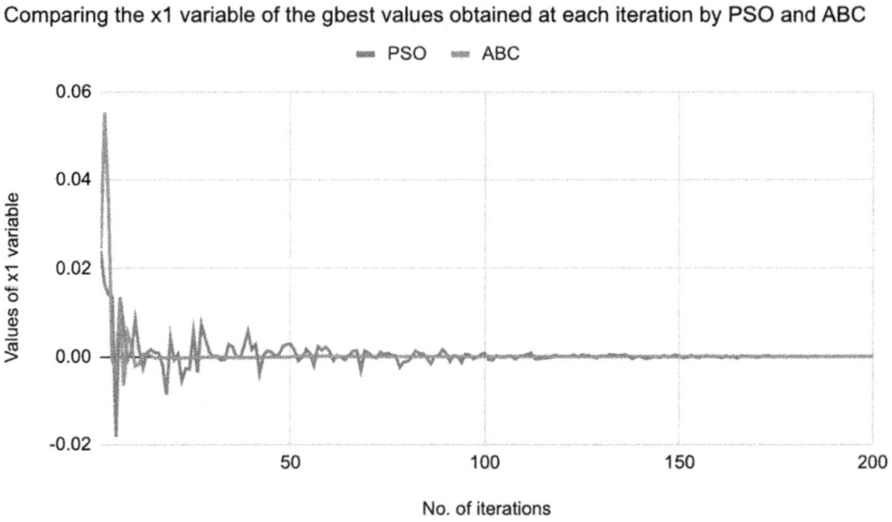

Fig. 1.9 Comparing best x_1 values attained over 30 runs with 200 iterations

6 Conclusion

The chapter offers a thorough overview of SI-based algorithms by highlighting its key features and points of merit and demerits and detailing and demonstrating the stages involved in implementing PSO and ABC to optimize unconstrained problems. The chapter also provides the readers with a blueprint for comparing algorithms by laying out the steps and requirements involved in conducting fixed interaction tests.

It is worth noting that both the algorithms attained an accurate optimal solution with their original structure, but their full potential can be unlocked only when necessary, and modifications are made to their structure. Hybridization of ABC with an evolutionary framework, stochastic methods, or deterministic methods can make

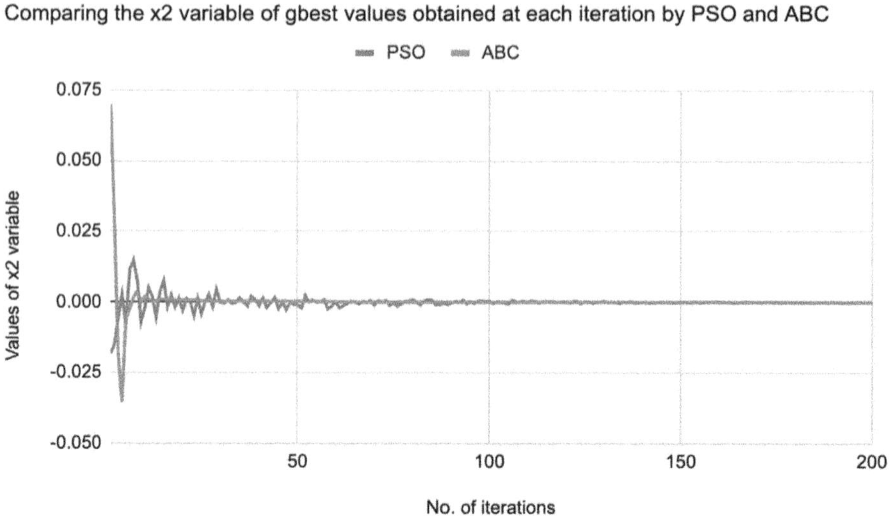

Fig. 1.10 Comparing best x_2 values attained over 30 runs with 200 iterations

the algorithm more efficient in the search process and allow parallel processing for time-saving. In order to improve the convergence rate of ABC, modifications in the production of new neighbor can be proposed. The search pool can be diversified with new strategies in the scout production phase. New selection strategies can also enhance the performance of ABC. On the other hand, hybridization of PSO with an evolutionary algorithm like genetic algorithm (GA) where the population of one algorithm is used as the initial population for the other one, instead of random population generation, produced finer results [28]. Adoption of new strategies of updating the velocity and particle position can lead to an increased efficiency of PSO. Along with this, further research can be conducted on fine parameter tuning for both PSO and ABC, since the results of the algorithms are heavily dependent on their parameters.

PSO and ABC have been evolving with time. The enhanced versions of the two algorithms have found them a place in a large number of applications. They have a huge scope in the field of neural networks [14], image and video analysis [4, 7], bioinformatics and medical applications [27], data mining [29], and much more [19].

While PSO and ABC are the most common examples of SI optimization algorithms, several other SI-based techniques of optimizations have been introduced in the recent years such as bacterial foraging [26], cat swarm optimization [6], artificial immune system [2], and glowworm swarm optimization [21, 22]. It should be interesting to realize that all these algorithms take inspiration from nature and help simulate an environment to solve real-world problems. At the same time, this very reason makes SI algorithms relatively weaker, because there exists an inadequacy of the theoretical analysis. The study of SI algorithms seems to be at an early stage, but with their growing popularity, one can believe that research and depth analysis will only improve the state of SI algorithms in the future.

References

1. Ahmed, H., Glasgow, J.: Swarm Intelligence: Concepts, Models and Applications. School of Computing, Queens University Technical Report (2012)
2. Bakhouya, M., Gaber, J.: An immune inspired-based optimization algorithm: application to the traveling salesman problem. Adv. Model. Optim. **9**(1), 105–116 (2007)
3. Bela, M., Gaber, J., El-Sayed, H., Almojel, A.: Swarm Intelligence. In: Handbook of Bio-inspired Algorithms and Applications, CRC Computer & Information Science, vol. 7. Chapman & Hall (2006)
4. Benala, T.R., Villa, S.H., Jampala, S.D., Konathala, B.: A novel approach to image edge enhancement using artificial bee colony optimization algorithm for Hybridized Smoothening Filters. In: World Congress on Nature & Biologically Inspired Computing, pp. 1071–1076. IEEE (2009
5. Bonabeau, E., Meyer, C.: Swarm intelligence: a whole new way to think about business. Harv. Bus. Rev. **79**(5), 105–115 (2001)
6. Buck, F.: Cooperative Problem Solving with a Distributed Agent System-Swarm Intelligence. (2007)
7. Chu, S.C., Tsai, P.W., Pan, J.S.: Cat swarm optimization. In: Pacific Rim International Conference on Artificial Intelligence, pp. 854–858. Springer (2006)
8. Das, S., Abraham, A., Konar, A.: Spatial information based image segmentation using a modified particle swarm optimization algorithm. In: 6th International Conference on Intelligent Systems Design and Applications, vol. 2, pp. 438–444. IEEE (2006)
9. Das, S., Abraham, A., Konar, A.: Swarm intelligence algorithms in bioinformatics. In: Computational Intelligence in Bioinformatics, pp. 113–147. Springer (2008)
10. Del Valle, Y., Venayagamoorthy, G.K., Mohagheghi, S., Hernandez, J.C., Harley, R.G.: Particle swarm optimization: basic concepts, variants and applications in power systems. IEEE Trans. Evol. Comput. **12**(2), 171–195. IEEE (2008)
11. Dorigo, M.: Optimization, Learning and Natural Algorithms (1992)
12. Dorigo, M.: Editorial. Swarm Intell. J. **1**(1) (2007)
13. Eberhart, R., Kennedy, J.: A new optimizer using particle swarm theory. In: MHS'95 Proceedings of the Sixth International Symposium on Micro Machine and Human Science, pp. 39–43. IEEE (1995)
14. Engelbrecht, A.P.: Computational Intelligence: An Introduction. Wiley (2007)
15. Irani, R., Nasimi, R.: Application of artificial bee colony-based neural network in bottom hole pressure prediction in underbalanced drilling. J. Petrol. Sci. Eng. **78**(1), 6–12. Elsevier (2011)
16. Karaboga, D.: An Idea Based on Honey Bee Swarm for Numerical Optimization. Technical report-TR06. Technical Report, Erciyes University (2005)
17. Karaboga, D., Akay, B.: Artificial bee colony algorithm for large-scale problems and engineering design optimization. J. Intell. Manuf. **23**, 1001–1014 (2010)
18. Karaboga, D., Basturk, B.: A powerful and efficient algorithm for numerical function optimization: artificial bee colony (ABC) algorithm. J. Glob. Optim. **39**(3), 459–471. Springer (2007)
19. Karaboga, D., Basturk, B.: On the performance of artificial bee colony (ABC) algorithm. Appl. Soft Comput. **8**(1), 687–697 (2008)
20. Karaboga, D., Gorkemli, B., Ozturk, C., Karaboga, N.: A comprehensive survey: Artificial Bee Colony (ABC) algorithm and applications. Artif. Intell. Rev. **42**(1), 21–57. Springer (2014)
21. Kennedy, J., Eberhart, R.: Particle swarm optimization. In: Proceedings of International Conference on Neural Networks, vol. 4, pp. 1942–1948. IEEE (1995)
22. Krishnanand, K., Ghose, D.: Glowworm swarm optimization for searching higher dimensional spaces. Innov. Swarm Intell. 61–75. Springer (2009)
23. Kulkarni, V.R., Desai, V.: ABC and PSO: a comparative analysis. In: IEEE International Conference on Computational Intelligence and Computing Research, pp. 1–7. IEEE (2016)
24. Lim, C.P., Dehuri, S.: Innovations in Swarm Intelligence, vol. 248. Springer Science & Business Media (2009)

25. Olivas, E.S., Guerrero, J.D.M., Martinez-Sober, M., Magdalena, B., Jose, R., Serrano, L.: Handbook of Research on Machine Learning Applications and Trends: Algorithms, Methods, and Techniques. IGI Global (2009)
26. Parsopoulos, K.E., Vrahatis, M.N.: Particle Swarm Optimization and Intelligence: Advances and Applications. IGI Global (2010)
27. Passino, K.M.: Biomimicry of bacterial foraging for distributed optimization and control. IEEE Control Syst. Magaz. **22**(3), 52–67. IEEE (2002)
28. Veeramachaneni, K., Osadciw, L.A., Varshney, P.K.: An adaptive multimodal biometric management algorithm. IEEE Trans. Syst. Man Cybern. C. Appl. Rev. **35**(3), 344–356. IEEE (2005)
29. Veeramachaneni, K., Peram, T., Mohan, C.K., Osadciw, L.A.: Optimization using particle swarms with near neighbor interactions. In: Genetic and Evolutionary Computation Conference, pp. 110–121. Springer (2003)
30. Wu, S., Lei, X., Tian, J.: Clustering PPI network based on functional flow model through artificial bee colony algorithm. In: 7th International Conference on Natural Computation, vol. 1, pp. 92–96. IEEE (2011)
31. Mirjalili, S.: Dragonfly algorithm: a new meta-heuristic optimization technique for solving single-objective, discrete, and multi-objective problems. Neural Comput. & Applic. **27**, 1053–1073 (2016)
32. Jevtić, A., Andina, D.: Swarm intelligence and its applications in swarm robotics. In: 6th WSEAS International Conference on Computational Intelligence, Man-Machine Systems and Cybernetics, pp. 41–46 (2007)
33. Shi, Y.: Feature article on particle swarm optimization. IEEE Neural Netw. Soc., 8–13 (2004)

Chapter 2
Particle Swarm Optimization and Its Applications in the Manufacturing Industry

Pinkey Chauhan and Shashi Barak

1 Introduction to Optimization

The term "optimization" entails the process of optimizing a given mathematical function or system's desirable properties while minimizing its undesirable characteristics. In the most basic sense, the optimization process tries to determine the best possible set of values to attain a given objective by satisfying various restrictions called constraints.

If we consider only one objective, then the problem is mathematically formulated as follows:

Minimize (or maximize)

$$f(x); \quad x = (x_1, x_2, \ldots, x_D) \tag{2.1}$$

subject to, usually defined by

$$F = \{x \in {}^D \mid h_i(x) = 0; \text{and}\, g_j(x) \geq or \leq 0\}$$
$$i = 1,2,\ldots,m \text{ and } j = m+1, m+2,\ldots,p$$

where $f, h_1, h_2, \ldots, h_m, g_{m+1}, g_{m+2}, \ldots g_p$ are real valued functions defined on $\Re^D$. The function $f(x)$ that is to be optimized (maximized or minimized) is called the "objective function." The equations $h_i(x) = 0$ for $i = 1, 2, \ldots, m$ are known as the equality constraints, and the inequalities $g_j(x) \geq or \leq 0$ for $j = m+1, m+2, \ldots, p$ are called inequality constraints. The independent variables $x_i^{'}s$ are called decision variables. A decision vector $x = (x_1, x_2, \ldots, x_D) \in \Re^D$ satisfying all the constraints is

P. Chauhan (✉) · S. Barak
Jaypee Institute of Information Technology, Noida, India

© The Author(s), under exclusive license to Springer Nature Switzerland AG 2022

D. Singh et al. (eds.), *Design and Applications of Nature Inspired Optimization*, Women in Engineering and Science, https://doi.org/10.1007/978-3-031-17929-7_2

called a "feasible point or solution." A feasible optimal solution is a possible solution that optimizes the objective function. It is intended to identify the independent variable values x_1, x_2, ..., x_D that optimize the objective function $f(x)$ without violating any of the constraints specified in problem (2.1)

The problem is known as a "linear programming problem (LPP)" when all of the functions $f(x)$, $h_i(x)$, $g_j(x)$ in the optimization problem are linear. The problem is known as a "nonlinear optimization problem" or a "nonlinear programming problem (NLPP)" if one or more of these functions are nonlinear. The model is termed an "integer programming problem" if the solution adds an extra constraint that the decision variables must be integers. The problem is known as a "mixed integer programming problem" when some of the variables are integers and others are real.

Local and Global Optimal Solution

The solution of an optimization problem is classified by the quality of the solution. The two types of solutions are referred to as local optima and global optima. An optimum $\overline{x}$ (local or global) is defined as follows: Let x be a solution vector of a given optimization problem that which satisfies all constraints. Now, let F be a set of all such solution vectors x, called feasible/solution space. Then, for a minimization problem, if for $\overline{x} \in F$, there exists an ε-neighborhood $N_\varepsilon(\overline{x})$ around $\overline{x}$ such that $f(x) \geq f(\overline{x})$ for each $x \in F \cap N_\varepsilon(\overline{x})$ and then $\overline{x}$ is called a "local minimum" of the given optimization problem. The functional value $f(\overline{x})$ will be called the local minimum value. If, however, $\overline{x} \in F$ and $f(x) \geq f(\overline{x})$ for all $x \in F$, then $\overline{x}$ is called a "global minimum" of the given optimization problem. The functional value $f(\overline{x})$ will be called the global minimum value. The local and global optima of a function are shown in Fig. 2.1.

If the problem is linear in nature, then the local solution will also play the role of a global optimum solution. The local optimum solution for an NLPP is guaranteed to be the global optimal solution, if the objective function for a minimization situation is convex and the domain of definition specified by the set of constraints is also convex. Figure 2.1 illustrates an example of a function with local and global optima. Figure 2.2 shows a function having a unique minimum (an example of a unimodal function), while Fig. 2.3 shows an example of a function having several local and global optima (multimodal function).

Algorithms that aim at determining the global solution are called global optimization algorithms. The practical necessity of global optima in real-life scenarios has motivated researchers to develop several global search methods for solving NLPP efficiently. Global search algorithms are categorized into two types: deterministic and probabilistic techniques. For exhaustively searching the solution space, deterministic approaches rely on a predetermined set of rules. Moreover, the solution found by a deterministic method always depends on the starting conditions and often be suboptimal. Probabilistic methods follow a stochastic approach to search the

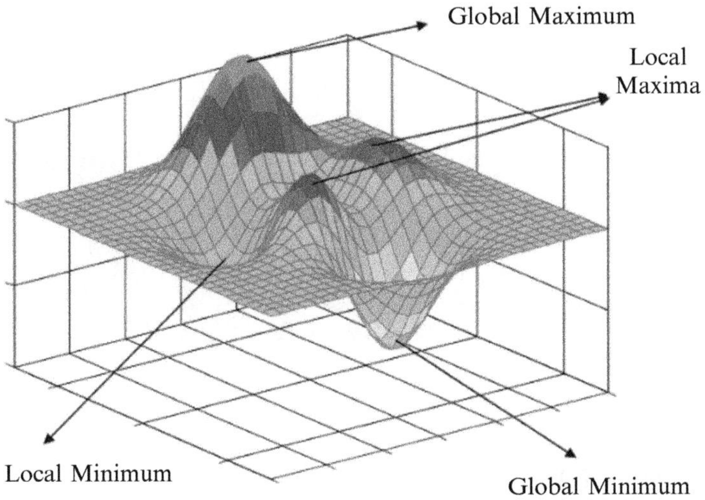

Fig. 2.1 Local optimum and global optimum

Fig. 2.2 Visualization of a unimodal function

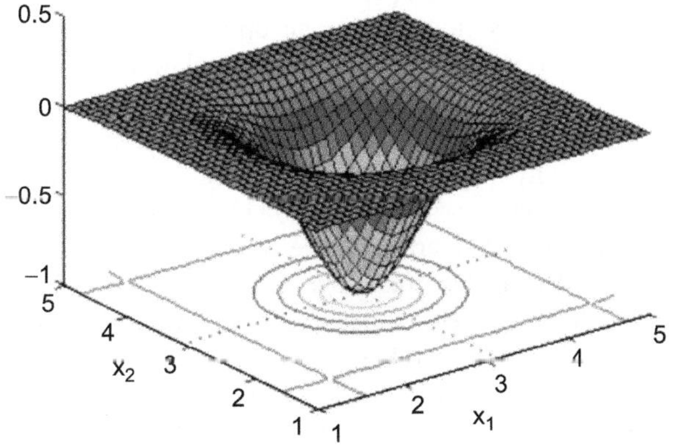

feasible space thoroughly for locating global optimal solutions. The deterministic techniques are applicable to a specific range of functions, such as differentiable or Lipschitz continuous functions, but Stochastic methods are applicable to a much broader range of functions. Despite the fact that probabilistic approaches do not guarantee global optima, they are occasionally recommended over deterministic methods due to their applicability to a broader class of functions. A detailed study of deterministic and stochastic methods could be found in [1–6]. A taxonomy of some global optimization methods is shown in Fig. 2.4

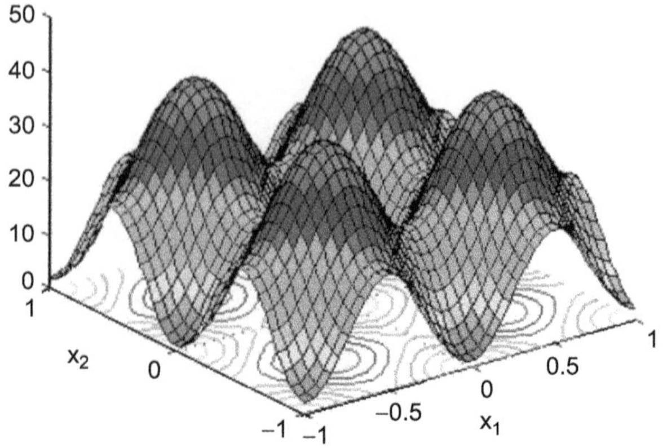

Fig. 2.3 Visualization of a multimodal function

Nature-Inspired Algorithms

Nature-inspired computing is a new computer paradigm that is based on self-organization and complex systems principles. Techniques that simulate an existing natural process to discover an optimum solution to a problem that seems to be resistant to conventional methods are known as nature-inspired optimization algorithms. The behavior or working of biological systems have been inspiring meta-heuristic search algorithms since its inception, for example, genetic algorithms [7], ant colony optimization [8, 9], tabu search [10], bacterial foraging optimization algorithm (BFOA) [11], differential evolution [12], central force optimization [13, 14], artificial bee colony optimization [15], glowworm swarm optimization [16], and particle swarm optimization [17]. The abovementioned methods have the advantage of being able to successfully address a variety of standard or application-based problems without any prior knowledge of the problem space. Furthermore, these algorithms are more capable of finding a problem's global optima. The scope of this chapter is limited to particle swarm optimization (PSO), which is considered an efficient, simple, and popular nature-inspired optimization approach. PSO is a swarm intelligence method, which is inspired by the behavior of fish schools and bird flocks for solving global optimization problems. The next section will present a detailed description of the simulation and parameters of PSO.

2 Particle Swarm Optimization

Particle swarm optimization (PSO) belongs to the category of swarm intelligence techniques, inspired from the well-informed social behavior of organisms. The foraging process of swarm analogies, such as bird flocks and fish schools, is simulated by PSO. This concept was firstly proposed as an efficient heuristic technique by Kennedy and Eberhart in 1995 [17]. The benefits of using PSO include

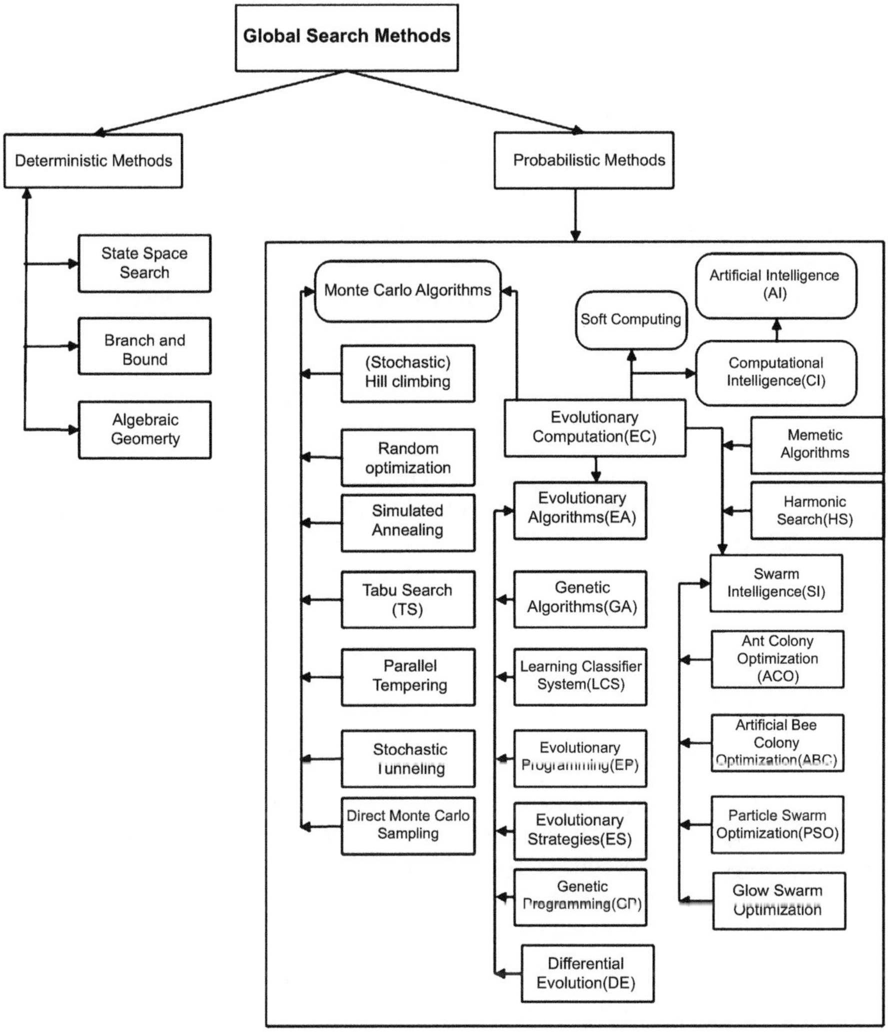

Fig. 2.4 Taxonomy of global optimization methods

fast convergence to the global optimum, a simple to implement code, as well as a complex computation-free environment. The searching process in PSO has better global searching capability at the start of the run and good local searching capability near the end. PSO is an efficient global optimizer that has gained great attention from academics since its inception. Because it is an efficient global optimizer, it may be viewed as an alternative to genetic algorithms (GA) and other evolutionary algorithms (EAs). PSO is an excellent option for dealing with a wide range of problems appearing in biology, economics, engineering, industry, and other real-world domains due to its simple and effective searching technique.

How PSO Works

For a D-dimensional search space, the ith particle of the swarm at time step t is represented by a D-dimensional vector, $x_i^t = \left(x_{i1}^t, x_{i2}^t, \ldots, x_{iD}^t\right)^T$. The velocity of this particle at time step t is represented by another D-dimensional vector, $v_i^t = \left(v_{i1}^t, v_{i2}^t, \ldots, v_{iD}^t\right)^T$. The previously best visited position of the *i*th particle at time step *t* is denoted as $p_i^t = \left(p_{i1}^t, p_{i2}^t, \ldots, p_{iD}^t\right)^T$. This is also called the personal best position or p_{best}.

The velocity of the *i*th particle is updated using the velocity update equation, given by

$$v_{id}^{t+1} = w^* v_{id}^t + c_1 r_1 \left(p_{id}^t - x_{id}^t\right) + c_2 r_2 \left(p_{gd}^t - x_{id}^t\right) \tag{2.2}$$

Here "g" is the index of the best particle in the swarm, and Pgd represents the best particle, i.e., the particle having the best fitness value. This is also called gbest, i.e., the global best.

The position updating rule is given below

$$x_{id}^{t+1} = x_{id}^t + v_{id}^{t+1} \tag{2.3}$$

where $d = 1, 2\ldots, D$ represents the dimension and $i = 1, 2, \ldots, S$ represents the particle index. *S* is the size of the swarm, and *c*1 and *c*2 are called cognitive and social acceleration constants, respectively, and constitute the parameters that have to be fine-tuned for the PSO to achieve convergence. *r*1 and *r*2 are uniform random numbers in the range [0, 1] and used to randomize the acceleration constants. Due to the stochastic effect introduced by these numbers, PSO trajectories should be considered stochastic processes. Equations (2.2) and (2.3) define the classical version of PSO algorithm with inertia weight (*w*).

In the velocity update Eq. (2.2), the new velocity v_{id}^{t+1} can be seen as the sum of three terms:

(i) *Momentum:* The first term $w^* v_{id}^t$ is momentum, which functions as memorization of the particle's prior flight direction. This concept restricts the particle from altering its path abruptly.
(ii) *Cognitive Component:* The second term $c_1 r_1 \left(p_{id}^t - x_{id}^t\right)$, related to local search, is proportional to the vector $\left(p_{id}^t - x_{id}^t\right)$ and leads back particle to its own best position. This factor, also known as the cognitive component of the velocity update equation, controls the step size in the direction of the particle's personal best position.
(iii) *Social Component:* The third term $c_2 r_2 \left(p_{gd}^t - x_{id}^t\right)$ is called social component, which is linked to the global search. This term is proportional to $\left(p_{gd}^t - x_{id}^t\right)$

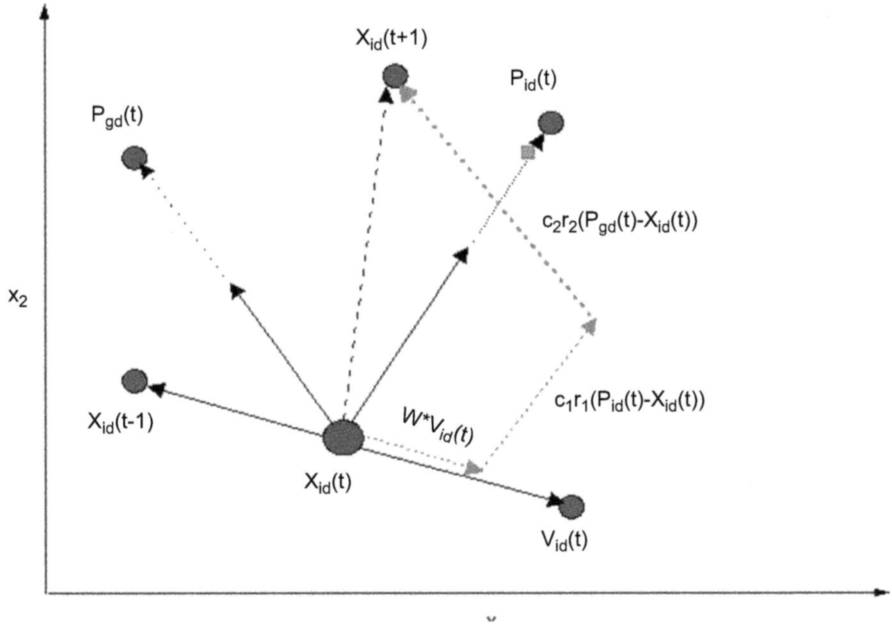

Fig. 2.5 Geometrical visualization of particle's movement in two-dimensional space

and points to the best position in the neighborhood. This term regulates maximum step size in the direction of global best particle.

In order to improve the resolution of the search, a constant, Vmax, is introduced in Eberhart et al. [18] to clamp the velocities of the particles in the range [−Vmax, Vmax]. The maximum velocity, Vmax, acts as a parameter to restrict the global exploration ability of a particle. The movement of a particle in two dimensional space can be visualized geometrically in Fig. 2.5.

The PSO paradigm follows the five basic principles of swarm intelligence [17, 19].

- Proximity principle: The proximity principle states that the population should be able to do simple spatial and time-related calculations.
- Quality principle: The population should be able to adapt to environmental quality variables.
- Principle of diverse response: The population should not commit its activities along excessively narrow channels.
- Stability principle: The population's behavior should not alter in response to changes in the environment.
- Principle of adaptability: The population must be able to adjust its behavior mode in response to the computational price.

The PSO's searching process is elaborated by the algorithm given below:

Algorithm: Basic PSO

```
Create and Initialize a D-dimensional swarm, S
    For t= 1 to the maximum bound on the number of iterations,
        For i=1 to S,
            For d=1 to D,
        Apply the velocity update equation (2)
        Update Position using equation (3)
            End- for-d;
        Compute fitness of updated position;
        If needed, update historical information for P_i and P_g;
        End-for-i;
     Terminate if P_g meets problem requirements;
    End-for-t;
```

Understanding PSO Parameters

The basic PSO has a number of parameters that should be fine-tuned to regulate the performance of the algorithm in a desired way. These parameters are briefly defined as follows [18, 20].

(i) *Swarm Size:* It refers to the number of random solutions generated initially to start the searching process. A good and diversified initial swarm leads the search in a better way, which may affect the performance of PSO significantly. The swarm size is problem dependent.

(ii) *Acceleration Coefficients.* These parameters are designated by $c1$ and $c2$, and they measure the stochastic impact of a particle's personal and social experiences on total velocity per iteration. With particle speed growing without control, the influence of these settings can make the PSO more or less "responsive" and possibly even unstable. Usually, $c1$ and $c2$ are taken as the following: $c1 = c2 = 2.0$; $c1 = 1.3$, $c2 = 2.8$ and $c1 = 2.8$, $c2 = 1.3$.

(iii) *Velocity Clamping (Vmax).* The concept of velocity clamping was introduced to limit velocities to the range [−Vmax, +Vmax] for each component of v_{id}. The value of parameter Vmax is carefully chosen, because it has a significant impact on the exploration-exploitation trade-off. Vmax's ideal value is problem-specific, and there is no fair rule of thumb.

(iv) *Inertia Weight (w):* Shi and Eberhart [21] introduced it as an explicit parameter to alter the momentum of a particle to a certain extent. The inertia weight governs the contribution of the previous velocity so that particles do not change their directions drastically and head toward good regions. When $w>1.0$, the particle will accelerate to its maximum velocity Vmax (or −Vmax) and then jump off the feasible space, while a value $w<1.0$ will force the particles to slow down until its velocity drops to zero, resulting in localized stagnation. Therefore, the value of w in the range [0.4, 1.0] is preferred more often.

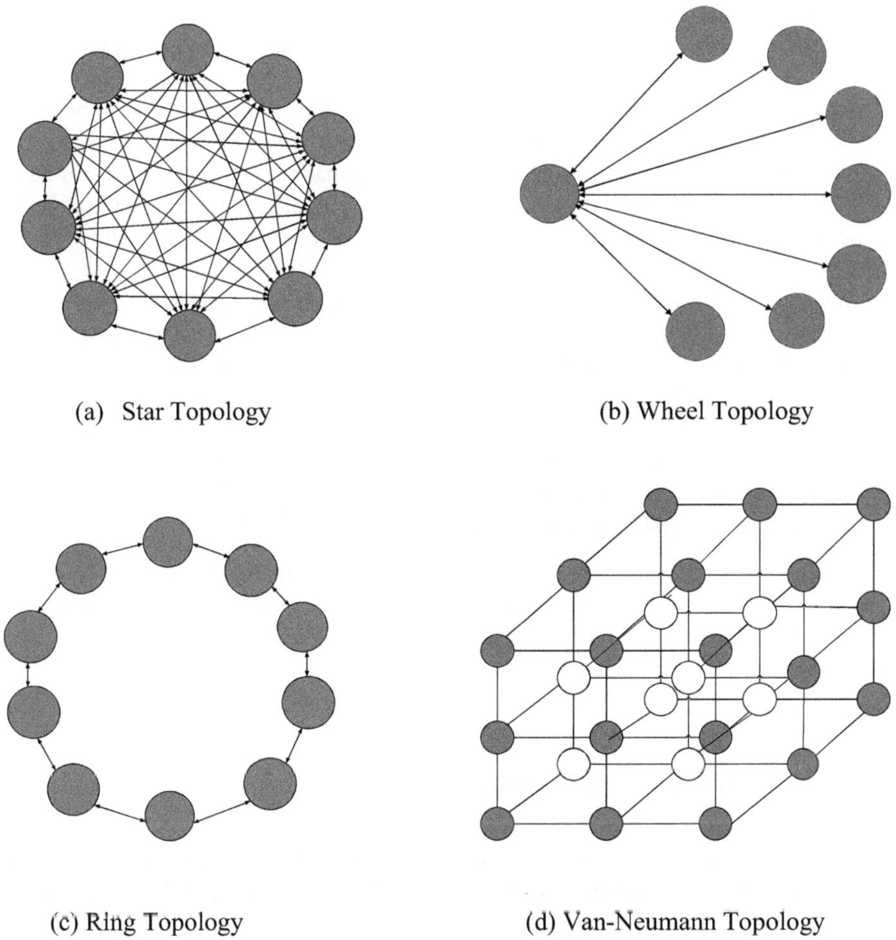

Fig. 2.6 Social networks for particle-to-particle interaction

(v) Particle's Social Interaction: The interaction methods show how the particles are interconnected with each other for information exchange. Some common structures are given below and are illustrated in Fig. 2.6.

- Star Topology: The star social structure is shown in Fig. 2.6, in which all particles are linked to each other and hence the communication occurs within the entire swarm. In this situation, every particle is drawn to the optimal solution traced by the entire swarm. As a result, each particle mimics the overall ideal solution. The "gbest PSO" is the initial version of the PSO, which utilized a star network structure. It has been observed that the gbest PSO converges more quickly than other communication networks but is more prone to becoming stuck in local minima. The "gbest PSO" shows better performance for problems having single optima.

- Ring or Circle Topology: The ring social structure is shown in Fig. 2.6c. The communication between each particle and its closest neighbors occurs within the ring social structure. By advancing toward the neighborhood's best solution, each particle makes an effort to emulate its best neighbor. Due to the link between limited number of particles, the convergence occurs more slowly as compared to star structure, but a bigger portion of the search space is covered in this structure. The above quality of ring social structure recommends it for multimodal problems. The first implementation of PSO using ring structure was named "lbest PSO."
- Wheel Topology: The wheel social structure isolates individuals living in a neighborhood from one another. As shown in Fig. 2.6b, one particle serves as the focal point, via which all information is transmitted. The focus particle evaluates all of the neighbors' performances and shifts its position toward the best neighbor. If the focal particle's changed position leads to improved performance, then the entire neighborhood is informed about the improvement.
- Von Neumann or Square Topology: The von Neumann social structure, as shown in Fig. 2.6d, has particles connected in a grid pattern.

There is no single structure that works best for all problems. It has been observed [20] that ring topology performs better for unimodal problems and star topology provides better results for multimodal problems. Particle indices are commonly used to define neighborhood size.

Binary Particle Swarm Optimization

PSO was originally developed for continuous optimization problems, but it has now been expanded to discrete and binary-valued problem spaces. Kennedy and Eberhart [22] created the first discrete version of PSO for binary issues as a result of their initiative. The core particle searching mechanism is the same in binary PSO as in the continuous version, with the exception of a change in the position update equation, which in the case of binary PSO becomes a binary number generator. To determine whether x_{id}, the dth component of x_i, should be evaluated as "0" or "1," the velocity is employed as a probability threshold. A mapping rule, from vid to a probability in the range [0, 1] must be defined for each $v_{id} \in \mathfrak{R}$. This is accomplished by squashing velocities into a range of [0, 1] using a function called "sigmoid function." The sigmoid function is defined by the following mathematical equation:

$$sigm(v_{id}) = \frac{1}{1 + \exp(-v_{id})} \tag{2.4}$$

The shape of the sigmoid function resembles the shape of the letter "S" as shown below in Fig. 2.7. The sigmoid function trajectory serves the purpose of a probability generating function for deciding a bit (from 0 to 1 and vice versa).

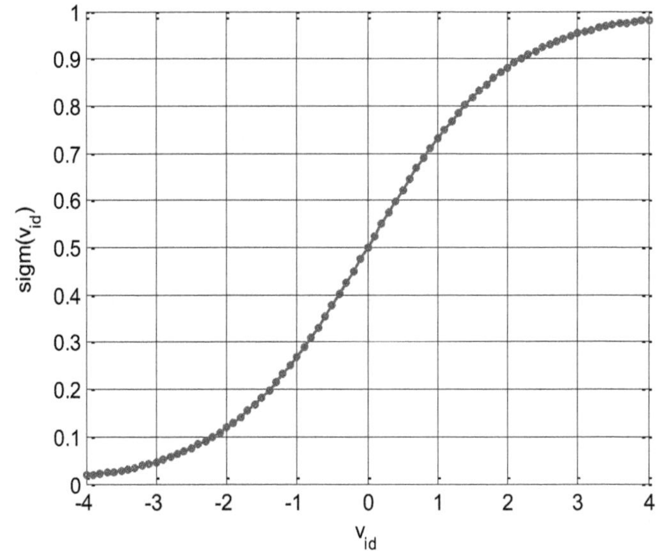

Fig. 2.7 Visualization of sigmoid function

In BPSO, the particle velocities (v_{id}) are fed as input to the sigmoid function, which normalizes them to be produced in the range [0, 1]. The generated values are further employed as the probability threshold for selecting bits 0 or 1. The binary PSO (BPSO) position update equation is now a probabilistic update equation:

$$x_{id}^{t+1} = \begin{cases} 1 & \text{if } U(0,\ 1) < sigm\left(v_{id}^{t}\right) \\ 0 & \text{otherwise} \end{cases} \tag{2.5}$$

where is a quasi-random number generated from a uniform distribution with values between 0 and 1. If sigm (vid) = 0, xid will remain 0 as shown in Eq. (2.5) (for convenience, the time scripts are dropped). This occurs when either $\mathrm{v_{id}} < -10$ or vid $>$ 10 [23]. To overcome this situation, it has been advised to set v_{id} in the range $[-4, 4]$ and to use velocity clamping with Vmax = 4. set vid and employ velocity clamping with Vmax = 4.

Research Developments in PSO

PSO, like several other population-based methods, faces problems while dealing with a certain class of problems, e.g., multimodal and complex real-world problems having a large number of decision variables. Two common drawbacks/shortcomings detected are as follows: premature convergence, when the algorithm converges to a solution which is not optimum; stagnation, when the algorithm shows no improvement in the fitness value although new particles are generated. These issues arise when the swarm enters a suboptimal state in which the algorithm is no longer capable of producing solutions that improve to the desired accuracy. The main reason behind the occurrence of these problems is the loss of diversity which in turn arises due to an imbalance between exploration (exploring different parts of the search space in order to find a good optimum) and exploitation (ability to narrow down a search to a feasible region in order to fine-tune a potential solution). The focus of this thesis is to develop improved PSO variants so that they can be applied to different problems arising in process industries.

According to the literature, the modification strategies for developing improved PSO variants may be broadly classified as:

(i) Hybridizing PSO with ideas borrowed from other heuristics or traditional methods
(ii) Disturbing the searching process of PSO by introducing some dynamics, e.g., chaotic maps
(iii) Proposing new strategies for parameter selection in PSO

A brief introduction on the developments of PSO using different strategies is presented below:

Mutation Embedded PSO Variants The idea of mutation was originally suggested for genetic algorithms to create perturbation in the population. The work of a mutation operator is to perturb the individuals so as to increase the diversity of the population and to pull out the particles, which are probably stuck in some local optimizer. Many mutation operators have been implemented in PSO so far, including Gaussian, Cauchy, Uniform, Levy, Power, and others [24, 25], to improve its performance and the notion reportedly provided satisfactory results.

Inertia Weight-Based PSO Variants In order to improve PSO's performance, Shi and Eberhart [26] added a new parameter called "inertia weight" to the original PSO, which was designed to manage the swarm's exploration and exploitation abilities by weighting particle motion. In addition, Shi and Eberhart [26] empirically analyzed the effects of inertial weight and maximum velocity on PSO performance, taking into account various parameter settings. Early studies suggested a constant inertial weight throughout the search, whereas later research focused on dynamic changes in inertial weight that dynamically regulated search capabilities. The various inertial weight approaches can be categorized as follows:

Linear Strategy: During a run, an inertia weight that decreases linearly from a reasonably large value to a small value has more global searching capacity at the start and more local searching ability near the finish. Several investigations [27–29] have documented the linear method to choose inertia weight, which depends on time.

Nonlinear Strategy: A nonlinear strategy that changes dynamically over time or iterations, based on the performance of a swarm or particle, was tested in several experiments and shown to be superior to the linear strategy. This approach gave better results with fewer iterations [30, 31].

Exponential Strategy: Exponential functions, which are faster and decreasing than linear and nonlinear functions, have attracted a lot of attention as a possible alternative for a lowering inertia weight strategy [32, 33]. The findings of the experiments reveal that exponential techniques converged faster than linear strategies early in the search process and produced better solutions.

Adaptive or Self-Adaptive Strategies: Choosing an inertia weight that adjusts to the needs of the particle is seen to be a preferable alternative, and researchers have presented a number of adaptive and self-adaptive ways for choosing an inertia weight that considerably improves PSO performance [32, 34, 35].

Fuzzy Rules-Based Strategy: A fuzzy system-based technique for dynamically adjusting inertia weight as developed by [36]. The input variables are the current best performance evaluation and the current inertia weight, whereas the output variable is the change in inertia weight. [37] developed another fuzzy-based technique in which the inertia weight is dynamically changed using fuzzy sets and rules.

Distribution-Based Random Adjustments: Some implementations used tactics based on probability distribution functions, which were found to be beneficial on a number of levels. Pant et al. [38] proposed a new Gaussian-based inertia weight based on the absolute value of half of the Gaussian random number, as well as discussing the likelihood of utilizing Gaussian and exponential distributions for producing the initial swarm. When the algorithm is likely to be stuck in local optima, Zhu et al. [39] developed a random adjustment for determining inertia weight with an adaptive initialization technique. The modified version was then used to solve the path planning problem for UAVs (unmanned aerial vehicles) and produced effective results.

Chaotic Inertia Weight Strategies: Some methods [40, 41] took advantage of dynamic systems to determine an adaptive inertia weight that would improve swarm diversity and convergence speed of method. The strategies incorporated chaotic terms as an additional parameter to increase randomness and, as a result, population diversity.

Some review reports have also been published by researchers [32, 42, 43] to analyze various existing inertia weight strategies and their performances. These review studies are always been very helpful to researchers, when selecting an existing strategy or proposing a new one.

Chaotic PSO Variants Chaos is a bounded unstable dynamic phenomenon in nonlinear systems that is sensitive to initial conditions and comprises infinite unstable periodic motions. It occurs in a deterministic nonlinear system under deterministic conditions, despite the fact that it appears to be stochastic. Chaos was introduced by many researchers as a disturbance term to enhance the capability of PSO for finding global optima. Chaos was added for handling premature convergence [44, 45], parameter adaptation [46], enhancing exploitation, maintaining population diversity [47], and preventing stagnation phenomena [48]. Many researchers [49–51] have also developed application-based variants of PSO by adding chaos at suitable points.

Binary PSO Variants Binary PSO was introduced by Kennedy and Eberhart [22] for handling binary and mixed integer problems. Binary PSO has the same searching process as its continuous version, therefore, having issues of premature convergence, and stagnation as well. To overcome the above shortcomings in binary PSO, researchers had come up with new modifications intending to improve the performance of binary PSO. Basic binary PSO uses sigmoid function for generating binary numbers. Some researchers have employed other functions as linear probability function [52], Boolean function [53], and bit change mutation [54, 55]. The sigmoid function is substituted by the Gompertz function in the study by [56], which has characteristics of both sigmoid and linear functions. The computational results shows that the novel approach is efficient over binary PSO and turns out as an efficient and handy algorithm for solving binary-valued problems.

Binary PSO has been extended in a number of studies [57–59] to solve integer or combinatorial optimization problems that arise in a variety of sectors, including science, engineering, and industry.

3 Application of PSO Manufacturing Industry

Large-scale, high-dimensional, nonlinear, and extremely unpredictable nature are all characteristics of industrial problems. Complex optimization problems are frequently solved using traditional methods such as "trial and error." Due to intrinsic limitations in describing and exploiting the available problem information, these methods frequently produce suboptimal results. In addition, the exploration of design space is restricted. Nature-inspired optimization approaches are gaining popularity for tackling real-world issues due to its stochastic features and wider applicability to a variety of functions (without any condition of continuity or differentiability). These methods are capable of delivering high-quality solutions and resolving some of the more complicated issues that arise in real-world problems. Some examples where PSO and other have been applied to different problems occurring in industries are given in a tabular form in Table 2.1.

4 Conclusion

The basic need in different spheres of life is seeking a better solution if possible. Therefore, finding a global optimal solution for real-life problems is required for exploiting available resources to its best without wasting available human resources, money, natural resources, etc. Since most of the problems arising in various industries can be modeled as optimization problems, therefore efficient techniques are

Table 2.1 Application of PSO in manufacturing industry

Application of PSO in product processing using machining		
Production process	**Objective**	**References and methods**
Hard turning	Finding optimal value of cutting speed and feed rate, depth of cut in hard turning	[60] (NSGA-II and PSO- NN); [61] (PSO); [62] PSO)
Milling	Finding the optimal value of rotation speed, feed rate, and depth of cutting	[63] (ABC, PSO, SA); [64, 65] (PSO)
Multi-pass turning, facing, and drilling	Finding the optimal value of cutting speed, feed rate, and depth of cut	[66] (EC); [49] (PSO)
Grinding	Finding the optimal value of wheel speed, work speed, traverse speed, in feed, dress depth, and dressing lead	[67] (PSO, GSA, SCA); [68] (PSO)
High-speed machining	Finding the optimal value of bonding wear, feed per tooth, and axial depth of cut	[69] (PSO), [70] (PSO-BP neural network), [71] (PSO)
Drilling	Finding optimal value of Cutting speed, feed rate, and cutting environment	[72] (PSO); [73] (PSO)
Multi-pass turning	Finding the optimal value of cutting speed, feed rate, and depth of cut	[74] (PSO); [75] (PSO); [49] (Chaotic PSO)
Application of PSO in the paper industry		
Problem	**Objective**	**References and methods**
Paper making process	Minimizing energy cost and production rate with constrained environment. Optimizing paper making process	[76] (Advanced GA) [77] (Advanced GA); [78] (Advanced GA)
Paper making process	Minimizing trim loss and production cost	[79] (2007) (SA-PSO), [34, 80] (PSO)
Application of PSO in the production industry		
Problem	**Objective**	**References and methods**
Scheduling	Optimal scheduling of polymer batch plants; scheduling of complex products with multiple resource constraints and deep product structure; optimal power generation to short-term hydrothermal scheduling; multi-objective job-shop scheduling; trust worthy workflow scheduling in a large-scale grid with rich service resources; optimal generation schedule of the real operated cascaded hydroelectric system	[81] (PSO); [82] (PSO); [83] (Fuzzy PSO); [84] (Rotary PSO); [85] (PSO)
Production planning	Optimal production planning to meet time-varying stochastic demand; optimizing the cost of the filter, filters loss, the total demand distortion of harmonic currents, and total harmonic distortion of voltages at each bus simultaneously; assembly sequence planning of complex products; production and distribution planning of a multi-echelon unbalanced supply chain	[86] (SQP-PSO); [87] (CPSO); [88] (PSO)

needed to deal with these problems irrespective of their mathematical nature. The present study starts with a general introduction of optimization and then leads to the introduction of PSO along with its parameters, some developments, and applications in the manufacturing industry. The manufacturing industry focuses on optimizing the production processes which further benefits it in different aspects, such as increasing profits and minimizing costs/waste material. As the field is very wide, the present study covers a brief review of optimization problems arising in various industries with the aim of paving a path for implementing PSO and other nature-inspired techniques in the concerned field.

The current study is making an effort of offering research direction in the process industry using nature-inspired algorithms. The review highlights processes, objectives, process parameters, and implemented algorithms. The objectives of this chapter in brief are:

(i) To discuss the scope of particle swarm optimization algorithms for obtaining the global optimal solution of continuous as well as binary optimization problems
(ii) Developments in PSO over the decades
(iii) To provide information on various industrial processes along with objectives and parameters

References

1. Rao, S.S.: Engineering Optimization Theory and Practice, 4th edn. Wiley, Hoboken (2009)
2. Taha, H.A.: Operations Research: An Introduction, 10th ed. University of Arkansas, Fayetteville. Global Edition published by Pearson Education, England (2017)
3. Mohan, C., Deep, K.: Optimization Techniques. New Age (2009)
4. Ravindran, A., Phillips, D.T., Solberg, J.J.: Operations Research: Principles and Practice, 2nd edn. Wiley, Hoboken (2009)
5. Deb, K.: Optimization for Engineering Design: Algorithms and Examples, 2nd edn. Prentice-Hall of India Private Limited, New Delhi (1995)
6. Himmelblau, D.M.: Applied Nonlinear Programming. McGraw-Hill, New York (1972)
7. Holland, J.H.: Adaptation in Natural and Artificial System. The University of Michigan Press, Ann Arbor (1975)
8. Colorni, A., Dorigo, M., Maniezzo, V.: Distributed optimization by ant colonies. In: Proceedings of European Conference on Artificial Life (ECAL-91). Elsevier Publishing, Amsterdam (1991)
9. Dorigo, M., Maniezzo, V., Colorni, A.: The Ant System: An Autocatalytic Optimizing Process, Technical Report TR91-016, Politecnico di Milano (1991)
10. Glover, F., Kochenberger, G.A.: Critical event tabu search for multidimensional knapsack problem. In: Osman, I.H., Kelly, J.P. (eds.) Meta-Heuristics: Theory and Applications, pp. 407–427. Kluwer Academic Publishers, New York (1996)
11. Passino, K.M.: Biomimicry of bacterial foraging for distributed optimization and control. IEEE Control. Syst. Mag. **52–67** (2002)
12. Storn, R., Price, K.: Differential Evolution – A Simple and Efficient Adaptive Scheme for Global Optimization over Continuous Spaces, Technical Report TR-95-012, Berkeley (1995)
13. Formato, R.: Central force optimization: a new nature inspired computational framework for multidimensional search and optimization. In: Nature Inspired Cooperative Strategies for

Optimization (NICSO-2007), Italy, Series: Studies in Computational Intelligence, Springer, vol. 129, pp. 221–238 (2008)
14. Formato, R.: Central force optimization: a new deterministic gradient-like optimization metaheuristic. OPSEARCH. **46**(1), 25–51 (2009)
15. Karaboga, D.: An Idea Based on Honey Bee Swarm for Numerical Optimization, Technical Report-TR06, Erciyes University, Engineering Faculty, Computer Engineering Department (2005)
16. Krishnanand, K.N., Ghose, D.: Glowworm swarm based optimization algorithm for multimodal functions with collective robotics applications. Multiagent Grid Syst. **2**(3), 209–222 (2006)
17. Kennedy, J., Eberhart, R.C.: Particle swarm optimization. In: Proceedings of IEEE International Conference Neural Networks, vol. 4, pp. 1942–1948 (1995)
18. Eberhart, R.C., Simpson, P.K., Dobbins, R.W.: Computational Intelligence PC Tools, 1st edn. Academic Press Professional, Boston (1996)
19. Clerc, M.: Think Locally, Act Locally: The Way of Life of Cheap-PSO, An Adaptive PSO, Technical Report (2001)
20. Engelbrecht, A.P.: Computational intelligence: An introduction. John Wiley and Sons, Ltd (2007)
21. Shi., Y., Eberhart, R. C.: Parameter selection in particle swarm optimization. In: Proceedings of the Seventh Annual Conference on Evolutionary Programming, New York, pp. 591–600 (1998)
22. Kennedy, J.,Eberhart, R.C.: A discrete binary version of the particle swarm algorithm. In: IEEE International Conference on Systems, Man, and Cybernetics, Computational Cybernetics and Simulation, vol. 5, pp. 4104–4108 (1997)
23. Bergh, F., Engelbrecht, A.: A study of particle swarm optimization particle trajectories. Inform. Sci. **176**, 937–971 (2006). https://doi.org/10.1016/j.ins.2005.02.003
24. Pant, M., Thangaraj, R., Abraham, A.: Particle swarm optimization using adaptive mutation. In: Proceedings of 19th International Workshop on Database and Expert Systems Application (DEXA-2008), pp. 519–523 (2008)
25. Pant, M., Thangraj, R., Singh, V.P., Abraham, A.: Particle swarm optimization using sobol mutation. In: Proceedings of International Conference on Emerging Trends in Engineering and Technology, India, pp. 367–372 (2008)
26. Shi, Y., Eberhart, R.C.: Empirical study of particle swarm optimization. In: Proceedings of the Congress on Evolutionary Computation (CEC-1999), vol. 3, pp. 1945–1950 (1999)
27. Ratnaweera, A., Halgamuge, S., Watson, H.: Particle swarm optimization with self-adaptive acceleration coefficients. In: Proceedings of the First International Conference on Fuzzy Systems and Knowledge Discovery, pp. 264–268 (2003)
28. Suganthan, P.N.: Particle swarm optimiser with neighbourhood operator. In: Proceedings of the IEEE Congress on Evolutionary Computation, pp. 1958–1962 (1999)
29. Yoshida, H., Fukuyama, Y., Takayama, S., Nakanishi, Y.: A particle swarm optimization for reactive power and voltage control in electric power systems considering voltage security assessment. In: Proceedings of IEEE International Conference on Systems, Man, and Cybernetics, vol. 6, pp. 497–502 (1999)
30. Peram, T., Veeramachaneni, K., Mohan, C.K.: Fitness-distance-ratio based particle swarm optimization. In: Proceedings of IEEE Swarm Intelligence Symposium, pp. 174–181 (2003)
31. Venter, G., Sobieszczanski-Sobieski, J.: Multidisciplinary optimization of a transport aircraft wing using particle swarm optimization. Struct. Multidiscip. Optim. **26**(1–2), 121–131 (2003)
32. Chauhan, P., Deep, K., Pant, M.: Novel inertia weight strategies for particle swarm optimization. Memetic Comput. **5**, 229–251 (2013)
33. Chen, G., Huang, X., Jia, J., Min, Z.: Natural exponential Inertia weight strategy in particle Swarm Optimization. In: Proceedings of 6th World Congress on Intelligent Control, pp. 3672–3675 (2006)
34. Deep, K., Chauhan, P., Pant, M.: New hybrid discrete PSO for solving non convex trim loss problem. Int. J. Appl. Evol. Comput. (IJAEC). **3**(2), 19–41 (2012)

35. Deep, K., Arya, M., Bansal, J.C.: A non-deterministic adaptive inertia weight in PSO. In: Proceedings of 13th Annual Conference on Genetic and Evolutionary Computation (GECCO-2011), ACM, New York, pp. 1155–1162 (2011)
36. Shi, Y. Eberhart, R.C., Fuzzy adaptive particle swarm optimization. In: Proceedings of IEEE Congress on Evolutionary Computation, vol. 1, pp. 101–106 (2001)
37. Liu, C., Ouyang, C., Zhu, P., Tang, W.: An adaptive fuzzy weight PSO algorithm. In: Proceedings of Fourth International conference on Genetic and Evolutionary Computing, pp. 8–10 (2010)
38. Pant, M., Thangraj, R., Singh, V.P., Particle swarm optimization using Gaussian inertia weight. In: Proceedings of International Conference on Computational Intelligence and Multimedia Applications, vol. 1, pp. 97–102 (2007)
39. Zhu, H., Zheng, C., Hu, X., Li, X.: Adaptive PSO using random inertia weight and its application in UAV path planning. In: Proceedings of Seventh International Symposium on Instrumentation and Control Technology: Measurement Theory and Systems and Aeronautical Equipment (SPIE), 7128, pp. 1–5 (2008)
40. Chen, J.Y., Shen, J.J.: Structure learning of Bayesian network using a chaos-based PSO. Adv. Mater. Res. **2292–2295** (2012)
41. Feng, Y., Yao, Y.M., Wang, A.: Comparing with chaotic inertia weights in particle swarm optimization. In: Proceedings of International Conference on Machine Learning and Cybernetics, pp. 329–333 (2007)
42. Bansal, J.C., Singh, P.K., Saraswat, M., Verma, A., Jadon, S.S., Abraham, A.: Inertia weight strategies in particle swarm optimization. In: Proceedings of Third World Congress on Nature and Biologically Inspired Computing (NaBIC-2011), pp. 633–640 (2011)
43. Nickabadi, A., Ebadzadeh, M.M., Safabakhsh, R.: A novel particle swarm optimization algorithm with adaptive inertia weight. Appl. Soft Comput. **11**(4), 3658–3670 (2011)
44. Deep, K., Chauhan, P., Pant, M.: Totally disturbed chaotic Particle Swarm Optimization. In: 2012 IEEE Congress on Evolutionary Computation, pp. 1–8 (2012)
45. Xie, X., Zhang, W., Yang, Z.: A dissipative particle swarm optimization. In: Proceedings of IEEE Congress on Evolutionary Computation (CEC-2002), pp. 1456–1461 (2002)
46. Alatas, B., Akin, E., Ozer, A.B.: Chaos embedded particle swarm optimization algorithms. Chaos, Solitons Fractals. **40**(4), 1715–1734 (2009)
47. Liu, B., Wang, L., Jin, Y.H., Tang, F., Huang, D.X.: Improved particle swarm optimization combined with chaos. Chaos, Solitons Fractals. **25**(5), 1261–1271 (2005)
48. He, Q., Han, C.: An improved particle swarm optimization algorithm with disturbance term. ICIC. **3**, 100–108 (2006)
49. Chauhan, P., Pant, M., Deep, K.: Parameter optimization of multi-pass turning using chaotic PSO. Int. J. Mach. Learn. Cybern. **6**, 319–337 (2015)
50. Li, C., Zhou, J., Kou, P., Xiao, J.: A novel chaotic particle swarm optimization based fuzzy clustering algorithm. Neurocomputing **83**, 98–109 (2012)
51. Mukhopadhyay, S., Banerjee, S.: Global optimization of an optical chaotic system by chaotic multi swarm particle swarm optimization. Expert Syst. Appl. **39**(1), 917–924 (2012)
52. Deep, K., Bansal, J.C.: A modified binary particle swarm optimization for knapsack problems. Appl. Math. Comput. **218**(22), 11042–11061 (2012)
53. Marandi, A., Afshinmanesh, F., Shahabadi, M., Bahrami, F.: Boolean particle swarm optimization and its application to the design of a dual-band dual-polarized planar antenna. In: Proceedings of IEEE Congress on Evolutionary Computation (CEC-2006), pp. 3212–3218 (2006)
54. Singh, Y., Chauhan, P.: New mutation embedded generalized binary PSO. In: Sathiyamoorthy, S., Caroline, B., Jayanthi, J. (eds.) Emerging Trends in Science, 2012, Engineering and Technology Lecture Notes in Mechanical Engineering, pp. 705–715. Springer, New Delhi (2012)

55. Lee, S., Park, H., Jeon, M.: Binary Particle swarm optimization with bit change mutation. In: IEICE Transactions on Fundamentals of Electronics, Communications and Computer Sciences, E90-A:10, pp. 2253–2256 (2007)
56. Chauhan, P., Pant, M., Deep, K.: Novel binary PSO for continuous global optimization problems. In: Proceedings of the International Conference on Soft Computing for Problem Solving (SocProS 2011) December 20–22, p. 130 (2011)
57. Deep, K., Chauhan, P., Pant, M.: Multi task selection including part mix, tool allocation and process plans in CNC machining centers using new binary PSO. In: 2012 IEEE Congress on Evolutionary Computation, pp. 1–8 (2012)
58. Chauhan, P., Pant, M., Deep, K.: Gompertz PSO variants for Knapsack and Multi-Knapsack problems. Appl. Math. J. Chin. Univ. **36**, 611–630 (2021)
59. Unler, A., Murat, A.: A discrete particle swarm optimization method for feature selection in binary classification problems'. Eur. J. Oper. Res. **206**(3), 528–539 (2010)
60. Bouacha, K., Terrab, A.: Hard turning behavior improvement using NSGA-II and PSO-NN hybrid model. Int. J. Adv. Manuf. Technol. **86**, 3527–3546 (2016)
61. Omkar, M., Chinchanikar, S., Gadge, M.: Multi-performance optimization in hard turning of AISI 4340 steel using particle swarm optimization technique. Mater. Today Proc. **5**(11 Part 3), 24652–24663 (2018)
62. Mishra, R.R., Kumar, R., Panda, A., Pandey, A., Sahoo, A.K.: Particle swarm optimization of multi-responses in hard turning of D2 steel. In: Das, H., Pattnaik, P., Rautaray, S., Li, K.C. (eds.) Progress in Computing, Analytics and Networking. Advances in Intelligent Systems and Computing, vol. 1119. Springer, Singapore (2020)
63. Rao, R.V., Pawar, P.J.: Parameter optimization of a multi-pass milling process using non-traditional optimization algorithms'. Appl. Soft Comput. **10**(2), 445–456 (2010)
64. Bahirje, S., Potdar, V.: Review paper on implementation of particle swarm optimization for multi-pass milling operation. Int. J. Eng. Res. Technol. (IJERT). **9**(9), 237–239 (2020)
65. Farahnakian, M., Razfar, M.R., Moghri, M., Asadnia, M.: The selection of milling parameters by the PSO-based neural network modeling method. Int. J. Adv. Manuf. Technol. **1–12** (2011)
66. Sankar, R.S., Asokan, P., Saravanan, R., Kumanan, S., Prabhaharan, G.: Selection of machining parameters for constrained machining problem using evolutionary computation. Int. J. Adv. Manuf. Technol. **32**(9–10), 892–901 (2007)
67. Shin, T., Adam, A., Abidin, A.: A comparative study of PSO, GSA and SCA in parameters optimization of surface grinding process. Bull. Electr. Eng. Inf. **8**(3), 1117–1127 (2019)
68. Pawar, P.J., Rao, R.V., Davim, J.P.: Multiobjective optimization of grinding process parameters using particle swarm optimization algorithm. Mater. Manuf. Process. **25**(6), 424–431 (2010)
69. Abbas, A.T., Sharma, N., Anwar, S., Hashmi, F.H., Jamil, M., Hegab, H.: Towards optimization of surface roughness and productivity aspects during high-speed machining of Ti–6Al–4V. Materials. **12**(22), 3749 (2019)
70. Zheng, J.X., Zhang, M.J., Meng, Q.X.: Tool cutting force modeling in high speed milling using PSO-BP neural network. In: Key Engineering Materials, vol. 375, pp. 515–519. Trans Tech Publications, Ltd. (2008)
71. Cus, F., Zuperl, U., Gecevska, V.: High speed end-milling optimisation using Particle Swarm Intelligence. J. Achieve. Mater. Manuf. Eng. **22**(2), 75–78 (2007)
72. Kumar, S.M.G., Jayaraj, D., Kishan, A.R.: PSO based tuning of a PID controller for a high performance drilling machine. Int. J. Comput. Appl. **1**(19), 12–18 (2010)
73. Gaitonde, V.N., Karnik, S.R.: Minimizing burr size in drilling using artificial neural network (ANN)-particle swarm optimization (PSO) approach. J. Intell. Manuf. **23**, 1783–1793 (2012)
74. Bharathi, R.S., Baskar, N.: Particle swarm optimization technique for determining optimal machining parameters of different work piece materials in turning operation. Int. J. Adv. Manuf. Technol. **54**(5–8), 445–463 (2011)
75. Yusup, N., Zain, A.M., Hashim, S.Z.M.: Overview of PSO for optimizing process parameters of machining. Proc. Eng. **29**, 914–923 (2012)

76. Santos, A., Dourado, A.: Global optimization of energy and production in process industries: a genetic algorithm application. Control. Eng. Pract. **7**, 549–554 (1999)
77. Wang, H., Borairi, M., Roberts, J.C., Xiao, H.: Modelling of a paper making process via genetic neural networks and first principle approaches. In: Proceedings of the IEEE International Conference on Intelligent Processing Systems, ICIPS, Beijing, pp. 584–588 (1997)
78. Borairi, M., Wang, H., Roberts, J.C.: Dynamic modelling of a paper making process based on bilinear system modelling and genetic neural networks. In: Proceedings of UKACC International Conference on Control, pp. 1277–1282 (1998)
79. Xianjun, S., Li, Y., Zheng, B., Dai, Z.: General particle swarm optimization based on simulated annealing for multi-specification one-dimensional cutting stock problem. In: Computational Intelligence and Security. Springer-Verlag Berlin, Heidelberg, LNAI, pp. 67–76 (2007)
80. Deep, K., Chauhan, P., Bansal, J.C.: Solving nonconvex trim loss problem using an efficient hybrid Particle Swarm Optimization. In: World Congress on Nature & Biologically Inspired Computing (NaBIC), pp. 1608–1611 (2009)
81. Hota, P.K., Barisal, A.K., Chakrabarti, R.: An improved PSO technique for short-term optimal hydrothermal scheduling. Electr. Power Syst. Res. **79**(7), 1047–1053 (2009)
82. Sha, D.Y., Lin, H.-H.: A multi-objective PSO for job-shop scheduling problems. Expert Syst. Appl. **37**(2), 1065–1070 (2010)
83. Liu, H., Abraham, A., Hassanien, A.E.: Scheduling jobs on computational grids using fuzzy particle swarm algorithm. Futur. Gener. Comput. Syst. **26**, 1336–1343 (2010)
84. Tao, Q., Chang, H., Yi, Y., Gu, C., Li, W.: A rotary chaotic PSO algorithm for trustworthy scheduling of a grid workflow. Comput. Oper. Res. **38**(5), 824–836 (2008)
85. Mahor, A., Rangnekar, S.: Short term generation scheduling of cascaded hydro electric system using novel self adaptive inertia weight PSO. Int. J. Electr. Power Energy Syst. **34**(1), 1–9 (2012)
86. Chang, Y.P.: Integration of SQP and PSO for optimal planning of harmonic filters. Expert Syst. Appl. **37**(3), 2522–2530 (2010)
87. Wang, Y., Liu, J.H.: Chaotic particle swarm optimization for assembly sequence planning. Robot. Comput. Integr. Manuf. **26**(2), 212–222 (2010)
88. Che, Z.H.: A particle swarm optimization algorithm for solving unbalanced supply chain planning problems. Appl. Soft Comput. **12**(4), 1279–1287 (2012)

Chapter 3
Role of Machine Learning in Bioprocess Engineering: Current Perspectives and Future Directions

Ashutosh Singh and Barkha Singhal

Abbreviations

AAD	Absolute average deviation
ANN	Artificial neural network
CNN	Convolutional neural networks
CT	Classification tress
DLAB	Deep learning for antibodies
GBSA	Generalized Born surface area
HER2	Human epidermal growth factor receptor 2
K_{cat}	Catalytic turnover number
Mabs	Monoclonal antibodies
ML	Machine learning
MM	Molecular mechanic
NIR	Near-infrared spectroscopy
RF	Random forest
RMSE	Root mean squared error
SAX	Symbolic aggregate approximation
SCM	Set covering machine
SG	Spatial graph
SSF	Simultaneous saccharification and fermentation
SVM	Support vector machine

A. Singh · B. Singhal (✉)
School of Biotechnology, Gautam Buddha University, Greater Noida, Uttar Pradesh, India
e-mail: barkha@gbu.ac.in

© The Author(s), under exclusive license to Springer Nature Switzerland AG 2022

D. Singh et al. (eds.), *Design and Applications of Nature Inspired Optimization*,
Women in Engineering and Science, https://doi.org/10.1007/978-3-031-17929-7_3

1 Introduction

The stupendous stride to achieve economic and environmental sustainability accelerates the rising demand for bioproducts [1]. The harnessing of bioproducts requires the understanding of holistic development of biological processes from raw materials to synthesis and purification of bioproducts and valorization of biowaste to make value-added products at an industrial scale [2, 3]. Therefore, for accomplishing at such height process, engineering principles integrating with natural sciences, such as physics, chemistry, biology with chemical, and system engineering, are playing a pivotal role in translating biological knowledge into making products of commercial importance. Bioprocess engineering is the thrust area that needs to be updated with technological innovations, though the past decade has envisaged significant developments in formulating extensive mechanistic and physiochemical empirical models for simulating the growth pattern of microbial biomass and product formation, calculating the fermented broth rheological parameters and dynamics for bioreactor scale-up, optimization of bioseparation unit designs, synthesis of new enzymes proteins, and analysis of metabolic flux ([4, 5]. However, the complexity of the biological system still posits certain inherent challenges that need to be addressed for industrial purposes [6].

As the fourth industrial revolution industry 4.0 has already gained momentum, there is a dire need for digitalization and inculcation of advanced process analytics and computational biology tools for accelerating the arena of bioprocess engineering. Currently, the paradigmatic shift from physical modeling to data-driven modeling using machine learning approaches contributed to the voluminous data generation in the bioindustry arena [7]. The elucidation of complex biological relationships in data form demonstrated great potential for the bioprocess research community and engineers to "scale up" as well as "scale down" the bioprocess for explicit commercial use. The arena of bioprocess engineering is quite vast constituting various branches from research and development to biomanufacturing consisting of metabolic engineering, bioreaction engineering, protein engineering, synthetic biology, biomaterials, and biocatalysis. The applications of ML are represented in Fig. 3.1. Currently, various ML algorithms have been utilized to circumvent the biological complexities during bioprocess optimization; thus, the accelerating pace of machine learning is invoking a renaissance in this area [8]. Therefore, the present chapter advocates various embodiments of machine learning applications in the bioprocess engineering sector and also predicate current challenges and future prospects. The technology is still evolving; therefore, this chapter doesn't cover the comprehensive aspects, but various dimensions of ML approaches has been described through various case studies of bioprocess engineering.

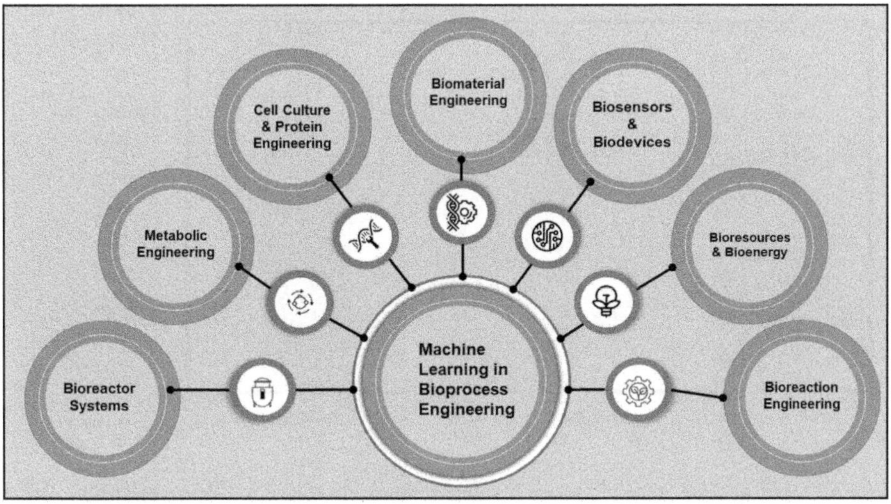

Fig. 3.1 Applications of machine learning is the arena of bioprocess engineering

2 Approaches of Machine Learning in Bioprocess Engineering

Bioprocess engineering is the application of interdisciplinary field to commercialize the bioproduct from lab to industry. The process seems to be quite heterogenous due to the complex requirement of living cells and their prevailed diversity. The commercialization of product various process parameters ingredients and their composition as well as interactions plays pivotal role. There are numerous challenges associated with mathematical modeling and simulations due to multi-parametric nature of biological data. Therefore, applications of ML methods have shown promising potential in tackling complex problems of bio-production at large scale. ML algorithms are categorized into four different learning categories, namely, supervised learning, unsupervised learning, semi-supervised learning, and reinforcement learning. This classification is based on configuration of various data set based on different problems on which ML algorithm will develop mathematical correlation to build a model followed by the solution of the defined problem. With rising technological advancements computational tools generate voluminous data of biological origin therefore past decade has seen massive growth of various algorithms of ML in the arena of development and manufacturing of bioproducts. The contribution of various ML algorithms in the arena of bioproduct development has been summarized in Fig. 3.2.

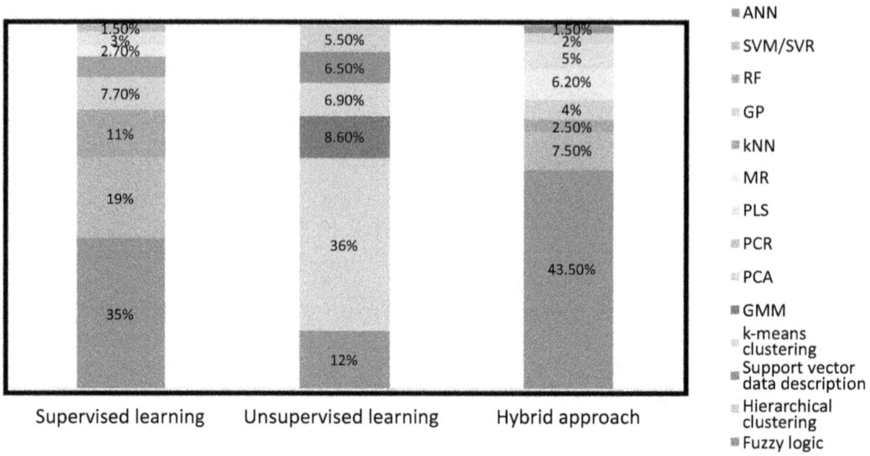

Fig. 3.2 Statistical coverage of various machine learning algorithms in bioprocess engineering

3 Why Machine Learning Strategies Are Needed in Bioprocess Engineering

The essence of bioprocess engineering is the scale-up of cellular factories for the overproduction of commercial metabolites. The scale-up is a multistep method commencing the fermentation and optimization of cells from bench scale (~250 mL–5 L) to pilot scale (~20–200 L) to industrial-scale processes (>1000 L). The fermentation of cells at a larger scale is considered to be a complex and multi-parametric process, in which different process variables, such as pH, temperature, aeration rate, media composition, mixing regime, fermentation time, and feed rate, is affecting the cell growth, product formation, and host cell physiology. Therefore, at industrial scale, the fermentation process is unpredictable; therefore, the central task of scale-up is to fine-tune all these process variables to perform the stable and robust production of desired bioproducts, because the slight change in any process variables confers significant impact on the overall productivity of cells [9, 10]. Thus, scale-up is a time-consuming and costly process; therefore, the industry needs advanced computational scientific methods for accelerating the fermentation process in bioreactors beyond the classical methods. The advent of automation, sensors for controlling, and monitoring the process parameters, comprehensive data collection, and archiving revolutionize the modern fermentation process [11]. Therefore, these huge data can be leveraged for various machine learning algorithms for better prediction, finding the bioprocess failure points, and improving the process outcomes in lieu of better product yield. However, the main bottlenecks of bioprocess data constituting heterogeneity in terms of collection of both online pH, oxygen uptake rate, dissolved oxygen, optical (cell) density, flow rate, off-gas production, etc.) and offline data (various metabolite concentrations, substrate consumption rates). Apart from that, certain data are binary or categorical

(ON/OFF nutrient feed setting), and some data such as the concentration of product has been collected at the final time point. The high variability in data sets with respect to fermentation time and fermentation runs necessitates the preprocessing of data for extracting temporal trends for training into machine learning premises [12, 13].

The research studies reported various preprocessing methods, such as wavelet decomposition methods [14], mean envelope filter methods, vector casting method [15], and Fourier transform and symbolic aggregate approximation (SAX) method, that represents temporal data profile as representative segments for the analysis through machine learning approaches [16]. Initially, decision trees, ANN, and genetic algorithm-based ML were applied for fermentative modeling and identification of optimum input variables by analyzing the data of 69 fed-batch fermentation for predicting the process output, including product concentration, biomass density, and volumetric productivity [17]. Similarly, ANN-based modeling followed by optimization through a genetic algorithm was reported for the production of xylitol. The predictive models for xylose consumption, biomass concentration, and xylitol production were based on analyzing the data of 27 fermentation batches with multiple inputs, and the product titer was enhanced from 59.4 to 65.7 g/L [18]. More recently, the advancement in bioreactor designing enables the generation of continuous online data that is being used for the optimum control and optimization of bioprocess by reinforcement learning. However, this method suffered the limitation of being built on fixed models while requiring continuous updates and improvement with respect to surplus data generation in automated fermentation systems [19]. Therefore, to improvise model-free reinforcement, learning methods have been developed and successfully applied for controlling final ethanol titers during yeast fermentations. Moreover, these methods have been instrumental in controlling coculture species biomass abundances, controlling reactor temperatures [20], optimizing product yields [21], and optimizing a downstream product separation unit [22]. However, the requirement of a large amount of data limits its wider utilization, but there is still a scope of improvement by seeing the marvelous credentials of ML approaches [23]. Thus, despite current challenges, the data of various fermentation systems gives an appealing opportunity to develop various ML algorithms for finding the most appropriate process conditions.

4 Applications of Machine Learning in Bioprocess Engineering (Case Studies)

Approaches of Machine Learning in Biorefinery: A Case Study

The rising demand of environmental pollution, reduction in fossil fuels, and increasing ecosystem resilience paved the way for finding various avenues for renewable energy sources. Among various sources, lignocellulosic biomass is offering the most promising feedstock for the development of the bioenergy paradigm. Though bioethanol and biodiesel are the most preferentially utilized product from the lignocellulosic biomass, the compositional variability among various biomass sources offers a diverse array of products that leads to the conception of multiproduct biorefinery [24]. The major operational bottleneck of the biorefinery is the natural heterogeneity and spatial variability of biomass. Recently, machine learning and data analytics has been envisaged as a prospective tool for predicting this biomass variability and easing the way of standardization of biomass properties that leads to the consistency in the biorefining process. Though advanced sophisticated analytical techniques, such as rapid near-infrared (NIR) spectroscopy and hyperspectral imaging, have been used for predicting the chemical composition of the biomass and its conversion performances, these techniques are unable to correlate a large amount of data and higher complexity of biomass [25]. Thus, a machine learning framework based on an ANN has been recently implied for correlating biomass chemical composition and their conversion performances and finding a correlation of physical properties of tissue powders along with handling and grinding performances [26]. It is envisioned that the predictive models will be used to produce conversion ready and highly flowable feedstock and provide decision centric view to researchers and multiple stakeholders. More recently, machine learning approaches, such as random forest, artificial neural networks (ANNs), and classification trees (CTs), have been used for alleviating one of the critical bottlenecks for bioethanol production that is enzymatic hydrolysis. The simultaneous saccharification and fermentation (SSF) process posit a prominent and feasible strategy for reducing the capital cost for the production of bioethanol from lignocellulosic biomass [29].

Thus, ML approaches have been used for visualizing the effects of time, temperature, inoculum size, and biomass on bioethanol fermentation in SSF.

ANN Based Model

An ANN-based model is used for predicting the yield of bioethanol by implementing three layers of data sets and finding optimum conditions using R software and AMORE library (http://cran.r-project.org/web/packages/AMORE/). The coefficient of determination (R) [2], reduction of root mean squared error (RMSE), and absolute average deviation (AAD) have been calculated by Eqs. (3.1), (3.2), and (3.3), respectively.

$$R^2 = 1 - \frac{\sum_{i=1}^{n}\left(Y_i^{\text{calc}} - Y_i^{\text{exp}}\right)^2}{\sum_{i=1}^{n}\left(Y_i^{\text{calc}} - Y_m\right)^2}, \tag{3.1}$$

$$\text{RMSE} = \left[\frac{1}{n}\sum_{i=1}^{n}\left(Y_i^{\text{calc}} - Y_i^{\text{exp}}\right)^2\right]^{\frac{1}{2}} = \sqrt{\text{MSE}}, \tag{3.2}$$

$$\mathrm{AAD} = \frac{1}{n}\sum\left|\frac{Y_i^{\mathrm{calc}} - Y_i^{\mathrm{calc}}}{Y_i^{\mathrm{calc}}}\right|, \tag{3.3}$$

where n = number of points, Y_i^{calc} = predicted value, Y_i^{exp} = experimental value, Y_m = average value of all experimental data, and MSE = mean square error.

Based on these equations, the optimal ethanol concentration and the optimal ethanol conversion value were found that lead to the determination of optimal volumetric productivity of ethanol by Eq. (3.4) [27],

$$I_j = \frac{\sum \frac{|W_{jm}^{ih}|}{\sum |W_{km}^{ih}|} \cdot |W_{mn}^{hO}|}{\sum\sum \frac{|W_{km}^{ih}|}{\sum |W_{km}^{ih}|} \cdot |W_{mn}^{hO}|}, \tag{3.4}$$

where I_j = relative importance of jth input variable on the ethanol conc.; N_{i} and N_{h} = number of input and hidden neurons, respectively; W_{s} = connection weights; subscripts i, h, and O refer to input, hidden, and output layers, respectively; and subscripts k, m, and n represent input, hidden, and output neurons, respectively.

Random Forest Model

This model has been used for predicting the effects of variables in SSF using the library of R language [28]. A total of 1000 RFs comprising different numbers of trees and variables in each of the branches has been assessed. The assessment of the optimal RF model was performed using two rando data sets having 2/3 for training and 1/3 for test, and the values of R[2], RMSE, and AAD have been calculated [29].

Classification Tress-Based Model

This model has been used for making decisions based on the entropy of the process. The current study includes the C5.0 script that has been used by utilizing the default library of R (http://cran.r-project.org/web/packages/C50/) for predicting the concentration of ethanol [29].

Thus, by the above discussion, it has been clearly seen that ML methodologies have tremendous potential to evaluate the various process parameters for bioethanol production without prior knowledge of kinetics and inhibition process. An overview of applications of ML approaches in biorefinery sector has been represented in Fig. 3.3. Thus, in the futuristic scenario, more comprehensive studies have been warranted for overcoming the various technical gaps for the commercialization of biorefineries.

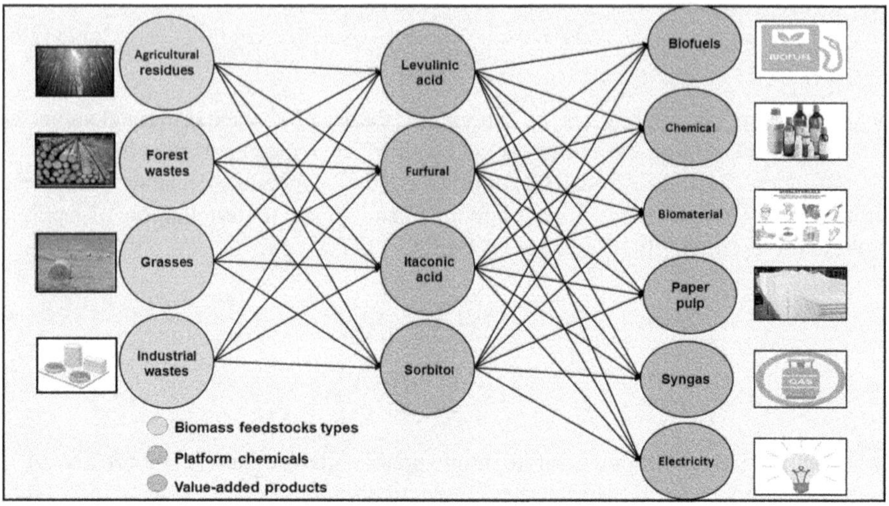

Fig. 3.3 An overview of applications of machine learning approaches in biorefinery

Approaches of Machine Learning in Monoclonal Antibody Production: A Case Study

The past decade has seen a stupendous ride in the production of biotherapeutics, more preferably monoclonal antibodies, for the treatment of a variety of chronic disorders like cancers and autoimmune and inflammatory diseases [30]. This continuous surge has been attributed to higher efficacy, specificity, reduced toxicity, and less side effects conferred by monoclonal antibodies. Apart from that, the production of monoclonal antibodies is considered to be a costly, time-consuming, and fastidious endeavor due to the requirement of the high standards and stability during production, storage, and transportation [31–34]. Due to the proteinaceous nature, these antibodies always remain susceptible to various physical and chemical degradation pathways with varied conditions encountered during the whole life cycle [35, 36]. Thus, there is a pressing need to overcome these challenges for the sustainable production of this important class of biotherapeutics. There are various avenues from the design and prediction of antigen specificity of monoclonal antibodies to the prediction of various liquid formulations for effective delivery of these compounds inside the body in which various domains of machine learning have been used. Recently, the structure-based deep learning for antibodies (DLAB) database has been developed for virtual screening and prediction of putative binding of antibodies against antigen as a target [37]. Based on this database, Reddy et al. reported the prediction of antigen specificity of therapeutic antibody trastuzumab against human epidermal growth factor receptor 2 (HER2) as an antigen. The studies involved the screening of thousands of lead molecules by analyzing 1×108

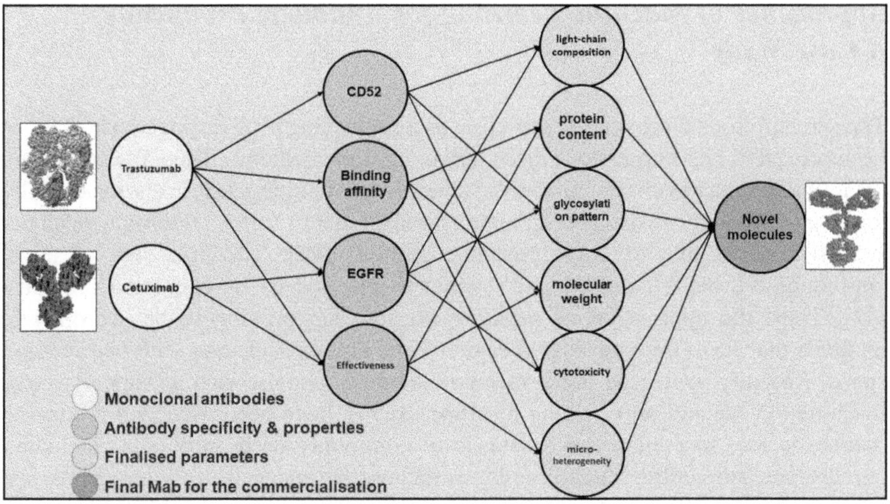

Fig. 3.4 Use of machine learning methods in commercial production of monoclonal antibodies

trastuzumab variants against 1 × 106 variants of HER2 based on viscosity, solubility, clearance, and immunogenicity [38]. Similarly, more comprehensive studies related to the determination of molecular descriptors affecting the viscosity of monoclonal antibodies have been reported by Trout et al. A decision tree-based machine learning framework has been used for predicting the net charge and high viscosity index of monoclonal antibodies [39].

That studies significantly contribute for the assessment of rheological behavior that affects the delivery of these therapeutic molecules. More recently, a Bayesian optimization algorithm has been developed for the screening of formulations of mAbs. The formulation comprises various excipients such as thermal stabilizers, amino acids buffering agents, surfactants and tonicity modifiers that imparts a significant effect on the stability of proteins and their storage [40]. Thus, this approach of ML leads to the acceleration in the design of formulations with optimum excipients and parallelization of operations in mAbs development. Figure 3.4 is representing the applications of ML algorithms in monoclonal antibody manufacturing.

Thus, based on the above discussion, it is conceivable to comprehend that ML approaches provide a novel, innovative, and accelerated platform for the discovery, development, and manufacturing of monoclonal antibodies and can be used for other biotherapeutics.

Approaches of Machine Learning for Antibiotic Production: A Case Study

The serendipitous discovery of penicillin as a life-saving drug during world war has been proved to be a cornerstone discovery in modern medicine. Then, the golden era of antibiotics has been visualized, but their overwhelming use leads to a deadly menace of antibiotic resistance, and it is estimated that by 2050, 10 million death per year will occur due to drug resistance diseases [41]. The discovery of novel antibiotics is from a natural source, which is plagued by dereplication problems [42]. Thus, the approaches of machine learning are proving to be eye-opening methods that have the capacity to search large amounts of data with accelerating speed. Recently, genotype-based machine learning models, such as support vector machine (SVM) and set covering machine (SCM), have been used as a promising diagnostic tool to predict the resistance of commonly used antibiotics, including tetracycline, ampicillin, sulfisoxazole, trimethoprim, and enrofloxacin, against the whole genome of 96 isolates of *Actinobacillus pleuropneumoniae* [43]. Moreover, halicin molecule was identified through the screening of 6000 chemical compounds that not only have the potency to treat diabetes but also found to exhibit strong activity against *Mycobacterium tuberculosis* and other hard-to-treat microbes [44]. ML is not only to accelerate the discovery of novel antibiotics, but different algorithms can be helpful for predicting the susceptibility towards antibiotics. Figure 3.5 represents the role of ML in antibiotic discovery for finding novel antimicrobials. Recently, the single centric study was performed to assess the eight algorithms of ML for predicting the resistance toward antimicrobials by taking

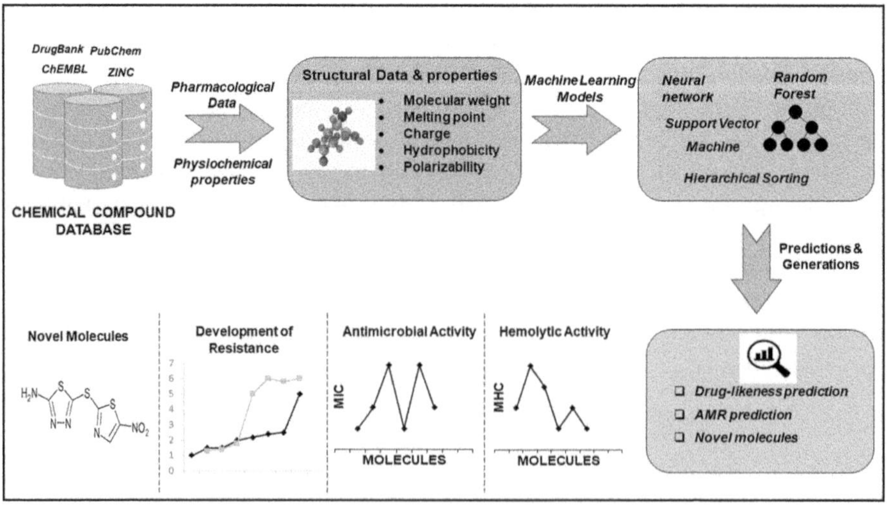

Fig. 3.5 Applications of machine learning methods in antibiotic production

demographic data from patients, gram staining, and site of infection [45]. These studies will be helpful for clinicians in the selection of appropriate antibiotic therapy. Thus, in the future ML holds tremendous potential to alleviate the global threat of antibiotic resistance and is helpful in maintaining the stewardship of antibiotics.

Machine Learning in Protein Engineering: A Case Study

The continuous surge in the production of bioproducts needs sustainable bioprocessing portfolios. The development of industrial strains requires a thorough understanding of genome organization, cellular metabolism, and enzymes. The overproduction of various products requires engineering of their biosynthetic pathway and enzymes that are still unknown to the scientific community. Thus, the development of novel biosynthetic pathways and the engineering of enzymes can spur the overproduction of industrially important metabolites. Recently, catalytic turnover (K_{cat}) of enzymes has been evaluated in *E. coli* through machine learning approaches. The diverse properties of enzymes, such as structural properties, network properties, assay conditions, and biochemical mechanism information, have been considered for generating ML models. This in vivo and in vitro prediction of K*cat* will be helpful for implementing the information of genome-scale metabolic models for correlating the expression of the proteome in *E. coli.* [46] Furthermore, the scope of substrate specificity of enzymes has also been predicted with ML models. Four machine learning models, along with molecular modeling and docking tools, namely, support vector machines, random forest, logistic regression, and gradient-boosted decision trees, have been developed for evaluating the substrate specificity of bacterial nitrilases that hydrolyzed the nitrile compounds to the corresponding carboxylic acids and ammonia. The accuracy of substrate prediction leads to a better catalytic activity of enzymes that facilitates the overproduction of metabolites [47]. Recently, the affinities of protein-ligand binding have been performed with deep learning ML models, including three-dimensional (3D)-convolutional neural networks (3D-CNNs), spatial graph neural networks (SG-CNNs), and their fusion models. These models predicted the binding free energies based on docking pose coordinates, docking scores, and molecular mechanic/generalized Born surface area (MM/GBSA) calculations. [48]. An overview of the utilization of ML methods in the realm of protein engineering has been summarized in Fig. 3.6. These studies will be playing a pivotal role in the drug discovery paradigm. Thus, based on the above discussion, enzyme engineering is the backbone in improving the bioprocess design and development and fosters the path for sustainable biomanufacturing.

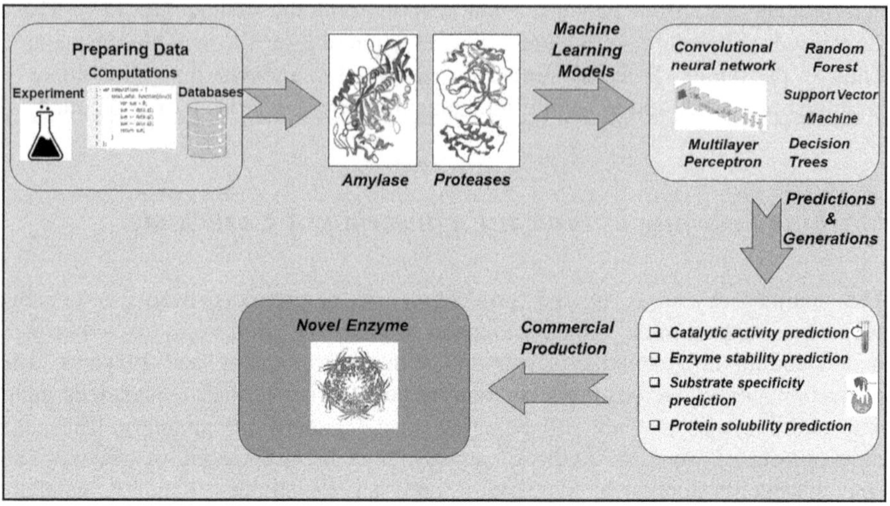

Fig. 3.6 An overview of applications of machine learning methods in protein engineering

5 Current Challenges and Future Prospects

The world is moving toward digitalization and bioproduct development, and manufacturing is no longer the exception for adoption of advanced technologies. Though machine learning methodologies have proven their mettle in other sectors in an efficient manner, biomanufacturing sector is still reluctant to adopt ML as the standardized tool for the development of bioprocess. The skepticism related to catastrophic consequences of defective products inhibited their wider adoption. There are technological challenges such as lack of representative datasets for development, eating, and validation of model limits their operability at commercial scale. The uncertainty of prediction due to the multi-parametric nature of biological data confers additional roadblock for the acceptance. The complexity of models further limits their correlation analysis with biological process. Inspite of these challenges, rising technological innovations in ML and computing will definitely overcome these challenges, and it is clearly envisioned that the ML approaches hold a bright future in upscaling the development of bioproducts through process engineering approaches.

6 Conclusion

Machine learning not only transformed the scientific paradigm but also leads to a gigantic leap in the productivity of industrial manufacturing. The digitalization accompanied with machine learning approaches creates novel history in the biomanufacturing too. The various approaches such as unsupervised and supervised models both are quite useful in various facets from process development to purification of bioproducts from living cells. The present chapter entails the current application of ML in various bioproducts and their commercial manufacturing through process engineering principles. The chapter represents various case studies of diversified bioproducts portfolios from high value to low value. The immersive applications of ML proved its utility in reducing the cost and time of industry that is considered to be a major economic consideration. The road of utilizing ML is not smooth currently, but in future, the vision of using these concepts for bringing the transformations in bioprocess engineering sector is certainly on horizon.

Acknowledgment The authors greatly endorsed the support of Gautam Buddha University for writing this chapter.

Conflicts of Interest/Competing Interests Authors declare that there is no conflict of interest in this work.

Glossary

Antibiotics	It is a class of antimicrobial substances that are used to kill infectious bacteria.
Antibiotic resistance	It is the type of resistance that is developed by microorganism against the effect of an antibiotic.
Biomanufacturing	It is a type of industrial production that utilizes biological systems to create commercially-important bioproducts.
Bioprocess engineering	A bioprocess is any method that uses living cells or their elements (e.g., enzymes, chloroplasts) to produce a product, whereas engineering is the science of coming up with complex machines or processes.
Bioreactor	It is an apparatus used to grow microorganisms in a controlled environment.
Docking	It is a tool for predicting the interaction, conformation, and orientation of a ligand in binding site of protein.
Entropy	It is a measurable property that is associated with the degree of randomness of a system.
Fermentation	Fermentation is the process by which molecules such as glucose are broken down into a simpler substance.
Hyperspectral imaging	It is a spectroscopic technique that captures and processes an image at very large number of wavelengths.
Monoclonal antibodies	These are laboratory-made proteins that can be used as substitutes for antibodies to enhance or modify the immune system.

Near-infrared spectroscopy	It is a spectroscopic technique that deals with the electromagnetic spectrum within the near-infrared area (780–2500 nm).
Protein engineering	It is the method of developing novel proteins with desired properties.
Scale-up	It is the process of increasing the scale of fermentation.
Scale-down	It is the process of decreasing the scale of fermentation.
Simultaneous saccharification and fermentation	It is a procedure that mixes enzymatic hydrolysis with fermentation to gain value-added products in an individual step.
Surfactants	These are the chemical compounds that are used to lower down the surface tension between two phases.
Synthetic biology	It is a multidisciplinary research area that involves engineering of organisms for producing novel useful substances.
Tonicity	It is the potential of a solution to change the water content surrounding the cell.
Viscosity	It is a measure of resistance of a fluid toward deformation by shear stress.

References

1. Gao, S., Song, W., Guo, M.: The integral role of bioproducts in the growing bioeconomy. Ind. Biotechnol. **16**(1), 13–25 (2020)
2. Petrides, D.: Bioprocess design and economics. Bioseparat. Sci. Eng., 1–83 (2000)
3. Chavan, S., Yadav, B., Atmakuri, A., Tyagi, R.D., Wong, J.W., Drogui, P.: Bioconversion of organic wastes into value-added products: a review. Bioresour. Technol. **344**, 126398 (2022)
4. Mears, L., Stocks, S.M., Albaek, M.O., Sin, G., Gernaey, K.V.: Mechanistic fermentation models for process design, monitoring, and control. Trends Biotechnol. **35**(10), 914–924 (2017)
5. Sakthiselvan, P., Meenambiga, S.S., Madhumathi, R.: Kinetic studies on cell growth. Cell Growth. **13** (2019)
6. Brooks, S.M., Alper, H.S.: Applications, challenges, and needs for employing synthetic biology beyond the lab. Nat. Commun. **12**(1), 1–16 (2021)
7. Montáns, F.J., Chinesta, F., Gómez-Bombarelli, R., Kutz, J.N.: Data-driven modeling and learning in science and engineering. Comptes Rendus Mécanique. **347**(11), 845–855 (2019)
8. Mowbray, M., Savage, T., Wu, C., Song, Z., Cho, B.A., Del Rio-Chanona, E.A., Zhang, D.: Machine learning for biochemical engineering: a review. Biochem. Eng. J. **172**, 108054 (2021)
9. Crater, J.S., Lievense, J.C.: Scale-up of industrial microbial processes. FEMS Microbiol. Lett. **365**(13), fny138 (2018)
10. Humphrey, A.: Shake flask to fermentor: what have we learned? Biotechnol. Prog. **14**(1), 3–7 (1998)
11. Carbonell, P., Radivojevic, T., Garcia Martin, H.: Opportunities at the intersection of synthetic biology, machine learning, and automation. ACS Synth. Biol. **8**(7), 1474–1477 (2019)
12. Cheung, J.Y., Stephanopoulos, G.: Representation of process trends—Part I. A formal representation framework. Comput. Chem. Eng. **14**(4–5, 495), –510 (1990a)
13. Cheung, J.Y., Stephanopoulos, G.: Representation of process trends—Part II. The problem of scale and qualitative scaling. Comput. Chem. Eng. **14**(4–5), 511–539 (1990b)

14. Bakshi, B.R., Stephanopoulos, G.: Representation of process trends—III. Multiscale extraction of trends from process data. Comput. Chem. Eng. **18**(4), 267–302 (1994)
15. Gebrekidan, M.T., Knipfer, C., Braeuer, A.S.: Vector casting for noise reduction. J. Raman Spectrosc. **51**(4), 731–743 (2020)
16. Charaniya, S., Hu, W.S., Karypis, G.: Mining bioprocess data: opportunities and challenges. Trends Biotechnol. **26**(12), 690–699 (2008)
17. Coleman, M.C., Buck, K.K., Block, D.E.: An integrated approach to optimization of Escherichia coli fermentations using historical data. Biotechnol. Bioeng. **84**(3), 274–285 (2003)
18. Pappu, S.M.J., Gummadi, S.N.: Artificial neural network and regression coupled genetic algorithm to optimize parameters for enhanced xylitol production by Debaryomyces nepalensis in bioreactor. Biochem. Eng. J. **120**, 136–145 (2017)
19. Qin, S.J., Badgwell, T.A.: MPC. 4th generation. MPC. Fig. 1 Approximate genealogy of linear MPC algorithms. Control. Eng. Pract. **11**, 733–764 (2003)
20. Xie, H., Xu, X., Li, Y., Hong, W., Shi, J.: Model predictive control guided reinforcement learning control scheme. In: 2020 International Joint Conference on Neural Networks (IJCNN), pp. 1–8. IEEE (2020)
21. Treloar, N.J., Fedorec, A.J., Ingalls, B., Barnes, C.P.: Deep reinforcement learning for the control of microbial co-cultures in bioreactors. PLoS Comput. Biol. **16**(4), e1007783 (2020)
22. Hwangbo, S., Sin, G.: Design of control framework based on deep reinforcement learning and monte-carlo sampling in downstream separation. Comput. Chem. Eng. **140**, 106910 (2020)
23. Shin, J., Badgwell, T.A., Liu, K.H., Lee, J.H.: Reinforcement learning–overview of recent progress and implications for process control. Comput. Chem. Eng. **127**, 282–294 (2019)
24. Ulonska, K., König, A., Klatt, M., Mitsos, A., Viell, J.: Optimization of multiproduct biorefinery processes under consideration of biomass supply chain management and market developments. Ind. Eng. Chem. Res. **57**(20), 6980–6991 (2018)
25. Schimleck, L., Dahlen, J., Yoon, S.C., Lawrence, K.C., Jones, P.D.: Prediction of Douglas-fir lumber properties: Comparison between a benchtop near-infrared spectrometer and hyperspectral imaging system. Appl. Sci. **8**(12), 2602 (2018)
26. Ighalo, J.O., Adeniyi, A.G., Marques, G.: Application of artificial neural networks in predicting biomass higher heating value: an early appraisal. Energy Sources. **10**(5), 933–944 (2020)
27. Garson, D.G.: Interpreting neural network connection weights. AI Expert. **6**(4), 46–51 (1991)
28. Breiman, L.: Random forests. Machine learning. J. Biomed. Sci. Eng. **45**(1), 5–32 (2001)
29. Fischer, J., Lopes, V.S., Cardoso, S.L., Coutinho, U., Cardoso, V.L.: Machine learning techniques applied to lignocellulosic ethanol in simultaneous hydrolysis and fermentation. Braz. J. Chem. Eng. **34**, 53–63 (2017)
30. Walsh, G.: Biopharmaceutical benchmarks 2018. Nat. Biotechnol. **36**(12), 1136–1145 (2018)
31. Elgundi, Z., Reslan, M., Cruz, E., Sifniotis, V., Kayser, V.: The state-of-play and future of antibody therapeutics. Adv. Drug Deliv. Rev. **122**, 2–19 (2017)
32. Chi, E.Y., Krishnan, S., Randolph, T.W., Carpenter, J.F.: Physical stability of proteins in aqueous solution: mechanism and driving forces in nonnative protein aggregation. Pharm. Res. **20**(9), 1325–1336 (2003)
33. Randolph, T.W., Carpenter, J.F.: Engineering challenges of protein formulations. AICHE J. **53**(8), 1902–1907 (2007)
34. Gentiluomo, L., Svilenov, H.L., Augustijn, D., El Bialy, I., Greco, M.L., Kulakova, A., Indrakumar, S., Mahapatra, S., Morales, M.M., Pohl, C., Roche, A.: Advancing therapeutic protein discovery and development through comprehensive computational and biophysical characterization. Mol. Pharm. **17**(2), 426–440 (2019)
35. Krause, M.E., Sahin, E.: Chemical and physical instabilities in manufacturing and storage of therapeutic proteins. Curr. Opin. Biotechnol. **60**, 159–167 (2019)
36. Jiskoot, W., Randolph, T.W., Volkin, D.B., Middaugh, C.R., Schöneich, C., Winter, G., Friess, W., Crommelin, D.J., Carpenter, J.F.: Protein instability and immunogenicity: roadblocks to clinical application of injectable protein delivery systems for sustained release. J. Pharm. Sci. **101**(3), 946–954 (2012)

37. Schneider, C., Buchanan, A., Taddese, B., Deane, C.M.: DLAB: deep learning methods for structure-based virtual screening of antibodies. Bioinformatics. **38**(2), 377–383 (2022)
38. Mason, D.M., Friedensohn, S., Weber, C.R., Jordi, C., Wagner, B., Meng, S.M., Ehling, R.A., Bonati, L., Dahinden, J., Gainza, P., Correia, B.E.: Optimization of therapeutic antibodies by predicting antigen specificity from antibody sequence via deep learning. Nature Biomed. Eng. **5**(6), 600–612 (2021)
39. Lai, P.K., Fernando, A., Cloutier, T.K., Gokarn, Y., Zhang, J., Schwenger, W., Chari, R., Calero-Rubio, C., Trout, B.L.: Machine learning applied to determine the molecular descriptors responsible for the viscosity behavior of concentrated therapeutic antibodies. Mol. Pharm. **18**(3), 1167–1175 (2021)
40. Narayanan, H., Dingfelder, F., Condado Morales, I., Patel, B., Heding, K.E., Bjelke, J.R., Egebjerg, T., Butté, A., Sokolov, M., Lorenzen, N., Arosio, P.: Design of biopharmaceutical formulations accelerated by machine learning. Mol. Pharm. **18**(10), 3843–3853 (2021)
41. O'Neill, J.: Antimicrobial resistance: tackling a crisis for the health and wealth of nations. Rev. Antimicrob. Resist. **2014**(4), 1–20 (2014)
42. Cox, G., Sieron, A., King, A.M., De Pascale, G., Pawlowski, A.C., Koteva, K., Wright, G.D.: A common platform for antibiotic dereplication and adjuvant discovery. Cell Chem. Biol. **24**(1), 98–109 (2017)
43. Liu, Z., Deng, D., Lu, H., Sun, J., Lv, L., Li, S., Peng, G., Ma, X., Li, J., Li, Z., Rong, T.: Evaluation of machine learning models for predicting antimicrobial resistance of Actinobacillus pleuropneumoniae from whole genome sequences. Front. Microbiol. **11**, 48 (2020)
44. Stokes, J.M., Yang, K., Swanson, K., Jin, W., Cubillos-Ruiz, A., Donghia, N.M., MacNair, C. R., French, S., Carfrae, L.A., Bloom-Ackermann, Z., Tran, V.M.: A deep learning approach to antibiotic discovery. Cell. **180**(4), 688–702 (2020)
45. Feretzakis, G., Loupelis, E., Sakagianni, A., Kalles, D., Martsoukou, M., Lada, M., Skarmoutsou, N., Christopoulos, C., Valakis, K., Velentza, A., Petropoulou, S.: Using machine learning techniques to aid empirical antibiotic therapy decisions in the intensive care unit of a general hospital in Greece. Antibiotics. **9**(2), 50 (2020)
46. Heckmann, D., Lloyd, C.J., Mih, N., Ha, Y., Zielinski, D.C., Haiman, Z.B., Desouki, A.A., Lercher, M.J., Palsson, B.O.: Machine learning applied to enzyme turnover numbers reveals protein structural correlates and improves metabolic models. Nat. Commun. **9**(1), 1–10 (2018)
47. Mou, Z., Eakes, J., Cooper, C.J., Foster, C.M., Standaert, R.F., Podar, M., Doktycz, M.J., Parks, J.M.: Machine learning-based prediction of enzyme substrate scope: application to bacterial nitrilases. Proteins Struct. Funct. Bioinf. **89**(3), 336–347 (2021)
48. Jones, D., Kim, H., Zhang, X., Zemla, A., Stevenson, G., Bennett, W.D., Kirshner, D., Wong, S. E., Lightstone, F.C., Allen, J.E.: Improved protein–ligand binding affinity prediction with structure-based deep fusion inference. J. Chem. Inf. Model. **61**(4), 1583–1592 (2021)

Chapter 4
Advanced Selection Operation for Differential Evolution Algorithm

Pravesh Kumar and Vanita Garg

1 Introduction

The term optimization refers to the process of identifying the most viable solution and thereby reaching the extreme point of the objective functions. The goal of identifying these optimal solutions is typically to design a problem to minimize total cost or to maximize probable reliability, among other things. Because of the high quality of optimal solutions, we place a high value on optimization approaches in scientific, engineering, and business decision-making situations. We can divide optimization approaches into two categories: classic and nontraditional methods.

Traditional methods may not be able to solve such issues due to the presence of nonlinearity, non-continuity, non-differentiability, and many local/global optimums.

Recently, many nature-inspired and evolutionary algorithms have been created to handle optimization challenges.

Genetic algorithms, ant colonies, particle swarm optimization, differential evolution algorithm, artificial bee colony, teaching learning-based algorithm, Jaya algorithms, and firefly algorithms are some of the most common algorithms in use today.

Biogeography-based optimization algorithm also comes in the category of nature-inspired algorithms. Garg and Deep have proposed LX-BBO in [47]. LX-BBO is extended for solving constrained optimization problems in [49]. The same algorithm is proposed after applying mutation strategies in [48].

Differential evolution (DE) algorithm was introduced by Storn and Price in 1997 [1]. It is a prominent, stochastic, and population-based optimization algorithm, where the population consists of many individuals, each of which represents a potential solution to the optimization problem. DE produces offspring solution by

P. Kumar
Rajkiya Engineering College Bijnor (AKTU Lucknow), Lucknow, Uttar Pradesh, India

V. Garg (✉)
Galgotias University, Greater Noida, Uttar Pradesh, India

© The Author(s), under exclusive license to Springer Nature Switzerland AG 2022

D. Singh et al. (eds.), *Design and Applications of Nature Inspired Optimization*, Women in Engineering and Science, https://doi.org/10.1007/978-3-031-17929-7_4

mutation, crossover, and selection operation, which are likely to be nearer to the optimal result.

A few of the advantages that DE has over other nature-inspired algorithms are that it is compact, has a small number of control parameters, and is easy to implement without requiring any special knowledge. Some of its more advanced capabilities include the capacity to handle nonlinear, discontinuous, non-differentiable, and multi-objective functions, among other aspects. Engineers and scientists have successfully used DE to solve a wide range of real-world problems in the engineering and science fields. Examples include the following: engineering design difficulties, pattern identification, power engineering, image processing, and noise detection.

Premature convergence or evolution stagnation, which is fatal to an algorithm that relies on population difference, is inevitable as the number of generations increases in a population. Control settings affect DE's performance as well [2]. In order to find the optimal value for these control parameters for various optimization problems, several trials must be performed.

A few of the modified variants of DE during recent years are as follows: trigonometric mutation-based DE (TDE) [3], fuzzy adaptive DE (FADE) [4], modified differential evolution (MDE) [5], DE with random localization (DERL) [6], self-adapting control parameter-based DE (jDE) [7], opposition-based DE (ODE) [8], accelerating differential evolution [9], mixed mutation strategy embedded DE [10], self-adaptive DE (SADE) [11], adaptive DE with optional external archive (JADE) [12], DE with neighborhood mutation [13], DE with Cauchy mutation (CDE) [14], clustering-based DE (CDE-Cai) [15], learning enhanced DE (LeDE) [16], DE with proximity-based mutation [17], enhanced mutation strategy (MRLDE) [18], DE with adaptive population tuning scheme [19], DE with dynamic parameters selection [20], control parameter and mutation-based DE (CDE) [21], multiple mutation strategies-based DE [22], multi-population-based DE [23], collective information-based DE [24], adaptive learning mechanism-based DE [25], novel DE for constrained [26], parameter adaptation schemes for DE (PaDE) [27], random perturbation modified DE [28], DE with dual preferred learning mutation [29], DE with neighborhood-based adaptive evolution mechanism [30], self-adaptive mutation DE with PSO [31], parameter adaptive-based DE [32], DE with adaptive multi-population inflationary [33], and dual-strategy-based DE (IDE) [34].

A well-prepared literature review of enhancement and applications of differential evolution algorithm can also be found in [35–38, 46].

In this chapter, a novel modification in selection operation for DE named "DE with advanced selection operator (DEaS)" is proposed. DEaS works in two ways: first, it reuses the rejected trial vectors by their superiority, and second, it operates selection operation in a single array strategy proposed by Babu and Angira in MDE [5].

Furthermore, this newly proposed selection operation is integrated with two other DE-enhanced variants such as DERL [6] and MRLDE [18] and named it DERLaS and MRLDEaS, respectively. The evaluation of proposed modifications has executed on benchmark problems as well as real-life applications. The numerical and statistical significance of proposed variants is discussed later in the chapter. Here, we would also like to mention that this work is an extended version of our previous studies carried out in [39, 40].

Organization of the chapter is as follows: The introduction of basic DE algorithm is given in Sect. 2. The proposed advanced selection operation and functioning of DERLaS and MRLDEaS are explained in Sect. 3. In Sect. 4, benchmark functions, real-life applications, and experimental settings are given.

The results and comparison of the algorithms is given in detail in Sect. 5, and the chapter is finally concluded in Sect. 6 with its future scope.

2 Basic Differential Evolution (DE)

In this section, the basic concept and working of differential evolution algorithm (DE/rand/1/bin) is illustrated. DE works in four steps, such as initialization, mutation, crossover, and selection operation, for which the details are presented as below:

(i) *Initialization Phase*: The first phase of DE algorithm is to initialize a uniform random set of solutions called population. Here, each solution is a d-dimensional vector also called an individual. Equation 4.1 generate the initial population $Pop= \{ P_i^{(gen)}, i=1,2,...N\}$ *of* d-dimensional N vectors.

$$P_i^{(0)} = P_{LB} + rand\,(0,\,1) \times [P_{UB} - P_{LB}] \tag{4.1}$$

Here:

- *rand (0, 1)* is the uniform random number between 0 and 1
- P_{UB} and P_{LB} are the upper and lower bound, respectively, of search space.

(ii) *Mutation Phase*: To perform the mutation operation, three mutually separate vectors, say $P_a^{(gen)}$, $P_b^{(gen)}$, and $P_c^{(gen}$, are selected at random from $Pop= \{P_i^{(gen)}, i=1,2,...N\}$ corresponding to a target vector P_i^{gen}, such that $a \neq b \neq c \neq i$, and then a new vector $M_i^{gen} =(m_{1,i}, m_{2,i}, \ldots, m_{d,i})$, also called mutant or perturbed vector, is generated by Eq. 4.2:

$$M_i^{(gen)} = P_a^{(gen)} + SF \times \left[P_b^{(gen)} - P_c^{(gen)}\right] \tag{4.2}$$

Here:

- SF is the scaling factor and use to controls the amplification of the difference $[P_b^{(gen)} - P_a^{(gen)}]$.
- It may have a value between [0 and 2] to as per suggested by Storn and Price.

(iii) *Crossover Phase*: In crossover operation, a trial vector $T_i^{(gen)} = (t_{1,I}, t_{2,i}, \ldots, t_{d,i})$ is generated corresponding to the target and mutant vector. It is defined in Eq. 4.2:

$$t_{j,i}^{(gen)} = \begin{cases} m_{j,i}^{(gen)}, \ if\ CR < rand_j \forall j = = I_j \\ p_{j,i}^{(gen)} \quad \text{otherwise} \end{cases} \tag{4.3}$$

Here,

- *CR* is the crossover constant having value between 0 and 1.
- $rand_j$ [0, 1] is the uniform random number between 0 and 1.
- I_j : randomly chosen index from 1, 2, …*d*. to make sure that at least one component of trial vector will pick from mutant vector.

(iv) *Selection Phase*: Selection operation is performed at the end of any generation of *DE* and ensures that fitter vector has chosen for next generation between trial vector and target vector. Equation 4.4 describes the selection operation between trail and target vector.

$$P_i^{(gen+1)} = \begin{cases} T_i^{(gen)}, \quad if\ fun\left(T_i^{(gen)}\right) < fun\left(P_i^{(gen)}\right) \\ P_i^{(gen)} \quad \text{otherwise} \end{cases} \tag{4.4}$$

3 Proposed Modification

Advance Selection Strategy

The basic selection technique of DE is based on a tournament selection between trail and target vector. The vector with the lowest fitness value is considered as a winner and goes to next-generation population. Here, it can be noticed that during this type of one-on-one competition, a rejected trial vector may have better fitness value than some other target vectors in the population, but there is no additional feature for such rejected trail vectors to prove their efficiency in the space. Also, every time-rejected trial vector takes up extra space in computer memory and may lead to low computer processor speed. Therefore, some additional inspection measures should be done so that more of these fitted trial vectors can be selected and also reduce extra space in memory. Our proposed advance selection approach offers such additional characteristic to the old selection operation of DE.

In advance selection operation, first we perform the old selection operation by comparing trail and target vector and chose the fittest vector for the next generation.

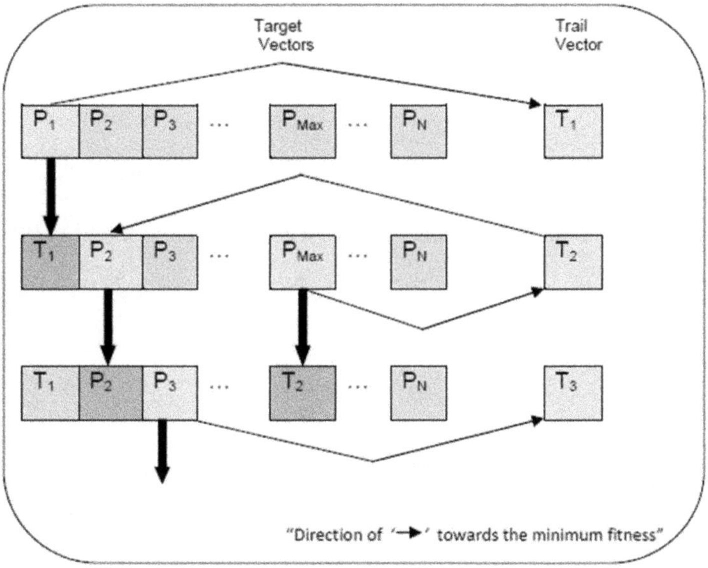

Fig. 4.1 Working design of advance selection operation

In case of rejection of trail vector, it further compares with the worst vector (having highest fitness value) of the population and swap on that place, if it has a lower fitness value than the worst vector. After updating the worst vector, this process will continue for the next trail vector.

Furthermore, a single array strategy proposed by Babu and Angira [5] also has employed with our modified selection technique. The single array strategy helps to reduce the memory space. Consequently, the proposed selection operation compresses the searching region in every generation, and hence it boosts up in the convergence speed to achieve the desire result.

The advance selection operation is demonstrated graphically in Fig. 4.1.

Pseudo Code of DEaS Algorithm

BEGIN

Generate uniformly distributed random population $Pop = \{P_i^{(gen)}, i=1,2,... N\}$.

FOR $i=1:N$

{

$P_i^{(0)} = P_{LB} + rand(0,1)*(P_{UB} - P_{LB})$

}/**END FOR* */

Evaluate $fun\{P_i^{(gen)}\}$

WHILE (Termination criteria is met)

(continued)

```
{
FOR i=1:N
  {
    Execute mutation operation by Eq-2
    Execute crossover operation and generate trial vector T_i^(gen)
    Evaluate fun(T_i^(gen))
//** Advance Selection Operation with Single Array strategy***////
    IF (fun(T_i^(gen))< fun(P_i^(gen)))
       {
    P_i^(gen+1)= T_i^(gen)
    }
  ELSE
{
    IF (fun(T_i^(gen))< fun(P_max^(gen)))
    {
       P_max^(gen)= T_i^(g)
    }
    Update P_max^(gen)
}
    }/* END FOR loop*/
} /* END WHILE loop*/
END
```

Proposed DERLaS and MRLDEaS

In order to verify the effect of proposed advance selection operation on other variants, it has embedded with DERL and MRLDE. A short description of DERL and MRLDE is given as below:

DERL [6]: It is a mutation-based enhanced variants of DE. Here, first three mutually separate vectors are select randomly from the population and then chose the best fitted vector among these three has used as a base vector in the mutation operation. A detail description and its effectiveness of can be read in its original paper [6].

MRLDE [18]: It is our previously proposed DE variant, which is also a mutation-based enhanced variant of DE. In MRLDE, the whole population is divided into three regions, and then the base vector is selected randomly from the region of the best individuals. A details explanation and effectiveness of MRLDE in solving various real-life optimization problems can be study in the literature [41–45].

The pseudo code of proposed DERLas and MRLDEaS is given below:

Pseudo Code of DERLaS and MRLDEaS Algorithm

```
BEGIN
   Generate uniformly distributed random population Pop= {P_i^(g), i=1,2,...
N}.
   WHILE (Termination criteria is met )
   {
   FOR i=1:N
       {
   /*Working of DERLaS*/
       Select three random vectors P_a^(gen), P_b^(gen) and P_c^(gen)
       Select best of P_a^(gen), P_b^(gen) and P_c^(gen) and use as base vector in
mutation
       operation.
   /*Working of MRLDEaS*/
       Divide Population in three sub-regions of N_1,N_2 and N_3 size of best,
medium
       and worst sub-region respectively according fitness.
       Select P_a^(gen), P_b^(gen) and P_c^(gen) from best, medium and worst
sub-region
       respectively.
       Execute Mutation Operation
       Execute crossover operation
       Execute Advance selection operation
          }/* END FOR loop*/
     } /* END WHILE loop*/
   END
```

4 Experimental Settings

In this section, selected benchmark problems, real-life applications, performance criteria, and parameter settings for the evaluation of proposed variants are given.

Test Functions

Fifteen traditional benchmark problems and three real-life applications are selected from the literature to test the effect of the proposed advance selection on DE, DERL, and MRLDE and also the comparison with the other enhanced DE variants. The mathematical models and properties of these are given in Appendix.

Performance Criteria

The following evaluation criterias are taken from various literatures [12, 16, 18], and to evaluate the performance and comparisons of our proposed algorithms

***Number of function evaluation (NFE)*:** The NFEs are obtained when a fixed accuracy (VTR) is attained before reaching the maximum NFE. That is, we set the termination criteria as $|F_{opt} - F_{globqal}| \leq VTR$ and record the average NFE of successful run over 50 runs.

Error: The average and standard deviation of the minimum error $f(P)\text{-}f(P^*)$ is observed after fixed maximum NFEs are attained of 50 runs.

Acceleration rate (AR): It is used to compare the convergence speeds of two algorithms. For two algorithms A and B, AR is defined as follows:

$$AR = \left(1 - \frac{NFE_{\mathrm{B}}}{NFE_{A}}\right)\%$$

Convergence graphs: The convergence graphs demonstrate the performance graphically in terms of fitness value with respect to iteration in any run.

Parameter Setting

In the study, similar parameter settings as per Table 4.1 have been taken for each algorithm for a fair evaluation and comparison.

All experiments are carried out on a computer with 2.66 GHz 10th Gen Intel® Core™ i3, 4GB of RAM, and software Dev-C++ was used to implement the programming.

Table 4.1 Parameter setting [12, 16, 18]

Size of population (N)	100
Dimension (d) for benchmark functions	30
Scale factor (SF) and	0.5
Crossover rate (CR)	0.9
Max NFE	500,000
Size of N_1, N_2, and N_3 for MRLDE and MRLDEaS	20%, 40%, and 40%, respectively
Total run	50

5 Result and Discussion

Result on Benchmark Problems

(a) *Effect of Advance Selection on DE, DERL, and MRLDE*

In this section, an analysis of the effect of proposed selection operation on DE, DERL, and MRLDE algorithm has been carried out. The results are given in numerical and statistical significance terms. The numerical results are given in terms of the average NFE and average error with a standard deviation of 50 runs in Tables 4.2 and 4.3, respectively, while the results for acceleration rate (AR) and statistical significance are given in Table 4.4.

From Table 4.2, it is clear that the algorithm with advance selection, i.e., DEaS, DERLaS, and MRLDEas, takes less NFEs compared to their original variants, respectively, for all function, except function F_8 and F_9. None of the algorithm has obtained the desired accuracy for function F_8 and F_9. The total NFEs obtained by DE, DERL, and MRLDE are 2142410, 1233200, and 768000, respectively, while the total NFEs obtained by DEaS, DERLaS, and MRLDEaS are 1886900, 985900, and 670000, respectively, for all function, except function F_8 and F_9.

Now from Table 4.3, it can be easily observed that results are more accurate obtained by algorithms with advance selection operation in terms of average error also. Here, we can obtain the results for function F_8 and F_9, also for which Deas and DERLaS give better results; however, MRLDE gives a minimum error than MRLDEas for function F_9. For function F_6, all algorithms perform the same.

In Table 4.4, results are given in terms of AR for NFEs given in Table 4.2 and statistical significance on average error and standard deviation obtained in Table 4.3.

Table 4.2 Numerical results in terms of the average NFEs of 50 runs

Fun	VTR	DE	DEaS	DERL	DERLaS	MRLDE	MRLDEaS
F_1	10^{-09}	105600	**94100**	54800	**46600**	40400	***33400***
F_2	10^{-09}	175400	**158800**	91900	**77600**	66900	***57800***
F_3	10^{-09}	404200	**389500**	215900	**188900**	156800	***136600***
F_4	10^{-03}	137900	**116600**	147200	**110500**	65200	***62500***
F_5	10^{-09}	440400	**376800**	271900	**184400**	138500	***122900***
F_6	10^{-09}	32680	**29500**	19000	**14500**	12900	***10400***
F_7	10^{-02}	200390	**146600**	92500	**77900**	38600	***33600***
F_8	10^{-03}	NA	NA	NA	NA	NA	NA
F_9	10^{-03}	NA	NA	NA	NA	NA	NA
F_{10}	10^{-09}	164600	**146400**	86200	**72400**	62600	***53900***
F_{11}	10^{-09}	108500	**95600**	58100	**48300**	40400	***35900***
F_{12}	10^{-09}	95600	**83400**	49400	**41600**	37100	***31900***
F_{13}	10^{-09}	102200	**93400**	55600	**47400**	39900	***33500***
F_{14}	10^{-09}	68400	**62300**	35600	**28600**	27900	***22700***
F_{15}	10^{-09}	106600	**93900**	55100	**47200**	40800	***34900***

Table 4.3 Numerical results in terms of the average error and standard deviation of 50 runs

Fun	Max NFE	DE	DEaS	DERL	DERLaS	MRLDE	MRLDEaS
F_1	150K	5.80E-13 (2.62E-14)	**5.80E-16 (2.62E-16)**	2.43E-29 (2.82E-29)	**5.80E-36 (2.62E-36)**	8.35E-43 (8.61E-43)	**1.67E-50 (2.31E-50)**
F_2	200K	3.06E-10 (6.70E-10)	**1.12E-11 (5.34E-12)**	1.15E-20 (4.08E-20)	**9.11E-25 (7.44E-25)**	5.15E-29 (6.61E-29)	**3.37E-34 (4.19E-34)**
F_3	500K	2.79E-11 (4.21E-11)	**3.56E-12 (3.12E-13)**	5.22E-25 (3.32E-25)	**2.88E-28 (5.43E-28)**	1.12E-37 (5.04E-38)	**4.25E-40 (3.13E-40)**
F_4	500K	2.41E-01 (9.45E-02)	**3.50E-03 (1.11E-03)**	4.83E-07 (2.64E-07)	**2.88E-10 (5.43E-10)**	2.56E-28 (2.23E-28)	**3.76E-31 (4.33E-31)**
F_5	200K	1.17E+01 (7.41E-01)	**5.75E+00 (2.13E-01)**	1.01E-03 (2.75E-03)	**6.22E-11 (4.45E-11)**	2.16E-19 (2.43E-19)	**3.12E-24 (1.43E-24)**
F_6	50K	**(0.0E+00) (0.0E+00)**	**(0.0E+00) (0.0E+00)**	**(0.0E+00) (0.0E+00)**	**(0.0E+00) (0.0E+00)**	**(0.0E+00) (0.0E+00))**	**(0.0E+00) (0.0E+00)**
F_7	300K	2.81E-02 (5.61E-03)	**4.91E-03 (4.88E-04)**	**2.41E-03 (4.81E-04)**	2.64E-03 (6.33E-04)	2.09E-03 (9.65E-04)	**2.01E-03 (5.47E-04)**
F_8	500K	6.96E+03 (1.18E +03)	**4.73E+03 (8.51E +02)**	1.11E+03 (6.20E +02)	**3.55E+02 (3.25E +02)**	6.95E+02 (8.21E +02)	**1.18E+02 (1.31E +02)**
F_9	500K	7.97E+01 (1.83E +01)	**6.09E+01 (2.23E +01)**	1.52E+01 (4.61E-01)	**1.06E+01 (3.66E +00)**	***9.01E+00 (4.16E +00)***	**1.62E+01 (9.38E-01**
F_{10}	50K	6.41E-02 (3.43E-03)	**2.25E-02 (2.61E-03)**	1.18E-04 (5.36E-06)	**1.23E-05 (3.36E-06)**	9.18E-06 (4.28E-07)	**9.96E-08 (2.45E-08)**
F_{11}	50K	2.11E-01 (1.40E-02)	**1.18E-02 (3.09E-03)**	2.88E-06 (3.21E-06)	**1.23E-09 (3.36E-09)**	1.60E-10 (2.08E-10)	**1.17E-14 (5.35E-14)**
F_{12}	50K	3.34E-03 (2.15E-03)	**1.12E-03 (1.05E-03)**	8.37E-08 (4.45E-08)	**3.42E-11 (4.56E-12)**	4.86E-13 (2.88E-13)	**1.59E-15 (3.46E-15)**
F_{13}	50K	2.45E-02 (1.25E-02)	**8.23E-03 (5.41E-03)**	9.19E-08 (3.53E-10)	**6.91E-10 (4.33E-10)**	1.11E-11 (2.05E-11)	**3.21E-14 (1.79E-14)**
F_{14}	50K	1.56E-06 (6.73E-06)	**3.81E-07 (4.53E-07)**	1.01E-11 (8.31E-12)	**8.83E-14 (1.25E-14)**	4.79E-16 (3.94E-16)	**2.20E-18 (1.52E-18)**
F_{15}	50K	3.18E-02 (7.91E-03)	**6.62E-03 (1.17E-03)**	2.79E-07 (1.07E-07)	**5.83E-10 (3.42E-10)**	1.07E-11 (6.5E-12)	**4.47E-14 (4.24E-14)**

From the table, we can see a fast convergent speed in terms of AR for each function by each algorithm with advance selection operation. The average AR of DEaS with respect to DE is 11.93%, AR of DERL with respect to DERLaS is 20.05%, and AR of MRLDEaS with respect to MRLDE is 12.76%. Here, AR of MRLDEas is also obtained with respect to DERLaS and DEaS, which are 64.49% and 32.04%, respectively.

The statistical significance of results is also presented in Table 4.4. DEaS performs statistical better than DE for all function, except F_6 and F_{14} for which there is no significance difference between the performances.

Similarly, DERLaS gives an equal performance for function F_6 and is significantly better for other functions compared with DERL.

Table 4.4 Numerical results in terms of acceleration rate (AR) and statistically significance

	DEaS/DE		DERLaS/ DERL		MRLDEaS/ MRLDE		MRLDEaS/ DEaS		MRLDEaS/ DERLaS	
Fun	AR	Sig.	AR	Sig	AR	Sig	AR	Sig.	AR	Sig
F_1	10.89	+	14.96	+	17.33	+	64.51	+	28.33	+
F_2	9.46	+	15.56	+	13.60	+	63.60	+	25.52	+
F_3	3.64	+	12.51	+	12.88	+	64.93	+	27.69	+
F_4	15.45	+	24.93	+	4.14	+	46.40	+	43.44	+
F_5	14.44	+	32.18	+	11.26	+	67.38	+	33.35	+
F_6	9.73	=	23.68	=	19.38	=	64.75	=	28.28	=
F_7	26.84	+	15.78	+	12.95	=	77.08	+	56.87	=
F_8	NA	+	NA	+	NA	+	NA	+	NA	+
F_9	NA	+	NA	+	NA	−	NA	+	NA	−
F_{10}	11.06	+	16.01	+	13.90	+	63.18	+	25.55	+
F_{11}	11.89	+	16.87	+	11.14	+	62.45	+	25.67	+
F_{12}	12.76	+	15.79	+	14.02	+	61.75	+	23.32	+
F_{13}	8.61	+	14.75	+	16.04	+	64.13	+	29.32	+
F_{14}	8.92	=	19.66	+	18.64	+	63.56	+	20.63	+
F_{15}	11.91	+	14.34	+	14.46	+	62.83	+	26.06	+
Avg *w/l/t*	11.93	**13/0/2**	20.05	**14/0/1**	12.76	**12/1/2**	64.49	**14/0/1**	32.04	**12/1/2**

"+", "−", and "=" mean significantly better, lower, and equal, respectively

MRLDEaS performs significantly better than MRLDE for all functions, except F_6, F_7, and F_9. In the case of F_6 and F_7, there is no significant difference between the performances of both, while MRLDE is significantly better than MRLDEaS in the case of function F9.

The last row of Table 4.4 shows the total number of *win/loss/tie* performance of algorithms on all functions. The *w/l/t* performance of DEaS *vs* DE is 13/0/2, DERLaS *vs* DERL is 14/0/1, MRLDEaS *vs* MRLDE is 12/1/2, MRLDEaS *vs* DEaS is 14/0/1, and MRLDEaS *vs* DERLas is 12/1/2.

(b) *Comparison of MRLDEaS with Other Enhanced DE Variants*

In this section, comparison of MRLDEas is discussed with some other well-known enhanced DE variants, such as jDE [7], ODE [8], CDE-Cai [15], and LEDE [16]. The comparison is given in Table 4.5 in terms of NFE. The results for ODE, jDE, CDE-Cai, and LeDE are taken from [16]. All parameter settings have also taken similar from [16] for fair comparison.

From the table, we can see that our proposed MRLDEaS takes less NFE for all benchmark function, except F_7, F_8, and F_9 for which CDE-Cai and JDE perform best from others. The corresponding rank is also given for each function in the table. The average rank of ODE, jDE, CDE-Cai, and LEDE is 4.54, 3.62, 2.92, and 2.15, respectively, while the rank of MRLDEaS is 1.77, which proved the effectiveness of it compared to all others.

Table 4.5 Comparison of MRLDEaS with ODE, jDE, CDE, and LEDE

	NFE					Function-wise ranks				
Fun	ODE	jDE	CDE-Cai	LeDE	MRLDEaS	ODE	jDE	CDE-Cai	LeDE	MRLDEaS
F_1	67524	60000	54121	49494	**33400**	5	4	3	2	**1**
F_2	140170	83000	84295	77464	**57800**	5	3	4	2	**1**
F_3	489210	340000	166545	140176	**136600**	5	4	3	2	**1**
F_4	145880	300000	177268	157499	**141400**	2	5	4	3	**1**
F_5	NA	NA	315282	282972	**122900**	4.5	4.5	3	2	**1**
F_6	25008	23000	17869	17123	**10400**	5	4	3	2	**1**
F_7	60230	100000	**33275**	33302	33600	4	5	**1**	2	3
F_8	147472	**89000**	115163	111013	NA	4	**1**	3	2	5
F_9	190604	**120000**	184371	187813	NA	4	**1**	2	3	5
F_{10}	106694	91000	84920	76111	**53900**	5	4	3	2	**1**
F_{11}	79888	63000	56868	50579	**35900**	5	4	3	2	**1**
F_{12}	63710	55000	45803	41384	**31900**	5	4	3	2	**1**
F_{13}	63202	60000	50720	*46529*	**33500**	5	4	3	2	**1**
Average rank						4.54	3.62	2.92	2.15	**1.77**

Table 4.6 Wilcoxon sign rank test for MRLDEaS vs ODE, jDE, CDE, and LEDE

Algorithms		$\sum R^+$	$\sum R^-$	*W value*	*Critical value at 5% level*	Significance
MRLDEaS *vs*	**ODE**	70	21	21	21	+
	jDE	66	25	25	17	+
	CDE-Cai	65	26	26	21	+
	LeDE	65	26	26	21	+

In Table 4.6, a nonparametric Wilcoxon sign rank test is also performed to check the pair-wise comparison of MRLDEas with another algorithm. From the table, we can see that our proposed MRLDEaS provides an overall significance superior performance than ODE, jDE, CDE-Cai, and LeDE.

Result on Real-Life Application

In this section, the evaluation of the proposed variants on real-life applications is discussed. In Table 4.7, the results are obtained in terms of worst, best, mean, and standard deviation of fitness value in 50 runs. The best results obtained by algorithms are given in bold cases. We can see that the proposed variants with advance selection operation perform better than their original variants in all terms. The statistical test value is also given in the table, which also proved the significance of proposed variants over the original variants, respectively.

Convergence Graphs

In this section, the convergence speed of algorithms is represented graphically by the convergence graphs in Fig. 4.2. Here, convergence graphs are given for function F_1, F_2, F_5, F_{10}, F_{11}, and F_{14}. RF_1 and RF_2. From Fig. 4.2, we can easily observe that DE, DERL, and MRLDE obtain a fast convergence speed when applying proposed advance selection operation with these algorithms. We can also see that MRLDEaS provides a faster convergence speed compared to all other variants.

6 Conclusions

In the present chapter, an advance selection strategy for DE algorithm named DEaS is proposed. This advance selection operation gives an additional opportunity to the rejected trail vectors to prove their efficiency over other target vectors. This approach

Table 4.7 Numerical and statistical results for real-life applications

Fun	Max NFE	Fitness	DE	DEaS	DERL	DERLaS	MRLDE	MRLDEaS
RF_1	30000	Worst	1.2E+01	**1.0E+01**	8.7E-10	**6.3E-14**	3.2E-10	***3.6E-17***
		Best	8.1E+00	**5.1E-03**	3.7E-14	**9.1E-18**	7.2E-22	***0.0E+00***
		Mean	1.0E+01	**3.9E+00**	3.1E-10	**1.2E-14**	8.1E-11	***7.3E-18***
		SD	8.3E+00	**1.2E+00**	4.2E-10	**2.5E-14**	1.6E-10	***1.4E-17***
		z-value	$z = 5.14$		$z = 5.22$		$z = 3.58$	
		Significance at 5% level	+		+		+	
RF_2	1000	Worst	4.19092	**4.20318**	4.20757	**4.20977**	4.20877	***4.20989***
		Best	4.20489	**4.21198**	4.21279	**4.21282**	4.21231	***4.21346***
		Mean	4.19942	**4.20852**	4.21139	**4.21186**	4.21076	***4.21238***
		SD	6.1E-03	2.9E-03	1.9E-03	1.2E-03	1.4E-03	*1.3E-03*
		z-value	$z = 9.53$		$z = 1.48$		$z = 6.0$	
		Significance at 5% level	+		=		+	
RF3	$d = 20$ MaxNFE = *100K*	Worst	3.7523	**2.1274**	1.7603	**0.9010**	0.8551	***0.8014***
		Best	2.3012	**2.0138**	1.5816	**0.6652**	0.6625	***0.6671***
		Mean	3.1328	**2.4820**	1.6321	**0.7877**	0.7523	***0.5423***
		SD	2.0435	**1.001**	1.4099	**0.0672**	0.0466	***0.0011***
		z-value	$z = 2.02$		$z = 4.23$		$z = 3.19$	
		Significance at 5% level	+		+		+	

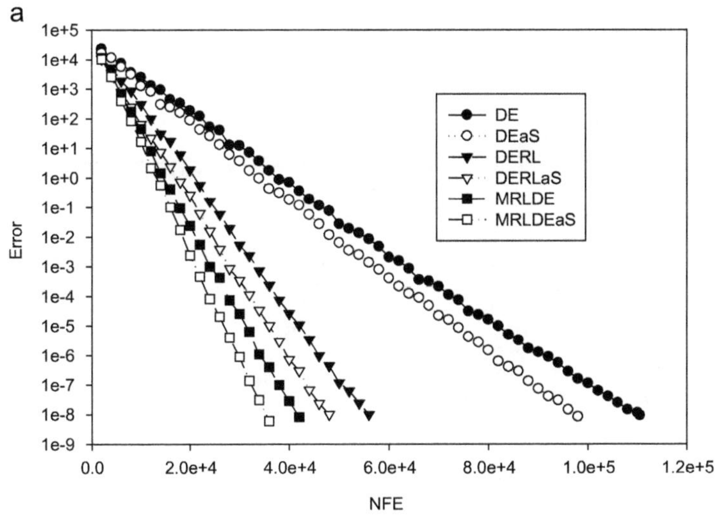

Function F_1

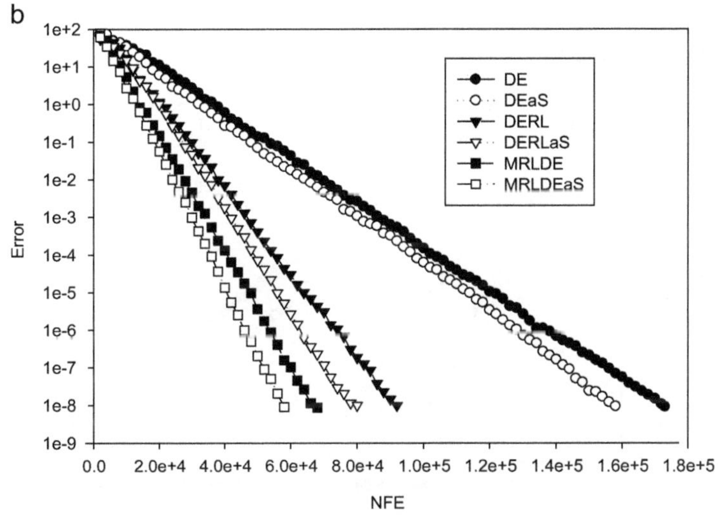

Function F_2

Fig. 4.2 Convergence graphs in terms of error and NFEs

condenses the searching space in every generation and helps to obtain better convergence speed as well as diminishes the redundant memory space.

Next, the proposed selection operation is embedded with other enhanced variants, named DERLaS and MRLDEaS.

The performances of proposed variants are evaluated on 15 traditional benchmark problems and 3 real-life applications. The numerical results for DEaS, DERLaS, and

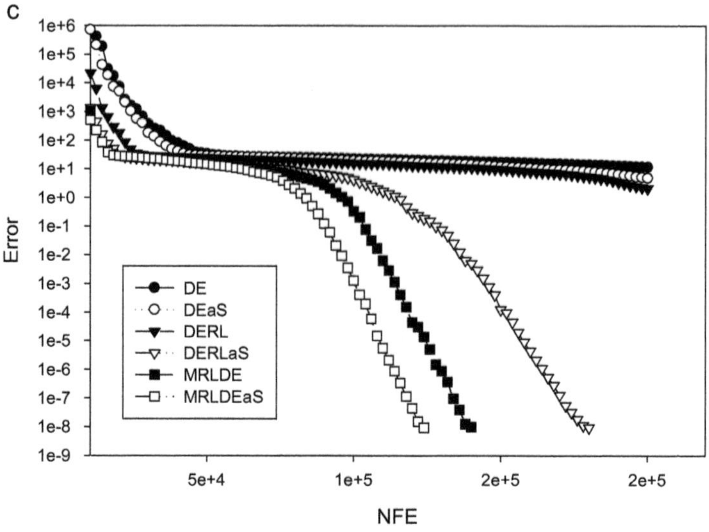

Function F_5

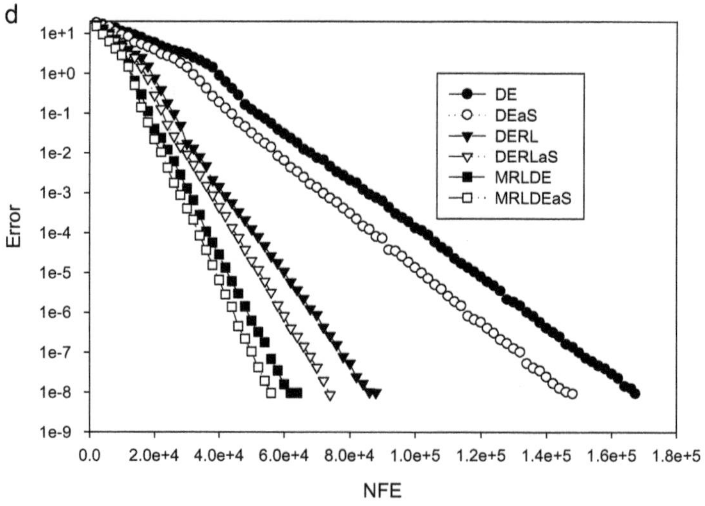

Function F_{10}

Fig. 4.2 (continued)

MRLDEaS are compared with the original variant DE, DERL, and MRLDE, respectively. Furthermore, the performance of MRLDEaS is also compared with other enhanced DE variants, such as ODE, jDE, CDE-Cai, and LeDE.

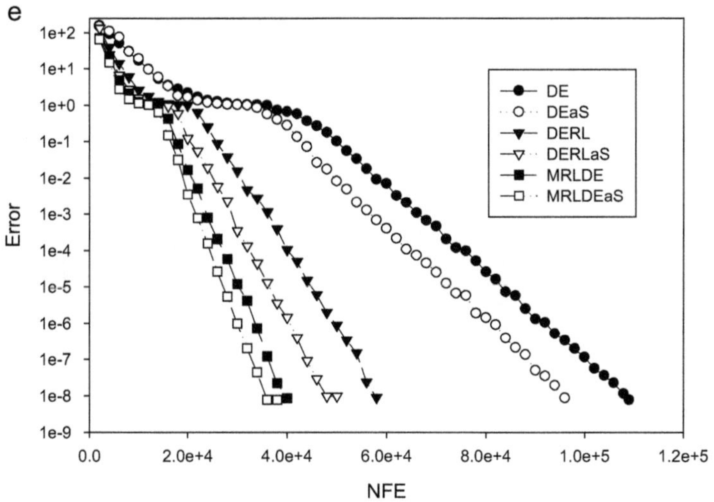

Function F_{11}

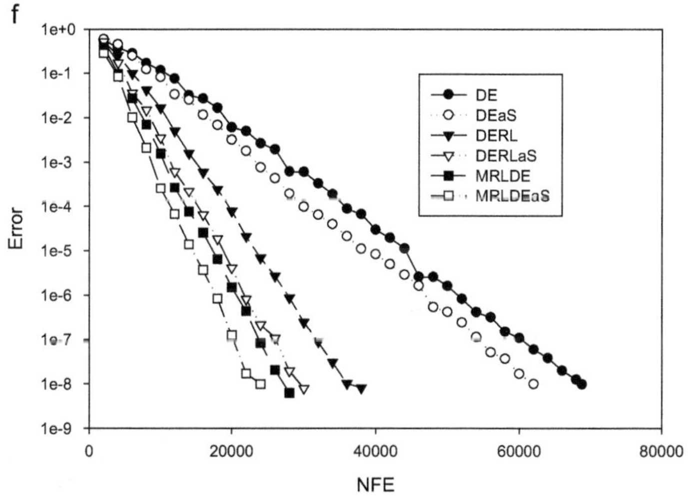

Function F_{14}

Fig. 4.2 (continued)

The numerical, statistical, and graphical results have proved the effectiveness and robustness of the proposed advance selection operation with DE and other variants DERL and MRLDE.

In future, the effect of this advance selection operation can be verified on other evolutionary algorithms for solving real-life optimization problems.

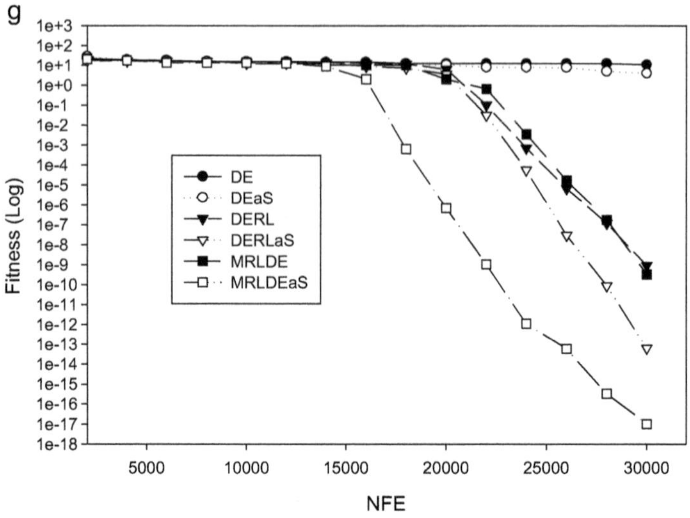

Real Life Application RF_1

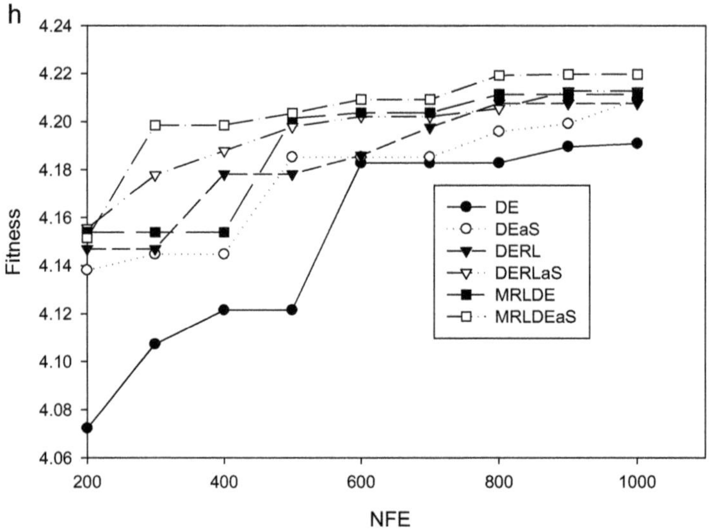

Real Life Application RF_2

Fig. 4.2 (continued)

References

1. Storn, R., Price, K.: Differential evolution – a simple and efficient heuristic for global optimization over continuous spaces. J. Glob. Optim. **11**(4), 341–359 (1997)
2. Karafotias, G., Hoogendoorn, M., Eiben, A.E.: Parameter control in evolutionary algorithms: trends and challenges. IEEE Trans. Evol. Comput. **19**(2), 167–187 (2015)
3. Fan, H., Lampinen, J.: A trigonometric mutation operation to differentia evolution. J. Glob. Optim. **27**, 105–129 (2003)

4. Liu, J., Lampinen, J.: A fuzzy adaptive differential evolution algorithm. Soft Comput. Fusion Found Meth. Appl. **9**(6), 448–462 (2005)
5. Babu, B.V., Angira, R.: Modified differential evolution (MDE) for optimization of non-linear chemical processes. Comput. Chem. Eng. **30**, 989–1002 (2006)
6. Kaelo, P., Ali, M.M.: A numerical study of some modified differential evolution algorithms. Eur. J. Oper. Res. **169**, 1176–1184 (2006)
7. Brest, J., Greiner, S., Boskovic, B., Mernik, M., Zumer, V.: Self adapting control parameters in differential evolution: a comparative study on numerical benchmark problems. IEEE Trans. Evol. Comput. **10**(6), 646–657 (2006)
8. Rahnamayan, S., Tizhoosh, H., Salama, M.: Opposition based differential evolution. IEEE Trans. Evol. Comput. **12**(1), 64–79 (2008)
9. Noman, N., Iba, H.: Accelerating differential evolution using an adaptive local Search. IEEE Trans. Evol. Comput. **12**(1), 107–125 (2008)
10. Pant, M., Ali, M., Abraham, A.: Mixed mutation strategy embedded differential evolution. In: IEEE Congress on Evolutionary Computation, pp. 1240–1246 (2009)
11. Qin, A.K., Huang, V.L., Suganthan, P.N.: Differential evolution algorithm with strategy adaptation for global numerical optimization. IEEE Trans. Evol. Comput. **13**(2), 398–417 (2009)
12. Zhang, J., Sanderson, A.: JADE: adaptive differential evolution with optional external archive. IEEE Trans. Evol. Comput. **13**(5), 945–958 (2009)
13. Das, S., Abraham, A., Chakraborty, U., Konar, A.: Differential evolution using a neighborhood based mutation operator. IEEE Trans. Evol. Comput. **13**(3), 526–553 (2009)
14. Ali, M., Pant, M.: Improving the performance of differential evolution algorithm using cauchy mutation. Soft. Comput. (2010). https://doi.org/10.1007/s00500-010-0655-2
15. Cai, Z., Gong, W., Ling, C., Zhang, H.: A clustering-based differential evolution for global optimization. Appl. Soft Comput. **11**(1), 1363–1379 (2011)
16. Cai, Y., Wang, J., Yin, J.: Learning enhanced differential evolution for numerical optimization. Soft Comput. (2011). https://doi.org/10.1007/s00500-011-0744-x
17. Epitropakis, M.G., Tasoulis, D.K., Pavlidis, N.G., Plagianakos, V.P., Vrahatis, M.N.: Enhancing Differential Evolution Utilizing Proximity-Based Mutation Operators. IEEE Trans. Evol. Comput. **15**(1), 99–11 (2011)
18. Kumar, P., Pant, P.: Enhanced mutation strategy for differential evolution. In: Proceeding of IEEE Congress on Evolutionary Computation (CEC-12), pp. 1–6 (2012)
19. Zhu, W., Tang, Y., Fang, J.-A., Zhang, W.: Adaptive population tuning scheme for differential evolution. Inf. Sci. **223**, 164–191 (2013)
20. Sarker, R.A., Elsayed, S.M., Ray, T.: Differential evolution with dynamic parameters selection for optimization problems. IEEE Trans. Evol. Comput. **18**(5), 689–707 (2014)
21. Singh, P., Chaturvedi, P., Kumar, P.: Control parameters and mutation based variants of differential evolution algorithm. J. Comput. Method Sci. Eng. **15**(4), 783–800 (2015)
22. Xiang, W.L., Meng, X.L., An, M.Q., Li, Y.Z., Gao, M.X.: An enhanced differential evolution algorithm based on multiple mutation strategies. Comput. Intell. Neurosci. **2015**, Article ID 285730, 15 pages (2015)
23. Wu, G., Mallipeddi, R., Suganthan, P.N., Wang, R., Chen, H.: Differential evolution with multi-population based ensemble of mutation strategies. Inf. Sci. **329**, 329–345 (2016)
24. Zheng, L.M., Zhang, S.X., Tang, K.S., Zheng, S.Y.: Differential evolution powered by collective information. Inf. Sci. **399**, 13–29 (2017)
25. Meng, Z., Pan, J.-S., Kong, L.: Parameters with adaptive learning mechanism (palm) for the enhancement of differential evolution. Knowl.-Based Syst. **141**, 92–112 (2018)
26. Singh, P., Chaturvedi, P., Kumar, P.: A novel differential evolution approach for constraint optimization. Int. J. Bio-Insp. Comput. **12**(4), 254–265 (2018)
27. Meng, Z., Pan, J.-S., Tseng, K.K.: PaDE: an enhanced differential evolution algorithm with novel control parameter adaptation schemes for numerical optimization. Knowl.-Based Syst. **168**, 80–99 (2019)

28. Wei, Z., Xie, X., Bao, T., Yu, Y.: A random perturbation modified differential evolution algorithm for unconstrained optimization problems. Soft. Comput. **23**(15), 6307–6321 (2019)
29. Duan, M., Yang, H., Liu, H., Chen, J.: A differential evolution algorithm with dual preferred learning mutation. Appl. Intell. **49**(2), 605–627 (2019)
30. Tian, M., Gao, X.: Differential evolution with neighborhood-based adaptive evolution mechanism for numerical optimization. Inf. Sci. **478**, 422–448 (2019)
31. Wang, S.H., Li, Y.Z., Yang, H.Y.: Self-adaptive mutation differential evolution algorithm based on particle swarm optimization. Appl. Soft Comput. **81** (2019)
32. Pan, J.S., Yang, C., Meng, F.J., Chen, Y.X., Meng, Z.Y.: A parameter adaptive DE algorithm on real-parameter optimization. J. Intell. Fuzzy Syst. **38**(1), 1–12 (2020)
33. Di Carlo, M., Vasile, M., Minisci, E.: Adaptive multipopulation inflationary differential evolution. Soft. Comput. **24**(5), 3861–3891 (2020)
34. Zhong, X., Cheng, P.: An improved differential evolution algorithm based on dual-strategy. Hindawi Math. Prob. Eng. (2020). https://doi.org/10.1155/2020/9767282
35. Plagianakos, V., Tasoulis, D., Vrahatis, M.: A review of major application areas of differential evolution. In: Advances in Differential Evolution, vol. 143, pp. 197–238. Springer, Berlin (2008)
36. Neri, F., Tirronen, V.: Recent advances in differential evolution: a survey and experimental analysis. Artif. Intell. Rev. **33**(1–2), 61–106 (2010)
37. Das, S., Suganthan, P.N.: Differential evolution: a survey of the state-of-the-art. IEEE Trans. Evol. Comput. **15**(1), 4–13 (2011)
38. Bilal, P.M., Pant, M., Zaheer, H., Garcia-Hernandez, L., Abraham, A.: Differential evolution: a review of more than two decades of research. Eng. Appl. Artif. Intell. **90**, Article 103479 (2020)
39. Kumar, P., Pant, M.: Modified single array selection operation for DE algorithm. In: Proceedings of Fifth International Conference on Soft Computing for Problem Solving, AISC, vol. 437, pp. 795–803 (2016)
40. Kumar, P., Pant, M., Astya, R., Ali, M.: Real life optimization problems solving by IUDE. In: International Conference on Computing, Communication and Automation (ICCCA), pp. 368–372 (2016)
41. Kumar, S., Kumar, P., Sharma, T.K., Pant, M.: Bi-level thresholding using PSO, Artificial Bee Colony and MRLDE embedded with Otsu method. Memetic Comput. **5**(4), 323–334 (2013)
42. Kumar, P., Pant, M., Singh, V.P.: Modified random localization based de for static economic power dispatch with generator constraints. Int. J. Bio-Insp. Comput. **6**(4), 250–261 (2014)
43. Kumar, P., Singh, D., Kumar, S.: MRLDE for solving engineering optimization problems. In: International Conference on Computing, Communication & Automation, pp. 760–764. https://doi.org/10.1109/CCAA.2015.7148512 (2015)
44. Kumar, P., Pant, M.: Recognition of noise source in multi sounds field by modified random localized based DE algorithm. Int. J. Syst. Assur. Eng. Manag. **9**(1), 245–261 (2016). https://doi.org/10.1007/s13198-016-0544-x
45. Kumar, P., Sharma, A.: MRL-Jaya: a fusion of MRLDE and Jaya Algorithm. Palestine J. Math. **11**, 65–74 (2022)
46. Dor, A.E., Clerc, M., Siarry, P.: Hybridization of differential evolution and particle swarm optimization in a new algorithm: DEPSO-2S. In: Proceeding of SIDE 2012 and EC 2012, LNCS 7269, , pp. 57–65. Springer, Berlin/Heidelberg (2012)
47. Garg, V., Deep, K.: Performance of Laplacian Biogeography-Based Optimization Algorithm on CEC 2014 continuous optimization benchmarks and camera calibration problem. Swarm Evol. Comput. **27**, 132–144 (2016)
48. Garg, V., Deep, K.: Constrained Laplacian biogeography-based optimization algorithm. Int. J. Syst. Assur. Eng. Manag. **8**(2), 867–885 (2017)
49. Garg, V., Deep, K.: Efficient mutation strategies embedded in Laplacian-biogeography-based optimization algorithm for unconstrained function minimization. Int. J. Appl. Evol. Comput. (IJAEC). **7**(2), 12–44 (2016)

Chapter 5
Profit Optimization of Two-Unit Briquetting System Using Grey Wolf Optimization Algorithm

Divesh Garg and Reena Garg

1 Introduction

Crop leftovers, timber, and its wastage, and animal wastes are all key sources of biofuels in underdeveloped nations. Biomass can be used to generate heat, electricity, and a variety of other forms of energy, which is a readily available natural resource. Because of its low levels of greenhouse and acidic gas emissions, biomass has emerged as a viable alternative to other forms of renewable energy. As nonrenewable resources are depleted and the impact of greenhouse gases continues to rise, scientists have taken a strong interest in bioenergy.

When tiny, loose particles are compressed into a hard monolith; the process is called briquette. Rural and semi-urban regions rely heavily on it since it's both cost-effective and environmentally benign. Due to densification, briquetting is more feasible and helpful as it results in a higher biomass density. To make low-cost briquette machines, a number of approaches have been put out in the literature [2]. Densification of various agricultural waste, such as sawdust, rice straw, palm oil mill, sugar cane leaves, rice husk, and rice bran, can be accomplished using electric or manual methods.

Analysis of the briquettes' calorific value, porosity, XRD, and final analysis was conducted by Raju et al. [1]. In addition, they found that almond leaf briquettes were the best of the three options. Shukla and Vyas [3] addressed bioenergy producing systems and also outlined the aspects that impact the overall performance of biomass waste. Tannery solid wastes, such as buffing dust, chrome shavings, and hairs, were studied by Onukak et al. [4] for the characterization and manufacturing of biomass briquettes. A new screw press briquetting machine was proposed by Sanap et al. [5] after a thorough investigation. A 65% reduction in production costs and a 30%

D. Garg (✉) · R. Garg
J.C. Bose University of Science and Technology, YMCA, Faridabad, India

© The Author(s), under exclusive license to Springer Nature Switzerland AG 2022

D. Singh et al. (eds.), *Design and Applications of Nature Inspired Optimization*, Women in Engineering and Science, https://doi.org/10.1007/978-3-031-17929-7_5

reduction in the initial moisture content were found. Higher-grade novel briquettes with decreased smoke production have been discovered. The viability of briquette manufacture in Iloilo City, Philippines, with the participation of the informal sector has been examined by Ramallosa and Kraft [6]. For on-site fuel generation, they decided to make biomass briquettes from municipal garbage. Charcoal briquettes manufactured from Madan wood and coconut shell were examined by Kongprasert et al. [10]. Results showed that the maximum calorific value was found in charcoal briquettes produced entirely of Madan wood, with 6622 cal/g.

For corn cob briquettes, Orisaleye et al. [15] looked at the density as a function of temperature, particle size, and pressure. They discovered that increasing these variables improved the briquettes' density. Using the response surface approach, Raudah and Zulkifli [16] improved the quality of coffee husk material for making briquettes. A pilot-scale briquetting and torrefaction facility was demonstrated by Severy et al. [17] to identify the optimal conditions for producing bioenergy from forest trash. Arevalo et al. [18] developed a sustainable energy strategy for the manufacturing of briquettes from agricultural waste in low-income communities. Using eucalyptus and *Pinus caribaea* wood sawdust, Ijah et al. [19] calculated the calorific value of the briquettes. They also came to the conclusion that adding starch to sawdust briquettes enhances their calorific value. An investigation into the combustion and physical qualities of biomass briquettes was conducted by Aliye et al. [22]. Kumar et al. [23] constructed and tested a low-pressure multi-briquette screw press machine. Despite the challenges of making and using briquettes, Shekhar [26] stated that there is a huge untapped market for this fuel source. Researchers found that agricultural biomass leaching significantly improved its fuel properties by reducing gaseous emissions and total suspended particles [27]. Using proportional groundnut shells and coffee and rice husks, Lubwama et al. [28] created and investigated a bio-composite briquette with various unique properties. This briquette outperforms other single-component briquettes in terms of performance. To compare the cost of producing heat using wood briquettes to alternative biomass and fossil fuels, Stolarski et al. [29] conducted research on the amount of energy needed to heat a detached dwelling. There is a significant need for alternative energy sources, and researchers are focusing on developing novel biomass briquettes from biomass wastes to meet that demand [21]. An alternative energy source, the briquetting process, might be an affordable choice for many homes instead of utilizing forest wood directly for fuel, as Ullah et al. [14] stated. The biomass briquette life cycle assessment model established by Muazu et al. [11] was used to examine the environmental implications of briquetting different biomass feeds using various technical alternatives.

Prior to pressing, feeding and holding pressure were altered to improve the briquette machine's design [20]. Models developed by Orisaleye and Ojolo [24] were used to investigate how pressure was distributed along with the die. Biomass briquette production systems with varying demands have been studied by Garg and Garg [25]. Singh and Jaiswal [9] built a mathematical model and examined dependability metrics for power production systems using the Boolean function approach, which required extensive computations. A number of system metrics, such as the busiest period, availability, MTSF, estimated number of repairmen visits, and profit, may be simply calculated using RPGT [12]. Garg et al. [30] optimized real-life problems by using a recently developed nature-inspired optimization algorithm.

Some of the recent works include analysis of system parameters of one-unit briquette machine under different major and minor faults [13]. Also, Briquette machine efficiency was studied by Garg and Garg [8] by looking at the performance of the machine with and without preventive maintenance, but the study of system profit and other parameters of two-unit briquette machines under major and minor faults are not discussed yet. To fill this gap, we are considering two units of briquette machines in which one unit will be working and one in standby mode. In case of minor or major faults, the other unit starts to work while the defected unit goes under maintenance. So, it is more effective than the one-unit briquette machine, where the urgent requirement of a repairman is necessary for the continuous functioning of the unit.

Structure of the current paper: Section 2 makes a point of outlining every one of the notes. Section 3 shows the unit's flow diagram. Section 4 calculates the average sojourn period and all possible transition probabilities for each state. Section 5 gives the numerical value of performance. measures Section 6 provides an overview of GWO. Section 7 summarizes the findings in tables and graphs. Section 8 concluded our work.

2 Introduction

O/O_{CS}	Unit operative/cold standby.
λ_1/λ_2	Machine minor/major fault rate.
$\alpha_1/\ \alpha_2/\ \alpha_3$	Repair rate of ordinary/expert repairmen.
η	Inspection rate.
$F_{min}/\ F_{maj}$	The failed unit is under minor/major repair.
$F_O/F_E/\ F_W$	The failed unit is under ordinary repairmen/expert repairmen/waiting.
$p_{i,\ j}$	p.d.f from regenerative state i to j.
$q_{i,\ j}$	Probability of transitioning from a regenerative state i to j.
$i(t)/I(t)$	Fault inspection time p.d.f/c.d.f.
$h(t)/H(t)$	p.d.f/c.d.f of time to inspecting major fault.
$g_1(t)/G_1(t)$	p.d.f/c.d.f of time to repair the unit under minor problems by ordinary repairmen.
$g_2(t)/G_2$(t)	p.d.f/c.d.f of time to repair the unit under minor problems by ordinary repairmen.
$g_3(t)/G_3(t)$	p.d.f/c.d.f of time to repair the unit under major problems by expert repairmen.

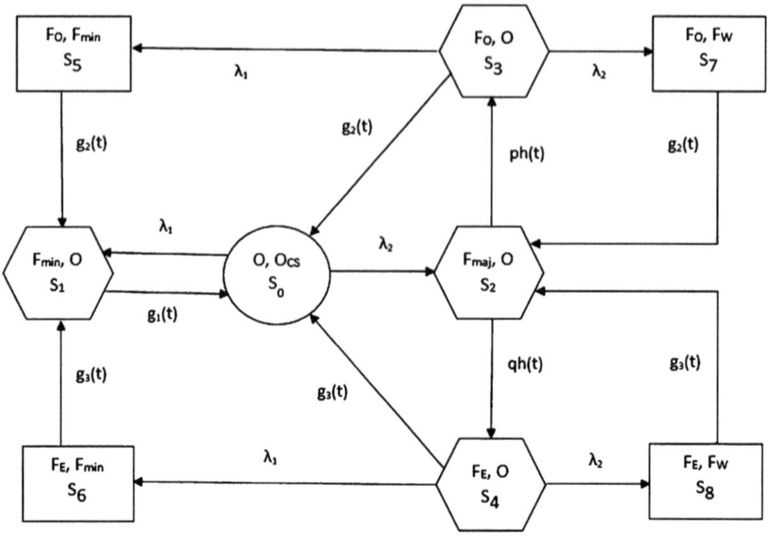

Fig. 5.1 State transition diagram

3 State Transition Diagram

As indicated in Fig. 5.1, S_O is the only fully operative state, and S_1, S_2, S_3, and S_4 are the partially failed state. Whereas S_5, S_6, S_7, and S_8 are the failed states. S_O is assumed to be the base state.

4 Transition Probabilities and Mean Sojourn Periods

Tables 5.1 and 5.2 indicate the probabilities of all transitions and the mean sojourn periods for each state transition.

$$p_{i,j}(t) = q_{i,j}^{*}(0)$$

The Laplace transformation is denoted by the symbol "*".

It is simple to verify that $p_{O,1} + p_{O,2} = 1, p_{2,3} + p_{2,4} = 1, p_{3,O} + p_{3,5} + p_{3,7} = 1$, and $p_{4,O} + p_{4,6} + p_{4,8} = 1$.

For determining the mean sojourn periods, the following formula was utilized:

Table 5.1 Transition probabilities

$q_{i,j}(t)$	$p_{i,j} = q_{i,j}^*(0)$
$q_{0,1} = \lambda_1 e^{-(\lambda_1+\lambda_2)t}$ $q_{0,2} = \lambda_2 e^{-(\lambda_1+\lambda_2)t}$	$p_{0,1} = \frac{\lambda_1}{(\lambda_1+\lambda_2)}$ $p_{0,1} = \frac{\lambda_1}{(\lambda_1+\lambda_2)}$
$q_{1,0} = g_1(t)$	$p_{1,0} = g_1^*(0)$
$q_{2,3} = ph(t)$ $q_{2,4} = qh(t)$	$p_{2,3} = ph^*(0)$ $p_{2,4} = qh^*(0)$
$q_{3,0} = g_2(t)e^{-(\lambda_1+\lambda_2)t}$ $q_{3,5} = \lambda_1 e^{-(\lambda_1+\lambda_2)t} G_2(t)$ $q_{3,7} = \lambda_2 e^{-(\lambda_1+\lambda_2)t} G_2(t)$	$p_{3,0} = g_2^*(\lambda_1 + \lambda_2)$ $p_{3,5} = \frac{\lambda_1}{(\lambda_1+\lambda_2)}\{1 - g_2^*(\lambda_1+\lambda_2)\}$ $p_{3,7} = \frac{\lambda_2}{(\lambda_1+\lambda_2)}\{1 - g_2^*(\lambda_1+\lambda_2)\}$
$q_{4,0} = g_3(t)e^{-(\lambda_1+\lambda_2)t}$ $q_{4,6} = \lambda_1 e^{-(\lambda_1+\lambda_2)t} G_3(t)$ $q_{4,8} = \lambda_2 e^{-(\lambda_1+\lambda_2)t} G_3(t)$	$p_{4,0} = g_3^*(\lambda_1 + \lambda_2)$ $p_{4,6} = \frac{\lambda_1}{(\lambda_1+\lambda_2)}\{1 - g_3^*(\lambda_1+\lambda_2)\}$ $p_{4,8} = \frac{\lambda_2}{(\lambda_1+\lambda_2)}\{1 - g_3^*(\lambda_1+\lambda_2)\}$
$q_{5,1} = g_2(t)$	$p_{5,1} = g_2^*(0)$
$q_{6,1} = g_3(t)$	$p_{6,1} = g_3^*(0)$
$q_{7,2} = g_2(t)$	$p_{7,2} = g_2^*(0)$
$q_{8,2} = g_3(t)$	$p_{8,2} = g_3^*(0)$

Table 5.2 Mean sojourn periods

$R_i(t)$	$\mu_i = R_i * (0)$
$R_0 = e^{-(\lambda_1+\lambda_2)t}$	$\mu_0 = \frac{1}{(\lambda_1+\lambda_2)}$
$R_1 = e^{-(\alpha_1)t}$	$\mu_1 = \frac{1}{\alpha_1}$
$R_2 = e^{-(\eta)t}$	$\mu_2 = \frac{1}{\eta}$
$R_3 = e^{-(\alpha_2+\lambda_1+\lambda_2)t}$	$\mu_3 = \frac{1}{(\alpha_2+\lambda_1+\lambda_2)}$
$R_4 = e^{-(\alpha_3+\lambda_1+\lambda_2)t}$	$\mu_4 = \frac{1}{(\alpha_3+\lambda_1+\lambda_2)}$
$R_5 = e^{-(\alpha_2)t}$	$\mu_5 = \frac{1}{\alpha_2}$
$R_6 = e^{-(\alpha_3)t}$	$\mu_6 = \frac{1}{\alpha_3}$
$R_7 = e^{-(\alpha_2)t}$	$\mu_7 = \frac{1}{\alpha_2}$
$R_8 = e^{-(\alpha_3)t}$	$\mu_8 = \frac{1}{\alpha_3}$

$$\mu_i = \int_0^\infty R_i(t)dt = R_i^*(0)$$

where $R_i(t)$ indicates the system's reliability at the given time t.

The following are the factors that affect the probability of a transition:

$$S_{0,0} = 1(\text{Verified})$$

$$S_{0,1} = p_{0,1} = \frac{\lambda_1}{(\lambda_1 + \lambda_2)}$$

$$S_{0,2} = p_{0,2} = \frac{\lambda_2}{(\lambda_1 + \lambda_2)}$$

$$S_{0,3} = p_{0,2}p_{2,3} = p\left(\frac{\lambda_2}{\lambda_1 + \lambda_2}\right)$$

$$S_{0,4} = p_{0,2}p_{2,3} = q\left(\frac{\lambda_2}{\lambda_1 + \lambda_2}\right)$$

$$S_{0,5} = p_{0,2}p_{2,3}p_{3,5} = p\left(\frac{\lambda_2}{\lambda_1 + \lambda_2}\right)\left(\frac{\lambda_1}{\alpha_2 + \lambda_1 + \lambda_2}\right)$$

$$S_{0,6} = p_{0,2}p_{2,4}p_{4,6} = q\left(\frac{\lambda_2}{\lambda_1 + \lambda_2}\right)\left(\frac{\lambda_1}{\alpha_3 + \lambda_1 + \lambda_2}\right)$$

$$S_{0,7} = p_{0,2}p_{2,3}p_{3,7} = p\left(\frac{\lambda_2}{\lambda_1 + \lambda_2}\right)\left(\frac{\lambda_2}{\alpha_2 + \lambda_1 + \lambda_2}\right)$$

$$S_{0,8} = p_{0,2}p_{2,4}p_{3,8} = p\left(\frac{\lambda_2}{\lambda_1 + \lambda_2}\right)\left(\frac{\lambda_2}{\alpha_3 + \lambda_1 + \lambda_2}\right)$$

5 System Effectiveness Measures

For the base state "S_0," the analysis of two-unit briquetting system parameters is as follows:

Mean Time to System Failure

As shown in the state transition diagram, S_0, S_1, S_2, and S_3 are the only operative states that can be passed through before arriving at the failed state. The MTSF per unit of time is shown in Table 5.3.

$$\text{MTSF} = \left(\frac{1}{\lambda_1 + \lambda_2}\right)\left[1 + \frac{\lambda_1}{\alpha_1} + \lambda_2\left(\frac{1}{\eta} + \frac{p}{\alpha_2 + \lambda_1 + \lambda_2} + \frac{q}{\alpha_3 + \lambda_1 + \lambda_2}\right)\right]$$

Table 5.3 MTSF

λ_1	$\alpha_1 = 0.75, \alpha_2 = 0.7, \alpha_3 = 0.8$	$\alpha_1 = 0.95, \alpha_2 = 0.7, \alpha_3 = 0.8$	$\alpha_1 = 0.75, \alpha_2 = 0.8, \alpha_3 = 0.8$	$\alpha_1 = 0.95, \alpha_2 = 0.8, \alpha_3 = 0.9$
0.002	11.42149	11.39597	11.34749	11.2824
0.004	8.549903	8.532359	8.481771	8.427376
0.006	7.020997	7.00763	6.958824	6.911477
0.008	6.063165	6.052369	6.006471	5.964395
0.01	5.402127	5.393072	5.350334	5.312458
0.012	4.915656	4.907859	4.868215	4.833811
0.014	4.540929	4.534083	4.497346	4.46588
0.016	4.242281	4.236178	4.202122	4.173185
0.018	3.99792	3.992416	3.960809	3.934074
0.02	3.793755	3.788742	3.759366	3.734568

Table 5.4 System availability

λ_2	$\alpha_1 = 0.75, \alpha_2 = 0.7, \alpha_3 = 0.8$	$\alpha_1 = 0.95, \alpha_2 = 0.7, \alpha_3 = 0.8$	$\alpha_1 = 0.75, \alpha_2 = 0.8, \alpha_3 = 0.8$	$\alpha_1 = 0.95, \alpha_2 = 0.8, \alpha_3 = 0.9$
0.1	0.98612	0.986089	0.98804	0.9889189
0.15	0.974067	0.974015	0.977491	0.9790785
0.2	0.960676	0.960604	0.965652	0.9679842
0.25	0.946733	0.946643	0.953214	0.956282
0.3	0.93271	0.932605	0.940607	0.9443776
0.35	0.918894	0.918775	0.928098	0.9325271
0.4	0.905452	0.905322	0.91585	0.9208907
0.45	0.89248	0.892341	0.903964	0.9095669
0.5	0.880027	0.879882	0.892495	0.8986135
0.55	0.868114	0.867963	0.88147	0.8880613

System Availability

A represents the likelihood that the system will be operating at time "t," which may be defined as the rate. According to the state transition diagram, only states S_0, S_1, S_2, S_3, and S_4 are operative, whereas all states are regenerative. System availability for different repair rate is shown in Table 5.4.

$$A = N/D$$

$$N = \left(\frac{1}{\lambda_1 + \lambda_2}\right)\left[1 + \frac{\lambda_1}{\alpha_1} + \lambda_2\left(\frac{1}{\eta} + \frac{p}{\alpha_2 + \lambda_1 + \lambda_2} + \frac{q}{\alpha_3 + \lambda_1 + \lambda_2}\right)\right]$$

$$D = \sum_{i=0}^{8} S_{0,i}\mu_i$$

$$= \left(\frac{1}{\lambda_1+\lambda_2}\right)\left[1 + \frac{\lambda_1}{\alpha_1} + \lambda_2\left\{\frac{1}{\eta} + \frac{p}{\alpha_2+\lambda_1+\lambda_2}\left(1 + \frac{\lambda_1}{\alpha_2} + \frac{\lambda_2}{\alpha_2}\right) + \frac{q}{\alpha_3+\lambda_1+\lambda_2}\left(1 + \frac{\lambda_1}{\alpha_3} + \frac{\lambda_2}{\alpha_3}\right)\right\}\right]$$

Table 5.5 Busy period

λ_2	$\alpha_1 = 0.75, \alpha_2 = 0.7, \alpha_3 = 0.8$	$\alpha_1 = 0.95, \alpha_2 = 0.7, \alpha_3 = 0.8$	$\alpha_1 = 0.75, \alpha_2 = 0.8, \alpha_3 = 0.8$	$\alpha_1 = 0.95, \alpha_2 = 0.8, \alpha_3 = 0.9$
0.01	0.2151	0.213367	0.208443	0.203169
0.02	0.287955	0.286529	0.279712	0.273885
0.03	0.348433	0.347239	0.339207	0.333073
0.04	0.399442	0.398428	0.389624	0.383339
0.05	0.443045	0.442173	0.432892	0.426559
0.06	0.480744	0.479986	0.470432	0.464118
0.07	0.513664	0.512999	0.503311	0.497059
0.08	0.542658	0.54207	0.532346	0.526185
0.09	0.56839	0.567866	0.558174	0.552122
0.1	0.59138	0.590911	0.581298	0.575366

Busy Period

The repairmen are working in states $j = 1$ to 8 according to the state transition diagram. As seen in Table 5.5, the base state "0" has a very busy period:

$$B = \frac{N_1}{D}$$

$$N_1 = \left(\frac{1}{\lambda_1 + \lambda_2}\right)$$
$$\times \left[\frac{\lambda_1}{\alpha_1} + \lambda_2 \left\{\frac{1}{\eta} + \frac{p}{\alpha_2 + \lambda_1 + \lambda_2}\left(1 + \frac{\lambda_1}{\alpha_2} + \frac{\lambda_2}{\alpha_2}\right) + \frac{q}{\alpha_3 + \lambda_1 + \lambda_2}\left(1 + \frac{\lambda_1}{\alpha_3} + \frac{\lambda_2}{\alpha_3}\right)\right\}\right]$$

$$D = \text{already discussed}$$

Expected Visits by Repairmen

Let "V" be the number of repairman visits that are scheduled to take place. A fresh round of repairs begins at $j = 1$ to 2, as indicated by the state transition diagram (Table 5.6).

$$V = \frac{S_{0,1} + S_{0,2}}{D} = \frac{1}{D}$$

Table 5.6 Visits

λ_2	$\alpha_1 = 0.75, \alpha_2 = 0.7, \alpha_3 = 0.8$	$\alpha_1 = 0.95, \alpha_2 = 0.7, \alpha_3 = 0.8$	$\alpha_1 = 0.75, \alpha_2 = 0.8, \alpha_3 = 0.8$	$\alpha_1 = 0.95, \alpha_2 = 0.8, \alpha_3 = 0.9$
0.01	0.086339	0.08653	0.087071	0.087651
0.02	0.113927	0.114155	0.115246	0.116178
0.03	0.136829	0.13708	0.138767	0.140055
0.04	0.156145	0.156409	0.158698	0.160332
0.05	0.172656	0.172926	0.175803	0.177767
0.06	0.186932	0.187205	0.190644	0.192918
0.07	0.199398	0.19967	0.203642	0.206206
0.08	0.210377	0.210648	0.215121	0.217955
0.09	0.220121	0.220388	0.225331	0.228418
0.1	0.228827	0.22909	0.234473	0.237795

Table 5.7 Profit

λ_1	$\alpha_1 = 0.75, \alpha_2 = 0.7, \alpha_3 = 0.8$	$\alpha_1 = 0.95, \alpha_2 = 0.7, \alpha_3 = 0.8$	$\alpha_1 = 0.95, \alpha_2 = 0.9, \alpha_3 = 0.8$	$\alpha_1 = 0.95, \alpha_2 = 0.9, \alpha_3 = 1$
0.01	386889.9	386866.5	388633.9	389437.8
0.02	375834.9	375791.5	378935.8	380378.3
0.03	363610.7	363548.6	368110	370223.3
0.04	350916.2	350837.6	356771.5	359546.8
0.05	338171.6	338078.7	345301	348708.6
0.06	325629.2	325524.3	333934.9	337935.2
0.07	313437.4	313322.5	322818.1	327367.8
0.08	301679.9	301556.7	312037.2	317092.7
0.09	290399.3	290269.4	301640.8	307160
0.1	279612.2	279476.8	291652.7	297596.2

Profit

We will consider a particular function with the aim of analyzing the system profit (Table 5.7).

$$P = P_1\,A - pP_2\,V - qP_3\,V - P_4\,B_0 - P_5, h(t) = \eta e^{\eta t}, g_1(t) = \alpha_1 e^{-\alpha_1 t}, g_2(t) = \alpha_2 e^{-\alpha_2 t}, \text{and } g_3(t) = \alpha_3 e^{-\alpha_3 t}.$$

where

P_1 = when the system is operating at full capacity, revenue is generated per unit time.

P_2 = the cost of repairs performed by an ordinary repairman.

P_3 = the cost of repairs performed by an expert repairman.

P_4 = the amount of money you lose as a result of the repair taking longer than expected.
P_5 = setup and related costs.

6 Grey Wolf Optimizer

Grey wolf optimizer is a stochastic nature-inspired optimization algorithm that is based on the food collection of grey wolves. Grey wolf optimizer when compared with an optimization algorithm, alpha, beta, and delta of grey wolf optimizer are the first three best solutions in the algorithm. Omega is those grey wolves who do not directly participate in the hunting process but help improve the solution or attach to the prey. Three steps in this algorithm are finding the prey, encircling the prey, and attacking the prey. This simulation is formulated in mathematical operators and termed a grey wolf optimizer [7] (Fig. 5.2 and Table 5.8).

For the different values of repair and failure rates, Table 5.9 shows the optimal values of the profit function.

Fig. 5.2 Pseudo code of the GWO algorithm

```
Initialize the grey wolf population Xi (i=1 to n)
Initialize a, A, and C
Calculate the fitness of each search agent
Xα = The best search agent
Xβ = The second-best search agent
Xδ = The Third-best search agent
while (t< Max number of iterations)
for each search agent
end for
Update a, A, and C
Calculate the fitness of all search agents
Update Xα, Xβ, and Xδ
t=t+1
end while
return Xα
```

Table 5.8 Failure, inspection, and repair rate parameters are subject to restrictions

Parameters	Min	Max
λ_1	0.001	0.1
λ_2	0.002	0.05
η	0	0.9
α_1	0.4	0.9
α_2	0.5	0.9
α_3	0.5	1

Table 5.9 Minimum, maximum, standard deviation, mean, and median of profit function by GWO

Minimum	398196.67
Maximum	398779.01
Mean	398586.20
Median	398655.72
Standard deviation	179.0002

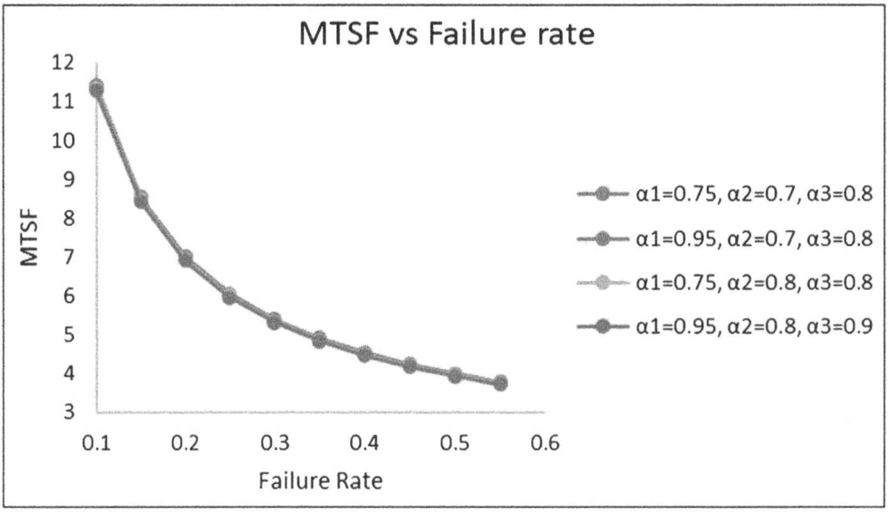

Fig. 5.3 MTSF vs failure rate

7 Graphical Results and Discussion

Figure 5.3 shows the impact of MTSF on the failure rate. It's easy to see that when the failure rate climbs, so does the availability and vice versa. Profit and failure rates are shown graphically in Figs. 5.4 and 5.5. As the failure rate grows, profit declines, but the overall picture remains the same. The increase in the failure rate ($\lambda 2$) from 0.02 to 0.04 results in a reduction of 25.14% in system failures in the interim (MTSF). When the failure rate ($\lambda 2$) increases from 0.1 to 0.55, the availability of the system decreases by 11.8%. As indicated in Table 6.4, an additional benefit of increasing repair rates ($\alpha 2$) and ($\alpha 3$) is that system availability is increased by 0.192% and 0.05189%, respectively, above baseline. In accordance with Table 5.5, the repairman's busy period increases by 33.7% when the failure rate is increased from 0.1% to 0.15% (approx.). According to Table 5.6, when the failure rate ($\lambda 2$) is increased from 0.01 to 0.1, the expected number of repairers increases by a factor of 8.55, which is a factor of 2.65. Another advantage of maintaining a consistent failure rate despite fluctuations in the repair rate is the reduction in the meantime to system failure.

To better illustrate each of these points, we've included graphs for profit, availability, and MTSF.

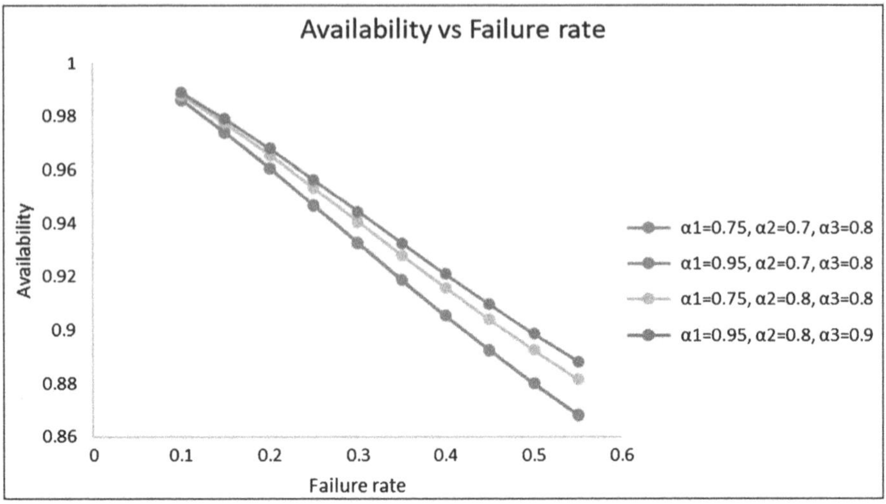

Fig. 5.4 Availability vs failure rate

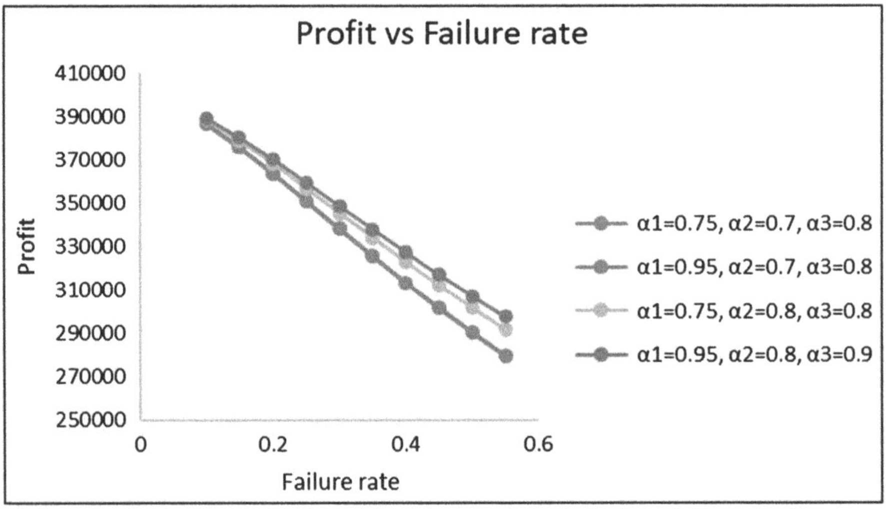

Fig. 5.5 Profit vs Failure rate

8 Conclusions

To learn more about how the two-unit biomass briquetting system works, a number of factors were taken into consideration. An increase in failure rates has a negative effect on availability, MTSF, and profit but has a positive effect on all three, as inspection rates grow. To maximize system profitability, the grey wolf optimization technique is utilized to simultaneously control failure, inspection, and repair rate parameters. There's the best value of 398779.01 for profit by GWO algorithm for repair and failure rate parameters ($\lambda 1$, $\lambda 2$, $\alpha 1$, $\alpha 2$, $\alpha 3$, η). As a result, the briquetting machine is a very successful business venture. To put it another way, biomass briquettes play a significant role in any coal or wood-burning appliance. The operational parameter needs to be adjusted in order to get the best results.

This manuscript failed to address the issues of ignored faults and periodic preventative maintenance. Preventive maintenance will be an important part of our future efforts to improve the profitability of our two-unit briquetting system.

References

1. Raju, C.A., Jyothi, K.R., Satya, M., Praveena, U.: Studies on development of fuel briquettes for household and industrial purpose. Int. J. Res. Eng. Technol. **3**(2), 54–63 (2014)
2. Sharma, M.K., Priyank, G., Sharma, N.: Biomass briquette production: a propagation of non-convention technology and future of pollution free thermal energy sources. Am. J. Eng. Res. (AJER). **4**(02), 44–50 (2015)
3. Shukla, S., Vyas, S.: Study of biomass briquettes, factors affecting its performance and technologies based on briquettes. J. Environ. Sci. Toxicol. Food Technol. **9**(11), 37–44 (2015)
4. Onukak, I.E., Mohammed-Dabo, I.A., Ameh, A.O., Okoduwa, S.I., Fasanya, O.O.: Production and characterization of biomass briquettes from tannery solid waste. Recycling. **2**(4), 17 (2017)
5. Sanap, R., Nalawade, M., Shende, J., Patil, P.: Automatic screw press briquette making machine. Int. J. Novel Res. Electr. Mech. Eng. **3**(1), 19–23 (2016)
6. Romallosa, A.R.D., Kraft, E.: Feasibility of biomass briquette production from municipal waste streams by integrating the informal sector in the Philippines. Resources. **6**(1), 12 (2017)
7. Mirjalili, S., Mirjalili, S.M., Lewis, A.: Grey wolf optimizer. Adv. Eng. Softw. **69**, 46–61 (2014)
8. Garg, D., Garg, R.: Performance analysis of the briquette machine considering aneglected faults with preventive maintenance. Int. J. Syst. Assur. Eng. Manag., 1–9 (2022)
9. Singh, J., Jaswal, R.A.: Evaluation of reliability parameter of thermal power plant by BFT. Int. J. Adv. Eng. Technol. **4**(3), 79–81 (2013)
10. Kongprasert, N., Wangphanich, P., Jutilarptavorn, A.: Charcoal briquettes from Madan wood waste as an alternative energy in Thailand. Proc. Manuf. **30**, 128–135 (2019)
11. Muazu, R.I., Borrion, A.L., Stegemann, J.A.: Life cycle assessment model for biomass fuel briquetting. Waste Biomass Valoriz. **13**(4), 2461–2476 (2022)
12. Kumar, A., Garg, D., Goel, P.: Mathematical modeling and behavioral analysis of a washing unit in paper mill. Int. J. Syst. Assur. Eng. Manag. **10**(6), 1639–1645 (2019)
13. Garg, D., Garg, R., Garg, V.: Inspecting briquette machine with different faults. Recent Adv. Comput. Sci. Commun. (Formerly: Recent Patents on Computer Science) **15**(4), 481–486 (2022)
14. Ullah, S., Noor, R.S., Gang, T.: Analysis of biofuel (briquette) production from forest biomass: a socioeconomic incentive towards deforestation. Biomass Convers. Biorefinery, 1–15 (2021)
15. Orisaleye, J.I., Jekayinfa, S.O., Adebayo, A.O., Ahmed, N.A., Pecenka, R.: Effect of densification variables on density of corn cob briquettes produced using a uniaxial compaction biomass briquetting press. Energy Sourcest A. Recov. Util. Environ. Effects. **40**(24), 3019–3028 (2018)
16. Raudah, Zulkifli: Optimization of binder addition and particle size for densification of coffee husks briquettes using response surface methodology. IOP Conf. Ser.: Mater. Sci. Eng. **334**, 012007 (2018)

17. Severy, M.A., Chamberlin, C.E., Eggink, A.J., Jacobson, A.E.: Demonstration of a pilot-scale plant for biomass torrefaction and briquetting. Appl. Eng. Agric. **34**(1), 85–98 (2018)
18. Arévalo, J., Quispe, G., Raymundo, C.: Sustainable Energy Model for the production of biomass briquettes based on rice husk in low-income agricultural areas in Peru. Energy Procedia. **141**, 138–145 (2017)
19. Ijah, A.A., Bubakar, S.A., Folabi, A.O., Yodele, J.T., Kanni-john, R., Lagunju, O.E., et al.: Determination of the calorific value of briquettes made from pinus caribaea and eucalyptus citirodora sawdust. J. Mater. Sci. Res. Rev. **6**(3), 46–50 (2020)
20. Yang, J., Wang, J., Li, J., Shi, L., Dai, X.: Optimum design of multidischarge outlet biomass briquetting machine. Complexity. (2020)
21. Wasfy, K.I., Awny, A.: Production of high-quality charcoal briquettes from recycled biomass residues. J. Soil Sci. Agric. Eng. **11**(12), 779–785 (2020)
22. Aliyu, M., Mohammed, I.S., Lawal, H.A., Dauda, S.M., Balami, A.A., Usman, M., et al.: Effect of compaction pressure and biomass type (rice husk and sawdust) on some physical and combustion properties of briquettes. Arid Zone J. Eng. Technol. Environ. **17**(1), 61–70 (2021)
23. Kumar, A.A., Jhansi, R., Vardhan, U.H., Gousia, S.M., Kumar, A.K.: Development and evaluation of low pressure multi briquetting machine. AMA Agric. Mech. Asia Africa Latin America. **50**(1), 48–56 (2019)
24. Orisaleye, J.I., Ojolo, S.J.: Mathematical modelling of pressure distribution along the die of a biomass briquetting machine. Int. J. Design Eng. **9**(1), 36–50 (2019)
25. Garg, D., Garg, R.: Reliability modelling and performance analysis of bio-coal manufacturing system with deviation in demand. Life Cycle Reliability Saf. Eng. **10**(4), 403–409 (2021)
26. Shekhar, N.: Popularization of biomass briquettes: a means for sustainable rural development. Asian J. Manage. Res. **2**(1), 457–473 (2011)
27. Ravichandran, P., Corscadden, K.: Comparison of gaseous and particle emissions produced from leached and un-leached agricultural biomass briquettes. Fuel Process. Technol. **128**, 359–366 (2014)
28. Lubwama, M., Yiga, V.A., Muhairwe, F., Kihedu, J.: Physical and combustion properties of agricultural residue bio-char bio-composite briquettes as sustainable domestic energy sources. Renew. Energy. **148**, 1002–1016 (2020)
29. Stolarski, M.J., Krzyżaniak, M., Warmiński, K., Niksa, D.: Energy consumption and costs of heating a detached house with wood briquettes in comparison to other fuels. Energy Convers. Manag. **121**, 71–83 (2016)
30. Garg, V., Singh, A., Garg, D.: Biogeography-based optimization algorithm for solving emergency vehicle routing problem in sudden disaster. In: Proceedings of International Conference on Scientific and Natural Computing, pp. 101–110. Springer, Singapore (2021)

Chapter 6
Solving Portfolio Optimization Using Sine-Cosine Algorithm Embedded Mutation Operations

Mousumi Banerjee, Vanita Garg, and Kusum Deep

1 Introduction

Portfolio optimization is the process in which investors receives appropriate guidance regarding the selection of assets from a variety of other option. The traditional asset location problem is that of an investor who wants to invest money in the stock market in such a way that individual can get a reasonable rate of return while minimizing risk. It is based on modern portfolio theory. MPT, first introduced by Markowitz in 1950, is also known as mean-variance analysis method, and this is a mathematical process which allows the investors to maximize returns for a given risk level. In a study by Zhai et al. [39], hybrid uncertainty, which mixes random returns and uncertain returns, is analysed using the chance theory. We explore the problem of optimizing a portfolio with an unknown random variable, which is the total return.

A new mean risk modal based on this criterion to optimization is proposed by Mehralizade et al. [28], along with a new risk criterion for uncertain random portfolio selection. To solve the portfolio selection problem with uncertain random returns, Ahmadzade et al. [2] used the idea of partial divergence metrics. Mehlawat et al. [27] study uses higher moments to investigate a multi-objective portfolio optimization issue in a chaotic, uncertain setting. We investigate a case with an asset universe, in which some assets have recently been listed assets that lack historical data while others have assets that have historical return data that is sufficient for modelling as random variables. We incorporate skewness (i.e. the third moment) in the portfolio optimization model and use mean absolute semi-deviation as a risk indicator. Ahmadzade and Gao [1] established a mean-variance-entropy model for uncertain random returns using the idea of covariance of uncertain random variables. Huang et al.'s [18] study offers the deterministic equivalents of a

---

M. Banerjee · V. Garg (✉) · K. Deep
Division of Mathematics, SBAS, School of Basic & Applied Sciences, Galgotias University, Greater Noida, Uttar Pradesh, India

© The Author(s), under exclusive license to Springer Nature Switzerland AG 2022

D. Singh et al. (eds.), *Design and Applications of Nature Inspired Optimization*, Women in Engineering and Science, https://doi.org/10.1007/978-3-031-17929-7_6

novel uncertain risk index model with background risk. Experts evaluate the security returns and backdrop asset returns with the assumption that they are uncertain variables. The portfolio problem between a risk-free and a risky asset in the presence of background risk was addressed by Brandtner et al. [6], using the convex shortfall risk measure.

Arhana and Iba [3] proposed a GA-based portfolio optimization method to generate an investment portfolio. Markowitz has used the mean-variance model and correlation variation model to present the expected return and risk of portfolio. This method calculated portfolio value when transaction cost is involved. Bonami and Lejeune [5] proposed portfolio optimization with PSO and solved the two types of risky portfolio, unrestricted and restricted. Ma et al. [24] solved the portfolio optimization problem with cardinally constraint method. Konno and Yamazaki [21] proposed a portfolio optimization model for huge-scale optimization problem on real-time basis. Solved the problem on a linear program as opposed to quadratic programme.

Shiang-Tai-Liu [34] proposed a method to solve the portfolio optimization problem with returns, a mean-absolute deviation risk function, and Zadeen's extension principles are used. Gupta et al. [17] presented the three stages of multiple decision-making portfolio in this study for financial and ethical criteria. GA presented an excellent meta-heuristic approach to solve this portfolio optimization problem [32] invented a interactive genetic algorithm (iGA) has been used to analyzed the nonlinear problem gives better result than GA. Zhang and Liu [37] endorse a hybrid version of fuzzy and genetic algorithm solving the fuzzy problems. It is feasible to solve multigoal issues by remodelling to a single goal. Zhang and Liu [31, 37] proposed a credibility multi-objective mean-semi entropy model with background risk for multi-period portfolio selection.

The importance of hybridization is to unite the benefits and to construct a strong model. Mansini et al. [25] proposed a solution to select a portfolio with fixed transaction cost and mixed integer linear programming model that used semi-deviation model to calculate the risk. Konno and Suzuki [22] proposed a mean-variance-skewness (MVS) portfolio optimization model; in this model, any decreasing utility function allows to maximize the third order approximation of the expected utility. Singh and Dharmendra [35] presented a credit risk optimization model using the l_∞ norm risk measure that is proposed for a portfolio of credit risky bonds.

Because the proposed model is written as a linear programming problem, it is computationally efficient for large portfolios. ZhongFeng [38] proposed a hybrid portfolio optimization and converted it to convex quadratic programming. Ertenlice and Kalayci [10] conducted swarm intelligence research for portfolio optimization, discussing algorithms and applications.

Hu et al. [19] studied the usage of evolutionary computation in the discovery of buying and selling policies in the set of rules of stock buying and selling. They proposed a hybrid technique that mixes the two styles of evaluation demonstrating via simulations that inventory optimization the use of economic indices (derived from essential evaluation) may be used to pick shares the pleasant organizations in phrases of operations with return. De Mighel et.al. [8] provided a general framework for identifying portfolios that perform well out of sample even in the presence of estimated error. This approach uses the sample covariance matrix to solve the standard minimum variance problem. Califore [7] proposed an opportunity to selection trees or pattern paths for multilevel portfolio allocation that results in specific convex confined quadratic programming fashions that may be solved globally and efficiently. The authors expand the multi-duration mean-variance version to cope with competing uncertainty eventualities and advocate a worst-case choice method that mixes a min-max approach with a stochastic optimization set of rules primarily based totally on situation trees. Pinar [30] and Takriti and Ahmed [36] proposed robust optimization in the context of two-stage planning system. An efficient variant of the L-shaped decomposition approach for classical stochastic linear programming can be used to solve a robust optimization model.

Advances in interior-point methods for some classes of nonlinear convex optimization have made heuristics based on repeated solution of a convex optimization problem possible. While these methods date back to the late 1960s (see, e.g. Fiacco and McCormick [11]), Karmarkar's interior-point method for linear programming [20], which was shown to be more efficient than the simplex method in terms of worst-case complexity analysis and in practice, ushered in the modern era.

Sharpe [33] proposed a linear goal programming model for open-end mutual fund portfolios selection. Orito et al. [29] proposed a new technique to initialize the population size using bordered Hessian that solved the problem with GA. Daun [9] proposed the traditional single-goal approach, including the suggest variance method, which solves the trouble by inclusive of one of the optimization goals withinside the goal characteristic and stifling the other. When an investor can promote securities quick in addition to purchase long and while an element and scenario model of covariance is assumed, the study by Levy and Markowitz [23] provides speedy algorithms for calculating mean-variance efficient frontiers.

In this study, an attempt is made to solve the Markowitz's classical mean-variance model using a recently introduced algorithm SCA and five versions of SCA. The result comapred with Laplacian BBO (LX-BBO). A brief literature study on BBO is done by Garg and Deep [15]. An improved variant of BBO called Laplacian BBO (LX-BBO) is developed for solving unconstrained optimization problems and is compared to the unconstrained version of blended BBO [13, 14, 16]. Laplacian BBO has proved its superiority over blended BBO for unconstrained optimization problems. Garg and Deep [12] solved the portfolio optimization problem using the Laplacian biogeography and variant blended biogeography method.

The rest of the paper is organized as follows: Sect. 2 describes the Markowitz model. The test problems, parameter settings, experimental results, and discussions are presented in Sect. 3. Section 4 presents briefly about the standard SCA and proposed approach of SCA. Analysis of result and comparison is presented in Sect. 6. Section 7 gives the conclusion of the present study.

2 Markowitz Model Based on Historical Stock Price Data

Markowitz Mean-Variance Model

Mean-Vriance Analysis technique to that investors choose which financial instruments to invest is based on the level of risk they are willing to take (Risk tolerance). Ideally, investors count on better returns after they spend money on riskier assets. When measuring peril, buyers shouldn't forget the ability deviation (i.e. the volatility of the yield generated through an asset) from that asset's anticipated yield. The evaluation of suggest variance basically checks the suggest variance of the anticipated return on an investment. The mean-variance model embraced with three main elements:

Rate of Return

Capital return is defined as the rate of return over a time interval or given period of time. The following equation is used to calculate capital return mathematically:

$$r_{i,t} = \frac{p_{i,t} - p_{i,t-1} + d_{i,t}}{p_{i,t-1}} \tag{6.1}$$

where $i = 1, 2, 3 - \ - -$variety of capitals,

$r_{i,\ t}$: returns on the capital over time t
$p_{i,\ t}$: during the time period t closing price i^{th} captial
$d_{i,\ t}$: during the time period t dividend price i^{th} captial

Expected Return

The second factor of mean-variance evaluation is anticipated return. This is the envisioned return that a protection is anticipated to produce, since it's a primarily based totally on historical data. The anticipated of return is not always 100% guaranteed. Mathematically expected return is stated as:

$$r(x_1, x_2, x_3, \ - - -, x_n) = E\left[\sum_{i=1}^{n} [R_i \middle| x_i]\right] = \sum_{i=1}^{n} E[R_i]x_i = \sum_{i=1}^{n} r_i x_i \tag{6.2}$$

where $[R_i]$ is the expectancy cost of random variable. Past data is used to calculate the value of R_i.

$$r_i = E[R_i] = \frac{1}{T}\sum_{t=1}^{T} r_{i,t} \tag{6.3}$$

Variance

Variance measures how remote or unfold the numbers in a statistics set are from the mean, or average. A massive variance shows that the numbers are in addition unfold out. A small variance shows a small unfold of numbers from the mean. The variance can also be zero, which shows no deviation from the mean. When studying a funding portfolio, variance can display how the returns of a safety are unfold out for the duration of a given period. Mathematically, the variance of the ith assets is stated as follows:

$$\sigma_i^2 = \delta(R_i) = E\left[(R_i - E[R_i])^2\right] = E\left[(R_i - r_i)^2\right] \tag{6.4}$$

The covariance σ_{ij} between asset return R_i and R_j is given as follows:

$$\sigma_{ij} = E\left[(R_i - E[R_i])\left(R_j - E\left[R_j\right]\right)\right] \tag{6.5}$$

Using the archivable data, covariance σ_{ij} is calculated as follows:

$$\sigma_{ij} = \frac{1}{T}\sum_{i=1}^{T}\left(r_{i,t} - r_i\right)\left(r_{i,j} - r_j\right) \tag{6.6}$$

σ_{ij} can also be expressed in terms of correlation coefficient (ρ_{ij}) as follows:

$$\sigma_{ij} = \rho_{ij}\sigma_i\sigma_j \tag{6.7}$$

As a result, the portfolio equation is defined by the equation:

$$\delta(x_1, x_2, \text{------}, x_n) = \sum_{i=1}^{n}\sum_{j=1}^{n} x_i x_j \sigma_{ij} \tag{6.8}$$

Portfolio Formulation

Markovitz [26] developed the modern portfolio theory as a financial framework via the trader's attempt to take minimum risks and attain most return to a given funding portfolio. The theory emphasizes that a higher return comes with a higher risk and that looking at the expected risk and return of a single asset is insufficient. An individual asset has a higher risk than an asset in a combined portfolio, as long as the risks of the various assets are not directly related.

The modern portfolio theory assumes that a rational investor wants the maximum return for a given level of risk and the least risk for a given level of expected return. As a result, the asset weight vector is the state variable in the asset allocation optimal solution, showing investors how much to invest in each asset in a given portfolio. Weight vector $x = [x_1, x_2, x_3 - - - - x_n]$ with x_i as the weight of asset i is the portfolio. The expected return for each asset in the portfolio is expressed in the vector form $r = [r_1 r_{2,} - - - r_n]$ with r_i as the mean return of assets i . The portfolio expected return is calculated using the weighted average of individual asset returns $= \sum_{i=1}^{n} x_i p_{i.}$

Statement of the Problem

The formulation of mean-variance method can be defined as:

Minimizing

$$\sum_{i=1}^{n} \sum_{j=1}^{n} x_i x_j \sigma_{ij} \tag{6.9}$$

Subject to

$$\begin{cases} \sum_{i=1}^{n} r_i = r_0 \\ \sum_{i=1}^{n} x_i = 1,\ x_i \geq 0 \ i = 1,\ 2......10 \end{cases} \tag{6.10}$$

3 Problem Description

The model is implemented using the stock market data obtained from the Indian National Stock Exchange, Mumbai, by selecting ten companies at random. The data is taken from the [12] paper proposed to solve the problem using the LX-BBO and blended BBO method and another variant blended biogeography method. The mean-variance model is shown in Table 6.9. The formulation of the ten-variable constrained optimization problem is as follows:

Problem 1

$$
\begin{aligned}
\text{Minimize } z = {} & 0.00338x_1^2 + 0.4225x_2^2 + 0.00615x_3^2 + 0.00429x_4^2 \\
& + 0.00686x_5^2 + 0.00260x_6^2 + 0.00275x_7^2 + 0.00224x_8^2 + 0.01036x_9^2 \\
& + 0.00178x_{10}^2 - 0.01584x_1x_2 + 0.00712x_1x_3 + 0.00404x_1x_4 \\
& + 0.00374x_1x_5 + 0.00294x_1x_6 + 0.00610x_1x_7 + 0.00170x_1x_8 \\
& + 0.00384x_1x_9 + 0.00192x_1x_{10} - 0.01350x_2x_3 - 0.00236x_2x_4 \\
& + 0.00614x_2x_5 + 0.00298x_2x_6 + 0.00236x_2x_7 + 0.00622x_2x_8 \\
& + 0.00384x_2x_9 + 0.00192x_2x_{10} + 0.00586x_3x_4 + 0.00456x_3x_5 \\
& + 0.00472x_3x_6 + 0.00182x_3x_7 + 0.00396x_3x_8 + 0.00648x_3x_9 \\
& + 0.00178x_3x_{10} + 0.00884x_4x_5 + 0.00516x_4x_6 + 0.00190x_4x_7 \\
& + 0.00464x_4x_8 + 0.01158x_4x_9 + 0.00288x_4x_{10} + 0.00696x_5x_6 \\
& + 0.00362x_5x_7 + 0.00530x_5x_8 + 0.0124x_5x_9 + 0.00384x_5x_{10} \\
& + 0.0017x_6x_7 + 0.0040x_6x_8 + 0.00766x_6x_9 + 0.00284x_6x_{10} \\
& + 0.00190x_7x_8 + 0.00324x_7x_9 - 0.00082x_7x_{10} + 0.00694x_8x_9 \\
& + 0.00180x_8x_{10} + 0.0054x_9
\end{aligned} \tag{6.11}
$$

$$
\begin{aligned}
\text{Subject to } r_0 = {} & 0.00728x_1 - 0.03613x_2 - 0.02414x_3 + 0.00706x_4 \\
& - 0.00458x_5 + 0.00372x_6 - 0.00461x_7 + 0.00413x_8 - 0.0248x_9 \\
& + 0.00562x_{10}
\end{aligned} \tag{6.12}
$$

$$x_1 + x_2 + x_3 + x_4 + x_5 + x_6 + x_7 + x_8 + x_9 + x_{10} = 1 \tag{6.13}$$

$$x_i \geq 0, i = 1,2, - - - - - - - - - - ,10. \tag{6.14}$$

The above optimization approach is solved using sine-cosine algorithm-based optimization.

Problem 2

The model is implemented using the stock market data (1 April 2020 to 31 March 2021) obtained from the Indian National Stock Exchange, Mumbai, by selecting ten companies at random. Table 6.18 shows the monthly asset return. According to the mean-variance model provided, Table 6.19 shows the expected returns calculated by

Eq. 6.3. Equation 6.4 is used to calculate the variance, and Eq. 6.5 is used to calculate the covariance.

$$\begin{aligned}\text{Minimize } z = {} & 0.087175x_1^2 + 0.03x_2^2 + 0.0061x_3^2 + 0.001x_4^2 + 0.0056x_5^2 \\ & + 0.0056x_6^2 + 0.003841x_7^2 + 0.010814x_8^2 + 0.0169x_9^2 + 0.005133x_{10}^2 \\ & - 0.0038x_1x_2 + 0.0013x_1x_3 + 0.005x_1x_4 + 0.00238x_1x_5 + 0.0022x_1x_6 \\ & + 0.0023x_1x_7 + 0.0041x_1x_8 + 0.00509x_1x_9 - 0.00259x_1x_{10} \\ & + 0.00398\,x_2x_3 - 0.0000000236x_2x_4 - 0.00250x_2x_5 - 0.000601x_2x_6 \\ & - 0.00088x_2x_7 + 0.00142x_2x_8 + 0.000841x_2x_9 + 0.000375x_2x_{10} \\ & - 0.00145x_3x_4 - 0.001x_3x_5 + 0.00114x_3x_6 + 0.00000332x_3x_7 \\ & + 0.00000361x_3x_8 - 0.0017x_3x_9 + 0.00026x_3x_{10} + 0.000202x_4x_5 \\ & + 0.000676x_4x_6 + 0.000706x_4x_7 + 0.002142x_4x_8 + 0.002336x_4x_9 \\ & + 0.00257x_4x_{10} - 0.00022x_5x_6 + 0.000192x_5x_7 + 0.000464x_5x_8 \\ & - 0.00336x_5x_9 - 0.00078x_5x_{10} + 0.000464x_6x_7 + 0.002499x_6x_8 \\ & + 0.007323x_6x_9 - 0.00336x_6x_{10} + 0.008177x_7x_8 + 0.005679x_7x_9 \\ & - 0.00593x_7x_{10} - 0.00418x_8x_9 - 0.00358x_8x_{10} - 0.00418x_9x_{10} \end{aligned} \tag{6.15}$$

$$\begin{aligned}\text{Subject to } r_0 = {} & 0.13036x_1 - 0.0265x_2 - 0.1065x_3 - 0.01833x_4 \\ & - 0.0200x_5 0.0252x_6 - 0.00038x_7 - 0.0153x_8 - 0.0412x_9 - 0.07308x_{10}\end{aligned} \tag{6.16}$$

$$x_1 + x_2 + x_3 + x_4 + x_5 + x_6 + x_7 + x_8 + x_9 + x_{10} = 1 \tag{6.17}$$

$$x_i \geq 0, i = 1, 2, - - - - - - - - - - , 10 \tag{6.18}$$

The above optimization problem is solved using sine-cosine algorithm-based optimization.

4 Sine-Cosine Algorithm

Sine-cosine is constructed on mathematical capabilities of sine-cosine function and discovering new feasible space using the two terms explore and exploit of search space. The SCA method is not usually tormented by the importance and nonlinear nature of the problem and even in other global strategies displays early convergence; the SCA reveals the best solution with more efficaciousness with a quicker convergence rate. The stability among the exploration and exploitation is the gain of this optimization technique. For this purpose, SCA makes use of trigonometric sine and cosine functions. At every step of the calculation, it updates the answers in line with the subsequent equations: The equation are as follows:

$$X_{ij}^{(t+1)} = \begin{cases} X_{ij}^{(t)} + r_1 \cos(r_2) |r_3 P_{ij}^{(t)} - X_{ij}^{(t)}|, \; r_4 \geq 0.5 \\ X_{ij}^{(t)} + r_1 \sin(r_2) |r_3 P_{ij}^{(t)} - X_{ij}^{(t)}|, \; r_4 \leq 0.5 \end{cases} \tag{6.19}$$

where $X_{ij}^{(t)}$ represents the current individual I at iteration t. $P_{ij}^{(\mathrm{t})}$ shows the best individual position at iteration t, and r_1, r_2, r_3, and r_4 are random parameters.

$$r_1 = a - \frac{ta}{T_{\max}} \tag{6.20}$$

where t denotes the iteration and r_1 is the main parameter that balances the exploration and exploitation phase, decreasing linearly from a constant value a to 0 by each iteration by Eq. 6.10, and r_2 and r_3 are random numbers.

The competency of SCA is different from other metaheuristic technique:

1. SCA works with a group of solution that benefit from the phenomenon of parallel exploration.
2. It simultaneously investigates several regions of solution space for sine and cosine function values outside the range [−1,1].
3. SCA investigates several promising solutions simultaneously during the exploratory process with sine-cosine value in the range [−1,1].
4. The best solution at a given point in the calculations is saved in a variable and becomes the problem's target ensuring that it never gets lost during the optimization phase.
5. The optimization process is convergent in nature (Table 6.1).

Table 6.1 Pseudo code of sine-cosine algorithm

```
Initiate {Evaluate the position X_i(i = 1, 2, — — — — n) and asses the objective function
Set the current best position P_i^t
Set T_max to the maximum number of iterations.
While T< T_max
for i = 1 : n
Update the parameter r_1, r_2,r_3 and r_4
Update X_i using equation (8)
   if (f(X_i^{t+1}) <f(X_i^t))
   refresh the current best position P_i^t
end if
end for
t = t + 1
end while
Return
the best solution P_i
```

Mutation

Mutation is a vital operator in genetic algorithms (GAs), because it ensures renovation of diversity in the evolving populations of GAs. It performs a crucial position in making the general search efficient. GAs are both simple and powerful in terms of computation, because they make no assumption about the solution space; genetic algorithm is an excellent tool for solving optimization problem.

The affinity of GAs is one of their advantages. GA uses a population of individual to search a solution space, making it less likely for them to become stuck in the local optimum. This comes at a price, which is the computational time. The longer runtime of Gas, on the other hand, can be reduced by terminating the evaluation earlier in order to obtain a satisfactory solution. Banerjee and Garg [4], incorporated five mutation operators power mutation, Polynomial mutation, Random mutation, Cauchy mutation & Gaussian mutation in SCA and presented a new version of SCA where cauchy & Random mutation performed better with constraint and unconstrained problems.

Power Mutation

Power mutation is a new form of SCA that incorporates the power mutation reported in (Banerjee and Garg). The power mutation p is set for 0.25 and $p = 0.50$. The mutation's strength is determined by the mutation's index (p). The smaller value of p should result in less fluctuation in the solution, while the larger value of p should result in more diversity. The mutation operator that has been proposed is based on power distribution. It's known as power mutation. Its distribution function is defined as follows:

$$f(x) = px^{p-1}, 0 \leq x \leq 1 \tag{6.21}$$

And the density function is presented by:

$$F(x) = x^p, 0 \leq x \leq 1 \tag{6.22}$$

The index of the distribution is denoted by p. The PM is used to generate a solution y near a parent solution z that follows the previously mentioned distribution. The mutated solution is then created using this formula below.

$$y = \begin{cases} x - z(x - x_l) & \text{if } r < t \\ x - z(x_u - x) & \text{if } r \geq t \end{cases} \tag{6.23}$$

Polynomial Mutation

Polynomial muatation (Banerjee & Garg 2022) presented incorporated in SCA. A new version of SCA in called Poly-SCA. To confound a solution in the neighbourhood of a parent, a polynomial probability distribution is used; the mutation operator adjusted the probability distribution to the left and right of a variable value so that no value outside the specific range $[a, b]$ is created. For a given parent solution $x\epsilon[x_l, x_u]$, mutated solution x' is constructed.

$$x' = \begin{cases} x+\delta_i(x-x_l) & \text{if} \quad u \leq 0.5 \\ x+\delta_i(x_u-x) & \text{if} \quad u > 0.5 \end{cases}, \tag{6.24}$$

Where $u\epsilon[0, 1]$ is a random number. The values δ_l and δ_r are computed as given by the formula.

$$\delta_l = (2u)^{\frac{1}{1+\rho}} - 1 \; u \leq 0.5$$

$$\delta_r = 1 - (2(1-u))^{\frac{1}{1+\rho}} \; u > 0.5$$

where $\rho_m \in [20, 100]$ is the user-defined parameter.

Random Mutation

Random mutation is incorporated in SCA.A new version of SCA is called Rand-SCA. Suppose x is any given solution, then a rand mutation operator is used as $x \in [x_l, x_u]$, and a random solution h is created using a neighbourhood of the replaced solution.

$$h = x_l + (x_u - x_l) * \text{rand} \tag{6.25}$$

where rand $\in[0, 1]$ represents a uniform distribution.

Gaussian Mutation

Gaussian mutation causes a small random change in the population. A random number from Gaussian distribution N (0,1) with parameter 0 as a mean and 1 as std. dev. is generated. $X(i,j)$ is chosen; then, find a new generated position.

$$z = X(i, j) + N_i(0, 1) \tag{6.26}$$

Cauchy Mutation

Cauchy mutation is defined in SCA as the same way as G-SCA. Suppose a random number is generated from the Cauchy distribution and defined by $\delta_i(t)$. The scale parameter is represented by t, where $t > 0$. Consider the value $t = 1$ as used in SCA-Cauchy. $X(i,j)$ is chosen; then, find a new generated position

$$z = X(i, j) + \delta_i(1) \tag{6.27}$$

5 Numerical Analysis of Results Obtained by the Proposed Version of SCA

Problem 1

The optimization problem described below is solved in two stages. The goal of the first stage is to figure out what the value of an unknown r_0 is in the restriction, given in Eq. 6.16. r_0 values are calculated for the upper and lower bounds, and this r_0 range is used in stage 2. The goal of stage 2 is to find the most cost-effective solution to the optimization problem. Different portfolios are created by considering various r_o values. These portfolios are then used to find the most cost-effective solution to the portfolio optimization problem.

Using SCA and variant of SCA, the value of undetermined r_0 is calculated in segment 1. The optimization problem is solved by removing the equality constraint in Eq. 6.17. r_0 min calculates the minimum value. The upper bound of r_0, denoted by $r_{\max}$, is calculated by investing all of one's money in the highest-returning asset. The r_0 values obtained are shown in Tables 6.2, 6.3, 6.4, 6.5, 6.6, and 6.7 for five the versions of SCA (Table 6.8).

In segment 2, five distinct portfolios are considered, namely, Portfolio 1, Portfolio 2, Portfolio 3, Portfolio 4, and Portfolio 5, in the same way that five different values r_0 are considered. These values of r_0 have to lie withinside the range $(r_{\min,}r_{\max})$ acquired in segment 1. The solution of those optimization problem using SCA and the variant of SCA is acquired with populace size 30, 50, and 100. Result obtained by the algorithms are tabulated in Tables 6.9, 6.10, 6.11, 6.12, 6.13, 6.14, 6.15, 6.16, and 6.17.

Table 6.8 depicts the expected rate of return is calculated over a specified range for different population sizes 30, 50, and100 and applied five versions of sine-cosine algorithm, compared the values with LX-BBO.

Result analysis for population size 30:

Figure 6.1 shows the Gaussian version of SCA gives an optimal portfolio with min risk 0.0012 for population size 30. The graph depicts that risk increases as return also increases while the difference between the maximum and minimum average

Table 6.2 For various population sizes, the range of r_0

The size of the population for SCA	risk_{min}	r_{min}	r_{max}
30	0.001428	0.000213	0.00612
50	0.0008	0.000312	0.00612
100	0.00033	0.00000003	0.0878

Table 6.3 For various population sizes, the range of r_0

The size of the population for PMSCA	risk_{min}	r_{min}	r_{max}
30	0.0012	0.0000000567	0.909
50	0.0006	0.00000343	0.00989
100	0.00055	0.001528	0.909

Table 6.4 For various population sizes, the range of r_0

The size of the population for Cauchy SCA	risk_{min}	r_{min}	r_{max}
30	0.0001256	0.00009	0.909
50	0.00065	0.000676	0.8889
100	0.00076	0.00009	0.89876

Table 6.5 For various population sizes, the range of r_0

The size of the population for Poly SCA	risk_{min}	r_{min}	r_{max}
30	0.001278	0.00009	0.909
50	0.00057	0.000676	0.8889
100	0.00039	0.00009	0.89876

Table 6.6 For various population sizes, the range of r_0

The size of the population for Gaussian SCA	risk_{min}	r_{min}	r_{max}
30	0.0012	0.0000765	0.9998
50	0.00055	0.000098	0.565
100	0.00058	0.000089	0.8988

Table 6.7 For various population sizes, the range of r_0

The size of the population for RM SCA	risk_{min}	r_{min}	r_{max}
30	0.0015	0.0000011	0.007
50	0.00082	0.000121	0.6789
100	0.0004	0.0000343	0.00564

Table 6.8 Comparison with other NIA

Algorithm	Population size	r_{min}	r_{max}
LX-BBO	30	0.000221	0.00728
	50	0.00518	0.00728
	100	−9E-06	0.0072
SCA	30	0.00213	0.00612
	50	0.000312	0.00612
	100	0.0000003	0.0878
PM-SCA	30	0.00000567	0.909
	50	0.00000343	0.00989
	100	0.001528	0.909
R-SCA	30	0.0000011	0.007
	50	0.000121	0.6789
	100	0.0000343	0.00564
C-SCA	30	0.0009	0.909
	50	0.00676	0.8809
	100	0.00009	0.89876
G-SCA	30	0.000765	0.9998
	50	0.000098	0.565
	100	0.000089	0.8988
Poly-SCA	30	0.00009	0.909
	50	0.000676	0.8989
	100	0.00009	0.89876

annual returns of the portfolio set decreases. The risk-reward trade-off is a trading principle that connects the high risk and high return. The best risk-return trade-off is determined by a number of factors, including the investor's risk tolerance and the ability to replace lost funds.

Result analysis for population size 50:

Figure 6.2 depicts SCA gives the best result with min risk 0.0005; it gives a set of optimal portfolios to strike a balance between an investment's expected return and its defined level of risk.

Result analysis for population size 100:

Poly-SCA variant of SCA anticipated range of expected return of different portfolio gives a good return with min risk 0.0013 for population size 100. Investing your money across a range of asset classes and securities to lower the portfolio's overall risk (Fig. 6.3 and Tables 6.18, 6.19, and 6.20).

Table 6.9 Efficient solution of portfolio optimization with population size 30 & 50 by SCA

	r_0	Risk	x_1	x_2	x_3	x_4	x_5	x_6	x_7	x_8	x_9	x_{10}
Portfolio 1	0.00023	0.001428	0	0	0.302	0.0256	0.250	0.002	0.102	0.003	0.210	0.100
Portfolio 2	0.00244	0.0017	0.05	0.012	0	0	0.235	0.0045	0.120	0.230	0.140	0.120
Portfolio 3	0.00449	0.00185	0.003	0.210	0.120	0.215	0.145	0	0	0.102	0.110	0.005
Portfolio 4	0.00551	0.00198	0	0.0543	0.4246	0.2405	0	0	0.0710	0	0.1230	0
Portfolio 5	0.00612	0.00620	0.00520	0.0020	0.001	0.102	0.203	0.403	0	0.006	0	0
Portfolio 1	0.00023	0.0008	0.005	0	0	0.208	0.310	0.008	0	0.025	0.30	0
Portfolio 2	0.00244	0.0012	0.0012	0.114	0.030	0.005	0.502	0	0	0.020	0.20	0
Portfolio 3	0.00449	0.0018	0.502	0.002	0	0.062	0.206	0.003	0.001	0.102	0	0.100
Portfolio 4	0.00551	0.002	0.302	0.133	0.123	0.007	0.159	0	0	0.162	0.0060	0
Portfolio 5	0.00620	0.00520	0.0020	0.001	0.102	0.203	0.403	0	0.0001	0.03	0.004	0

Table 6.10 Efficient solution of portfolio optimization with population 100 by SCA and 30 by PMSCA

	r_0	Risk	x_1	x_2	x_3	x_4	x_5	x_6	x_7	x_8	x_9	x_{10}
Portfolio 1	0.000748	0.0045	0.001	0.203	0.502	0.0002	0.310	0	0	0.020	0.30	0.003
Portfolio 2	0.00482	0.0055	0.402	0.004	0.0020	0.005	0	0	0.0023	0.010	0.200	0.004
Portfolio 3	0.006	0.06121	0	0.006	0.004	0.062	0.010	0.07	0.003	0	0.050	0.0020
Portfolio 4	0.0067	0.0912	1	0	0	0.007	0	0	0	0	0	0
Portfolio 5	0.8878	0.8878	0.09	0.01	0.502	0.203	0.001	0	0.05	0.002	0.01	0.004
Portfolio 1	0.0000343	0.0047	0.00528	0.003	0.502	0.007	0.008	0.009	0.001	0.002	0.055	0.101
Portfolio 2	0.00268	0.0052	0.00702	0.0004	0.00302	0.00702	0.0102	0.009	0.101	0.002	0.004	0.0404
Portfolio 3	0.0125	0.0056	0.0065	0.0054	0.00123	0.034	0.0045	0.0654	0.0006	0.0054	0.034	0.0054
Portfolio 4	0.100	0.0067	NAN	–	–	–	–	–	–	–	–	–
Portfolio 5	0.9298	0.9298	NAN	–	–	–	–	–	–	–	–	–

Table 6.11 Efficient solution of portfolio optimization with population size 50 and 100 by PMSCA

	r_0	Risk	x_1	x_2	x_3	x_4	x_5	x_6	x_7	x_8	x_9	x_{10}
Portfolio 1	0.00023	0.0006	0.001	0.203	0.502	0.0002	0.310	0	0	0.020	0.30	0.003
Portfolio 2	0.00244	0.001212	0.402	0.004	0.0020	0.005	0	0	0.0023	0.010	0.200	0.004
Portfolio 3	0.00449	0.001315	0	0.006	0.004	0.062	0.010	0.07	0.003	0	0.050	0.0020
Portfolio 4	0.00551	0.001517	1	0	0	0.007	0	0	0	0	0	0
Portfolio 5	0.00620	0.0052	0.09	0.01	0.502	0.203	0.001	0	0.05	0.002	0.01	0.004
Portfolio 1	0.001428	0.00055	0.00528	0.003	0.502	0.007	0.008	0.009	0.001	0.002	0.055	0.101
Portfolio 2	0.001202	0.00095	0.00702	0.0004	0.00302	0.00702	0.0102	0.009	0.101	0.002	0.004	0.0404
Portfolio 3	0.001109	0.0011	0.0065	0.0054	0.00123	0.034	0.0045	0.0654	0.0006	0.0054	0.034	0.0054
Portfolio 4	0.001025	0.00193	NAN	–	–	–	–	–	–	–	–	–
Portfolio 5	0.909	0.0015	NAN	–	–	–	–	–	–	–	–	–

Table 6.12 Efficient solution of portfolio optimization with population size 30 & 50 by RM- SCA

	r_0	Risk	x_1	x_2	x_3	x_4	x_5	x_6	x_7	x_8	x_9	x_{10}
Portfolio 1	0.00000011	0.0015	0.005	0.03	0.004	0.01	0.601	0.002	0.101	0.002	0.001	0.1
Portfolio 2	0.00230	0.0019	0.003	0.02	0.202	0.501	0.002	0.105	0	0.102	0	0
Portfolio 3	0.0250	0.0021	0.002	0.03	0.04	0.002	0.201	0.006	0.70	0	0	0.101
Portfolio 4	0.350	0.0022	NAN	–	–	–	–	–	–	–	–	–
Portfolio 5	0.70	0.004	NAN	–	–	–	–	–	–	–	–	–
Portfolio 1	0.000121	0.00082	0.003	0.04	0.05	0.05	0.001	0.045	0.501	0.001	0.30	0.001
Portfolio 2	0.00230	0.0015	0.04	0.005	0.06	0.06	0.01	0.05	0.001	0.02	0.04	0.5
Portfolio 3	0.00450	0.001567	0.003	0.05	0.7	0.7	0.001	0.05	0.001	0.20	0.02	0.001
Portfolio 4	0.00501	0.0016	0.04	0.05	0.07	0.7	0.001	0.1	0.002	0.20	0.40	0.001
Portfolio 5	0.6789	0.098	NAN	–	–	–	–	–	–	–	–	–

Table 6.13 Efficient solution of portfolio optimization with population size 100 by RM-SCA & 30 by Poly- SCA

	r_0	Risk	x_1	x_2	x_3	x_4	x_5	x_6	x_7	x_8	x_9	x_{10}
Portfolio 1	0.0000343	0.0004	0.005	0.03	0.004	0.01	0.601	0.002	0.101	0.002	0.001	0.1
Portfolio 2	0.000250	0.00085	0.003	0.02	0.202	0.501	0.002	0.105	0	0.102	0	0
Portfolio 3	0.00160	0.001167	0.002	0.03	0.04	0.002	0.201	0.006	0.70	0	0	0.101
Portfolio 4	0.00350	0.0015	NAN	–	–	–	–	–	–	–	–	–
Portfolio 5	0.00564	0.0020	NAN	–	–	–	–	–	–	–	–	–
Portfolio 1	0.00009	0.001278	0.003	0.001278	0.05	0.05	0.001	0.045	0.1	0.002	0.004	0
Portfolio 2	0.000890	0.001456	0.04	0.001456	0.06	0.06	0.01	0.005	0	0	0.065	0.043
Portfolio 3	0.000750	0.001628	0.003	0.001628	0.7	0.7	0.001	0	0.767	0.043	0	0
Portfolio 4	0.00501	0.001978	0.04	0.001978	0.07	0.7	0.001	0.004	0.0012	0.0023	0.0045	0
Portfolio 5	0.909	0.056	NAN	–	–	–	–	–	–	–	–	–

Table 6.14 Efficient solution of portfolio optimization with population size 50, 100 by Poly-SCA

	r_0	Risk	x_1	x_2	x_3	x_4	x_5	x_6	x_7	x_8	x_9	x_{10}
Portfolio 1	0.000676	0.00057	0.007	0.003	0.003	0.43	0.03	0.004	0.005	0.065	0.78	0
Portfolio 2	0.000350	0.00078	0.04	0.043	0	0.0032	0.005	0.002	0.87	0.006	0	0
Portfolio 3	0.00550	0.00098	NAN	–	–	–	–	–	–	–	–	–
Portfolio 4	0.0250	0.0015	NAN	–	–	–	–	–	–	–	–	–
Portfolio 5	0.8889	0.0022	NAN	–	–	–	–	–	–	–	–	–
Portfolio 1	0.00009	0.00039	0.001	0.0006	0.0054	0.0076	0.0043	0.03	0.43	0.34	0	0
Portfolio 2	0.00750	0.00078	0.43	0.0043	0.005	0.0054	0.00043	0.54	0.12	0	0.44	0
Portfolio 3	0.00550	0.001456	NAN	–	–	–	–	–	–	–	–	–
Portfolio 4	0.075	0.0018	NAN	–	–	–	–	–	–	–	–	–
Portfolio 5	0.89876	0.00165	NAN	–	–	–	–	–	–	–	–	–

Table 6.15 Efficient solution of portfolio optimization with population size 30 & 50 by Cauchy- SCA

	r_0	Risk	x_1	x_2	x_3	x_4	x_5	x_6	x_7	x_8	x_9	x_{10}
Portfolio 1	0.00009	0.001256	0.02	0.03	0.040	0.50	0.001	0.020	0.010	0.001	0.020	0
Portfolio 2	0.00150	0.001628	0.05	0.02	0	0	0.30	0.20	0.001	0.07	0	0.08
Portfolio 3	0.0080	0.001834	0.06	0.03	0.70	0.1	0.20	0.40	0.005	0	0.001	0.070
Portfolio 4	0.070	0.001928	0.1	0.01	0.10	0.02	0.20	0.050	0.070	0.050	0.021	0.10
Portfolio 5	0.909	0.0020	NAN	–	–	–	–	–	–	–	–	–
Portfolio 1	0.000676	0.00065	0.003	0.50	0.001	0.30	0.20	0.60	0.001	0.20	0.10	0.001
Portfolio 2	0.00249	0.00095	0.02	0.30	0.01	0.50	0.30	0.001	0.01	0.20	0.001	0.03
Portfolio 3	0.0060	0.001125	NAN	–	–	–	–	–	–	–	–	–
Portfolio 4	0.050	0.001356	NAN	–	–	–	–	–	–	–	–	–
Portfolio 5	0.889	0.0700	NAN	–	–	–	–	–	–	–	–	–

Table 6.16 Efficient solution of portfolio optimization with population size 100 by Cauchy-SCA & 30 by GA- SCA

	r_0	Risk	x_1	x_2	x_3	x_4	x_5	x_6	x_7	x_8	x_9	x_{10}
Portfolio 1	0.00009	0.00076	0.005	0.004	0.00056	0.004	0.005	0.065	0.076	0.0034	0.008	0.0034
Portfolio 2	0.00175	0.001267	0.03	0.5	0.006	0.0087	0.00654	0.05	0.005	0.006	0.03	0.03
Portfolio 3	0.0020	0.001834	0.05	023	0.008	0.65	0.9	0.087	0.65	0.56	0.004	0.04
Portfolio 4	0.040	0.001928	0.067	0.06	0.004	0.008	0.003	0.065	0.003	0.007	0.035	0.003
Portfolio 5	0.89876	0.0698	0.002	0.09	0.0087	0.05	0.8	0.004	0.004	0.0034	0.045	0.005
Portfolio 1	0.0000765	0.0012	0.0012	0.004	0.45	0.0043	0.0004	0.0065	0.87	0.0002	0.0067	0.0056
Portfolio 2	0.000560	0.0017	0.0017	0.0065	0.3	0.0056	0.0065	0.09	0.0054	0.34	0.23	0.07
Portfolio 3	0.00350	0.002123	0.002123	0.00054	0.1	0.0076	0.006	0.2	0.004	0.56	0.34	0.006
Portfolio 4	0.075	0.0022	0.0022	0.0006	0.076	0.87	0.112	0.45	0.54	0	0.002	0.001
Portfolio 5	0.9998	0.0076	0.878	NAN	–	–	–	–	–	–	–	–

Table 6.17 Efficient solution of portfolio optimization with population 50 & 100 by Gaussian- SCA

	r_0	Risk	x_1	x_2	x_3	x_4	x_5	x_6	x_7	x_8	x_9	x_{10}
Portfolio 1	0.000098	0.00055	0.003	0	0.004	0.007	0.0065	0.54	0.064	0.06	0	0
Portfolio 2	0.000878	0.00085	0.008	0	0.10	0.03	0.008	0.5	0.05	0	0	0
Portfolio 3	0.00780	0.0011	0.02	0.006	0.002	0.03	0.007	0	0.0045	0	0.007	0.0076
Portfolio 4	0.0850	0.0013	0.02	0.05	0.003	0.002	0.006	0.004	0	0	0.034	0.0054
Portfolio 5	0.565	0.0098	0.003	0.006	0.02	0.003	0.005	0	0		0	0.0056
Portfolio 1	0.000089	0.00058	0.007	0.05	0	0	0.10	0.03	0.008	0.5	0.05	0
Portfolio 2	0.00077	0.001176	0.0065	0.0045	0	0.006	0.002	0.03	0.007	0	0.0045	0
Portfolio 3	0.00617	0.001345	0.56	0	0	0.05	0.003	0.002	0.006	0.004	0	0
Portfolio 4	0.035	0.0016	NAN	–	–	–	–	–	–	–		–
Portfolio 5	0.8988	0.0020	NAN	–	–	–	–	–	–	–	–	–

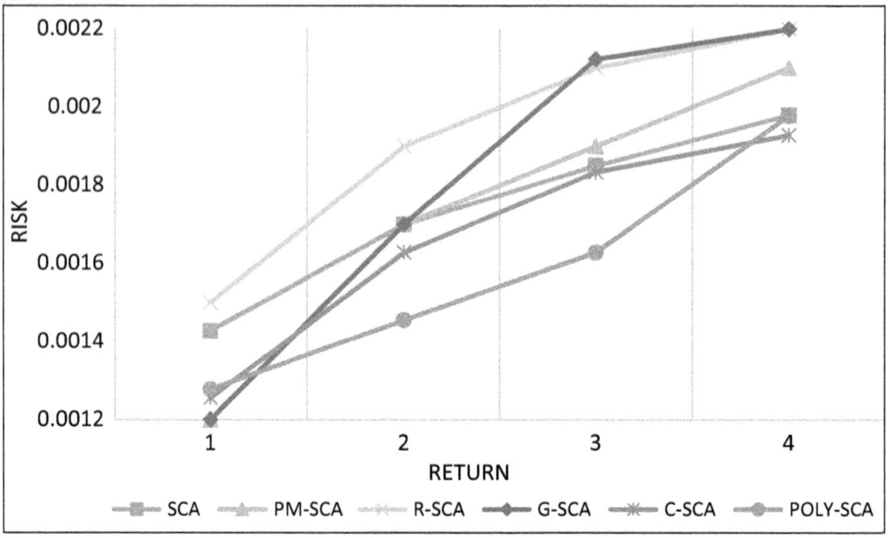

Fig. 6.1 Optimal portfolio for population size 30

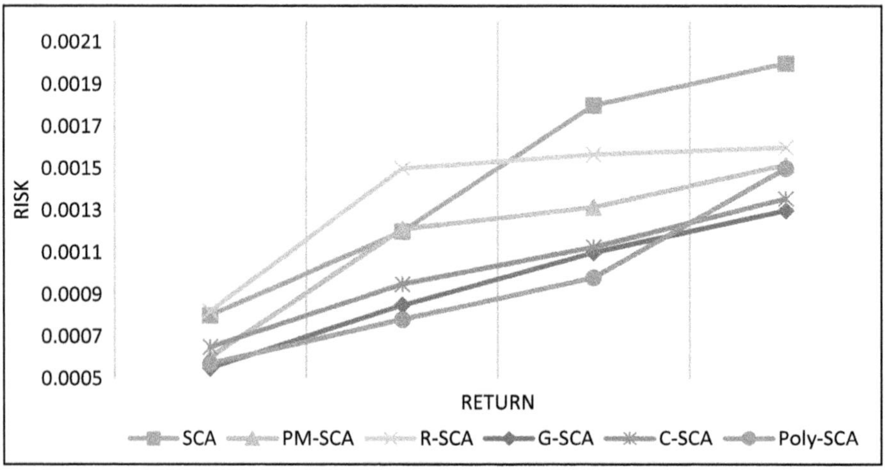

Fig. 6.2 Optimal portfolio for population size 50

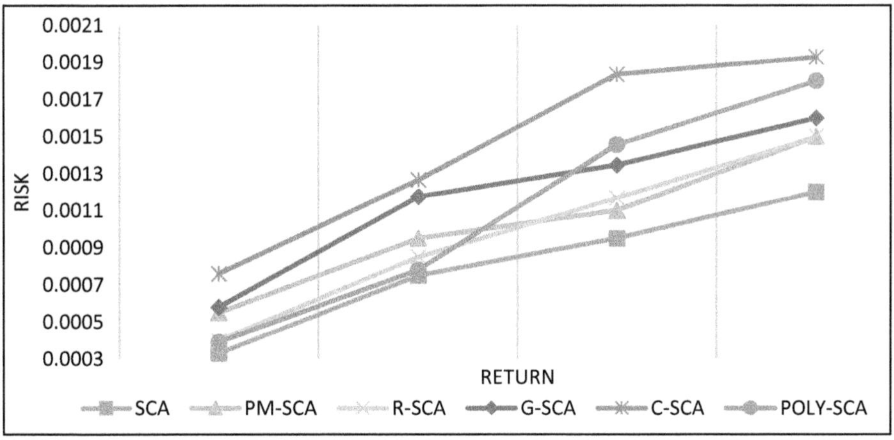

Fig. 6.3 Optimal portfolio for population size 100

Problem 2

The numerical analysis of the result is described similarly as in Sect. 5. Using SCA and the variant of SCA, the value of undetermined r_0 is calculated in segment 1. The optimization problem is solved by removing the equality constraint in Eq. 6.16. r_0 min calculates the minimum value. The upper bound of r_0, denoted by r_{max}, is calculated by investing all of one's money in the highest-returning asset. The r_0 values obtained are shown in Tables 6.21, 6.22, 6.23, 6.24, 6.25, and 6.26 for the five versions of SCA.

In segment 2, five distinct portfolios are considered, namely, Portfolio 1, Portfolio 2, Portfolio 3, Portfolio 4, and Portfolio 5, in the same way that five different values r_0 are considered. These values of r_0 have to lie withinside the range $(r_{min,} r_{max})$ acquired in segment I. The solution of those optimization problem using SCA and the variant of SCA is acquired with populace size 30, 50, and 100. The results obtained by the algorithms are tabulated in Tables 6.27, 6.28, 6.29, 6.30, 6.31, 6.32, 6.33, 6.34, 6.35, and 6.36.

Table 6.37 depicts the expected rate of return that is calculated over a specified range for different population sizes 30, 50, and100 and applied five versions of sine-cosine algorithm, which compared the values with LX-BBO.

Result analysis for population size 30:

PM-SCA and poly-SCA give the best convergence graph with min risk 0.0013 and 0.0022 for population size 30, which is shown in Fig. 6.4.

Result analysis for population size 50:

Table 6.18 Monthly assets return data from 1st April 2020 to 31st march 2021 of 10 companies

Security name	Apr_20	May_20	June_20	July_20	Aug_20	Sep_20	Oct_20	Nov_20	Dec_20	Jan_21	Feb_21	Mar_21
Asian Paints Ltd	1.055326	0.04299	0.002585	0.016623	0.107024	0.045969	0.113321	0.001718	0.247912	–0.12919	–0.05406	0.11426
Bajaj Auto Ltd	–0.03217	0.033241	–0.03217	–0.08645	0.029815	–0.00201	–0.09032	–0.07854	–0.14023	0.054515	0.034899	–0.04256
Cipla Ltd	–0.9033	0.012339	–0.11095	0.00925	–0.07893	0.026773	0.011937	–0.09068	–0.0072	0.0493	–0.03441	–0.0463
Grasim Industries Ltd	0.03	0.03	–0.02	–0.06	–0.09	–0.04	–0.011	–0.06	–0.012	–0.012	–0.017	0.03
Ambuja Cement Ltd	–0.10389	0.01059	–0.1204	0.04537	0.02972	–0.16442	–0.00517	0.049027	0.022601	0.11024	–0.11446	–0.00065
HDFC Bank Ltd	0.052698	–0.10714	0.032	–0.07443	0.034536	–0.08867	–0.17858	0.003168	0.032938	–0.09378	0.027282	0.05760
Hindustn Unilever Ltd	0.066906	–0.05626	–0.01353	0.04371	0.02374	–0.00147	–0.03129	–0.10737	0.058086	0.061842	–0.12315	0.03303
Kotak Mahindra Bank Ltd	0.108824	–0.1003	–0.00388	–0.0254	0.104991	–0.18043	–0.18861	–0.04435	0.165008	–0.03786	0.015602	0.00240
State Bank Ltd	0.181029	–0.09611	–0.0679	–0.0969	0.1434	–0.02034	–0.22518	–0.11166	–0.02535	–0.2769	0.07095	0.03055
Wipro Ltd	–0.10268	–0.03119	–0.21819	0.035569	–0.134	–0.07989	–0.02796	–0.09256	–0.07574	0.0185	–0.0093	–0.15951

Table 6.19 Expected return of individual stocks

Security name	Expected return
BAL	0.13036
CL	−0.0265
APL	−0.1065
GIL	−0.01833
ACL	−0.0200
HDFC	0.0252
HUL	−0.003811
KMBL	−0.01533
SBI	−0.0412
WL	−0.07308

Figure 6.5 depicts Cauchy-SCA gives the best result for population size 50.

Result analysis for population size 100:

This poly-SCA gives the best result with 100 population size in the year 2015–2016 and 2020–2021. As a result, portfolio optimization performed effectively with 100 population size (Fig. 6.6).

6 Result Analysis

A sensitivity analysis, performed with population size 30, 50, 100 and an algorithm, is applied in five different versions of SCA. Five different portfolios are presumed in the numerical problem for two data set year 2015–2016 and year 2020–2021. The convergence graphs for all of the cases derived with different population sizes. It is seen that portfolio theory attitude depends entirely on the size of the population. Because when the size of the population achieves 30, the risk goes up at the very same speed as the rates of return. Whenever the population size is placed to 50, the risk increases as the rates of return rise, but at a varying rates. When the size of the population reaches 100, the risk would be almost consistent as the rates of return enhance.

7 Conclusion

In this paper, we presented a novel attempt to solve the model of portfolio optimization for five variants of SCA. Portfolio diversification is one of the most important tenets of investing and is essential for risk management. Diversification has numerous advantages. It must, however, be done with caution. Modern investors do not concentrate their wealth in a single security or a single type of security; instead, they

Table 6.20 Covariance and variance for the month-to-month asset returns

Security name	APL	BAL	CL	GIL	ACL	HDFC	HUL	KMBL	SBI	WL
APL	0.087175	0.0003435	−0.07	0.004	−0.0004	0.0006	0.009911	0.009911	0.018284	−0.00269
BAL	0.0003435	0.003	−0.03	0.003	0.0010	0.0001	−0.00022	−0.00022	0.002033	0.00022
CL	−0.07	−0.003	0.0061	−0.003	0.0060	−0.08	−0.00442	−0.00442	−0.01932	0.005223
GIL	0.004	0.003	−0.003	0.001	−0.0005	0.0000046	0.000286	0.000286	4.8E-05	−0.00013
ACL	−0.0004	0.0010	0.006	−0.0005	0.0056	0.0013	0.0011	0.0011	−0.00516	0.002236
HDFC	0.0006	0.0001	−0.008	0.0000046	0.0013	0.0056	0.000464	0.000464	0.007322	−0.00336
HUL	0.009911	−0.00022	−0.00442	0.000286	0.0011	0.000464	0.003841	0.00234	0.000705	0.0003
KMBL	0.01039	−0.00022	−0.0111	−7.6E-05	0.00105	0.006361	0.002499	0.010814	0.008176	−0.00213
SBI	0.018284	0.002033	−0.01932	4.8E-05	−0.00516	0.007322	0.000705	0.008176	0.016923	−0.00417
WL	−0.00269	0.00022	0.005223	−0.00013	0.002236	−0.00336	−0.0003	−0.00213	−0.00417	0.005133

Table 6.21 For various population sizes, the range of r_0

The size of the population for SCA	$\text{risk}_{\min}$	$r_{\min}$	$r_{\max}$
30	0.0005	0.000323	0.323
50	0.0017	0.0000545	0.8878
100	0.0112	0.0000897	0.8878

Table 6.22 For various population sizes, the range of r_0

The size of the population for PMSCA	$\text{risk}_{\min}$	$r_{\min}$	$r_{\max}$
30	0.0013	0.0000343	0.9298
50	0.0013	0.000032	0.333
100	0.0025	0.0000434	0.5656

Table 6.23 For various population sizes, the range of r_0

The size of the population Cauchy SCA	$\text{risk}_{\min}$	$r_{\min}$	$r_{\max}$
30	0.0022	0.00011	0.7773
50	0.00085	0.0000343	0.323
100	0.0013	0.000088	0.7766

Table 6.24 For various population sizes, the range of r_0

The size of the population for Poly SCA	$\text{risk}_{\min}$	$r_{\min}$	$r_{\max}$
30	0.0022	0.000211	0.676
50	0.0011	0.00232	0.576
100	0.0013	0.0000656	0.576

Table 6.25 For various population sizes, the range of r_0

The size of the population for Gaussian SCA	$\text{risk}_{\min}$	$r_{\min}$	$r_{\max}$
30	0.0056	0.0000332	0.9998
50	0.0012	0.0011	0.4434
100	0.0012	0.00011	0.8988

Table 6.26 For various population sizes, the range of r_0

The size of the population for RM SCA	$\text{risk}_{\min}$	$r_{\min}$	$r_{\max}$
30	0.0037	0.000111	0.777
50	0.0056	0.000343	0.323
100	0.0012	0.00011	0.7766

Table 6.27 Efficient solution of portfolio optimization with population 30 & 50 by SCA

	r_0	Risk	x_1	x_2	x_3	x_4	x_5	x_6	x_7	x_8	x_9	x_{10}
Portfolio 1	0.00323	0.0026	0	0	0.302	0.0134	0.250	0.001	0.102	0.004	0.210	0.100
Portfolio 2	0.0050	0.0031	0.05	0.012	0	0	0.235	0.0045	0.120	0.230	0.140	0.120
Portfolio 3	0.0030	0.00332	0.003	0.210	0.120	0.215	0.145	0	0	0.102	0.110	0.005
Portfolio 4	0.0211	0.0041	0	0.0543	0.4246	0.2405	0	0	0.0710	0	0.1230	0
Portfolio 5	0.323	0.323	0.0070	0.212	0.0053	0.0213	0.423	0	0	0.006	0	0
Portfolio 1	0.000641	0.0049	0.005	0	0	0.208	0.310	0.008	0	0.025	0.30	0
Portfolio 2	0.00324	0.0055	0.0012	0.114	0.030	0.005	0.502	0	0	0.020	0.20	0
Portfolio 3	0.0125	0.0058	0.502	0.002	0	0.062	0.206	0.003	0.001	0.102	0	0.100
Portfolio 4	0.0100	0.0066	0.302	0.133	0.123	0.007	0.159	0	0	0.162	0.0060	0
Portfolio 5	0.8878	0.8878	0.0020	0.001	0.102	0.203	0.403	0	0.0001	0.03	0.004	0

Table 6.28 Efficient solution of portfolio optimization with population 100 by SCA and 30 by PMSCA

	r_0	Risk	x_1	x_2	x_3	x_4	x_5	x_6	x_7	x_8	x_9	x_{10}
Portfolio 1	0.000748	0.0045	0.001	0.203	0.502	0.0002	0.310	0	0	0.020	0.30	0.003
Portfolio 2	0.00482	0.0055	0.402	0.004	0.0020	0.005	0	0	0.0023	0.010	0.200	0.004
Portfolio 3	0.006	0.06121	0	0.006	0.004	0.062	0.010	0.07	0.003	0	0.050	0.0020
Portfolio 4	0.0067	0.0912	1	0	0	0.007	0	0	0	0	0	0
Portfolio 5	0.8878	0.8878	0.09	0.01	0.502	0.203	0.001	0	0.05	0.002	0.01	0.004
Portfolio 1	0.0000343	0.0047	0.00528	0.003	0.502	0.007	0.008	0.009	0.001	0.002	0.055	0.101
Portfolio 2	0.00268	0.0052	0.00702	0.0004	0.00302	0.00702	0.0102	0.009	0.101	0.002	0.004	0.0404
Portfolio 3	0.0125	0.0056	0.0065	0.0054	0.00123	0.034	0.0045	0.0654	0.0006	0.0054	0.034	0.0054
Portfolio 4	0.100	0.0067	NAN	–	–	–	–	–	–	–	–	–
Portfolio 5	0.9298	0.9298	NAN	–	–	–	–	–	–	–	–	–

Table 6.29 Efficient solution of portfolio optimization with population size 50 & 100 by PMSCA

	r_0	Risk	x_1	x_2	x_3	x_4	x_5	x_6	x_7	x_8	x_9	x_{10}
Portfolio 1	0.000032	0.00013	0.001	0.203	0.502	0.0002	0.310	0	0	0.020	0.30	0.003
Portfolio 2	0.000172	0.0015	0.402	0.004	0.0020	0.005	0	0	0.0023	0.010	0.200	0.004
Portfolio 3	0.00115	0.0019	0	0.006	0.004	0.062	0.010	0.07	0.003	0	0.050	0.0020
Portfolio 4	0.0105	0.002	1	0	0	0.007	0	0	0	0	0	0
Portfolio 5	0.332	0.332	0.09	0.01	0.502	0.203	0.001	0	0.05	0.002	0.01	0.004
Portfolio 1	0.0000434	0.0043	0.00528	0.003	0.502	0.007	0.008	0.009	0.001	0.002	0.055	0.101
Portfolio 2	0.000265	0.0056	0.00702	0.0004	0.00302	0.00702	0.0102	0.009	0.101	0.002	0.004	0.0404
Portfolio 3	0.00154	0.0059	0.0065	0.0054	0.00123	0.034	0.0045	0.0654	0.0006	0.0054	0.034	0.0054
Portfolio 4	0.065	0.0064	NAN	–	–	–	–	–	–	–	–	–
Portfolio 5	0.5656	0.5656	NAN	–	–	–	–	–	–	–	–	–

Table 6.30 Efficient solution of portfolio optimization with population 50 & 100 by PMSCA

	r_0	Risk	x_1	x_2	x_3	x_4	x_5	x_6	x_7	x_8	x_9	x_{10}
Portfolio 1	0.000032	0.00013	0.001	0.203	0.502	0.0002	0.310	0	0	0.020	0.30	0.003
Portfolio 2	0.000172	0.0015	0.402	0.004	0.0020	0.005	0	0	0.0023	0.010	0.200	0.004
Portfolio 3	0.00115	0.0019	0	0.006	0.004	0.062	0.010	0.07	0.003	0	0.050	0.0020
Portfolio 4	0.0105	0.002	1	0	0	0.007	0	0	0	0	0	0
Portfolio 5	0.332	0.332	0.09	0.01	0.502	0.203	0.001	0	0.05	0.002	0.01	0.004
Portfolio 1	0.0000434	0.0043	0.00528	0.003	0.502	0.007	0.008	0.009	0.001	0.002	0.055	0.101
Portfolio 2	0.000265	0.0056	0.00702	0.0004	0.00302	0.00702	0.0102	0.009	0.101	0.002	0.004	0.0404
Portfolio 3	0.00154	0.0059	0.0065	0.0054	0.00123	0.034	0.0045	0.0654	0.0006	0.0054	0.034	0.0054
Portfolio 4	0.065	0.0064	NAN	–	–	–	–	–	–	–	–	–
Portfolio 5	0.5656	0.5656	NAN	–	–	–	–	–	–	–	–	–

Table 6.31 Efficient solution of portfolio optimization with population size 30 & 50 by RM- SCA

	r_0	Risk	x_1	x_2	x_3	x_4	x_5	x_6	x_7	x_8	x_9	x_{10}
Portfolio 1	0.00011	0.0028	0.005	0.03	0.004	0.01	0.601	0.002	0.101	0.002	0.001	0.1
Portfolio 2	0.00562	0.00338	0.003	0.02	0.202	0.501	0.002	0.105	0	0.102	0	0
Portfolio 3	0.00268	0.0039	0.002	0.03	0.04	0.002	0.201	0.006	0.70	0	0	0.101
Portfolio 4	0.0142	0.0044	NAN	–	–	–	–	–	–	–	–	–
Portfolio 5	0.77	0.77	NAN	–	–	–	–	–	–	–	–	–
Portfolio 1	0.000343	0.005	0.003	0.04	0.05	0.05	0.001	0.045	0.501	0.001	0.30	0.001
Portfolio 2	0.00478	0.0053	0.04	0.005	0.06	0.06	0.01	0.05	0.001	0.02	0.04	0.5
Portfolio 3	0.00261	0.0058	0.003	0.05	0.7	0.7	0.001	0.05	0.001	0.20	0.02	0.001
Portfolio 4	0.0128	0.0066	0.04	0.05	0.07	0.7	0.001	0.1	0.002	0.20	0.40	0.001
Portfolio 5	0.323	0.323	NAN	–	–	–	–	–	–	–	–	–

Table 6.32 Efficient solution of portfolio optimization with population size 100 by RM-SCA & 30 by Poly- SCA

	r_0	Risk	x_1	x_2	x_3	x_4	x_5	x_6	x_7	x_8	x_9	x_{10}
Portfolio 1	0.00011	0.0044	0.005	0.03	0.004	0.01	0.601	0.002	0.101	0.002	0.001	0.1
Portfolio 2	0.00562	0.0048	0.003	0.02	0.202	0.501	0.002	0.105	0	0.102	0	0
Portfolio 3	0.00362	0.0053	0.002	0.03	0.04	0.002	0.201	0.006	0.70	0	0	0.101
Portfolio 4	0.0135	0.0058	NAN	–	–	–	–	–	–	–	–	–
Portfolio 5	0.7766	0.7766	NAN	–	–	–	–	–	–	–	–	–
Portfolio 1	0.000211	0.0033	0.003	0.04	0.05	0.05	0.001	0.045	0.1	0.002	0.004	0
Portfolio 2	0.00565	0.0037	0.04	0.005	0.06	0.06	0.01	0.005	0	0	0.065	0.043
Portfolio 3	0.0268	0.0044	0.003	0.05	0.7	0.7	0.001	0	0.767	0.043	0	0
Portfolio 4	0.0128	0.0048	0.04	0.05	0.07	0.7	0.001	0.004	0.0012	0.0023	0.0045	0
Portfolio 5	0.676	0.676	NAN	–	–	–	–	–	–	–	–	

Table 6.33 Efficient solution of portfolio optimization with population size 50 and 100 by Poly-SCA

	r_0	Risk	x_1	x_2	x_3	x_4	x_5	x_6	x_7	x_8	x_9	x_{10}
Portfolio 1	0.00232	0.0049	0.007	0.003	0.003	0.43	0.03	0.004	0.005	0.065	0.78	0
Portfolio 2	0.0468	0.0057	0.04	0.043	0	0.0032	0.005	0.002	0.87	0.006	0	0
Portfolio 3	0.0267	0.0068	NAN	–	–	–	–	–	–	–	–	–
Portfolio 4	0.0120	0.0071	NAN	–	–	–	–	–	–	–	–	–
Portfolio 5	0.576	0.576	NAN	–	–	–	–	–	–	–	–	–
Portfolio 1	0.0000656	0.0045	0.001	0.0006	0.0054	0.0076	0.0043	0.03	0.43	0.34	0	0
Portfolio 2	0.000568	0.0057	0.43	0.0043	0.005	0.0054	0.00043	0.54	0.12	0	0.44	0
Portfolio 3	0.00278	0.0071	NAN	–	–	–	–	–	–	–	–	–
Portfolio 4	0.0178	0.0078	NAN	–	–	–	–	–	–	–	–	–
Portfolio 5	0.576	0.576	NAN	–	–	–	–	–	–	–	–	–

Table 6.34 Efficient solution of portfolio optimization with population size 30 & 50 by Cauchy- SCA

	r_0	Risk	x_1	x_2	x_3	x_4	x_5	x_6	x_7	x_8	x_9	x_{10}
Portfolio 1	0.00011	0.0032	0.02	0.03	0.040	0.50	0.001	0.020	0.010	0.001	0.020	0
Portfolio 2	0.00782	0.0037	0.05	0.02	0	0	0.30	0.20	0.001	0.07	0	0.08
Portfolio 3	0.00684	0.0042	0.06	0.03	0.70	0.1	0.20	0.40	0.005	0	0.001	0.070
Portfolio 4	0.077	0.0046	0.1	0.01	0.10	0.02	0.20	0.050	0.070	0.050	0.021	0.10
Portfolio 5	0.7773	0.7773	NAN	–	–	–	–	–	–	–	–	–
Portfolio 1	0.0000343	0.0055	0.003	0.50	0.001	0.30	0.20	0.60	0.001	0.20	0.10	0.001
Portfolio 2	0.000436	0.0067	0.02	0.30	0.01	0.50	0.30	0.001	0.01	0.20	0.001	0.03
Portfolio 3	0.00320	0.0068	NAN	–	–	–	–	–	–	–	–	–
Portfolio 4	0.0105	0.0076	NAN	–	–	–	–	–	–	–	–	–
Portfolio 5	0.323	0.323	NAN	–	–	–	–	–	–	–	–	–

Table 6.35 Efficient solution of portfolio optimization with population size 100 by Cauchy-SCA & 30 by GA- SCA

	r_0	Risk	x_1	x_2	x_3	x_4	x_5	x_6	x_7	x_8	x_9	x_{10}
Portfolio 1	0.0000088	0.0044	0.005	0.004	0.00056	0.004	0.005	0.065	0.076	0.0034	0.008	0.0034
Portfolio 2	0.000728	0.0005	0.03	0.5	0.006	0.0087	0.00654	0.05	0.005	0.006	0.03	0.03
Portfolio 3	0.00620	0.0056	0.05	023	0.008	0.65	0.9	0.087	0.65	0.56	0.004	0.04
Portfolio 4	0.0158	0.0068	0.067	0.06	0.004	0.008	0.003	0.065	0.003	0.007	0.035	0.003
Portfolio 5	0.7766	0.7766	0.002	0.09	0.0087	0.05	0.8	0.004	0.004	0.0034	0.045	0.005
Portfolio 1	0.0000765	0.0027	0.007	0.004	0.45	0.0043	0.0004	0.0065	0.87	0.0002	0.0067	0.0056
Portfolio 2	0.000650	0.0032	0.07	0.0065	0.3	0.0056	0.0065	0.09	0.0054	0.34	0.23	0.07
Portfolio 3	0.00560	0.0037	0.45	0.00054	0.1	0.0076	0.006	0.2	0.004	0.56	0.34	0.006
Portfolio 4	0.0340	0.0046	0.006	0.0006	0.076	0.87	0.112	0.45	0.54	0	0.002	0.001
Portfolio 5	0.998	0.998	0.878	NAN	–	–	–	–	–	–	–	–

Table 6.36 Efficient solution of portfolio optimization with population size 50 & 100 by Gaussian- SCA

	r_0	Risk	x_1	x_2	x_3	x_4	x_5	x_6	x_7	x_8	x_9	x_{10}
Portfolio 1	0.000098	0.0048	0.003	0	0.004	0.007	0.0065	0.54	0.064	0.06	0	0
Portfolio 2	0.00068	0.0058	0.008	0	0.10	0.03	0.008	0.5	0.05	0	0	0
Portfolio 3	0.0052	0.0066	0.02	0.006	0.002	0.03	0.007	0	0.0045	0	0.007	0.0076
Portfolio 4	0.028	0.0071	0.02	0.05	0.003	0.002	0.006	0.004	0	0	0.034	0.0054
Portfolio 5	0.565	0.565	0.003	0.006	0.02	0.003	0.005	0	0		0	0.0056
Portfolio 1	0.000089	0.0047	0.007	0.05	0	0	0.10	0.03	0.008	0.5	0.05	0
Portfolio 2	0.000780	0.0005	0.0065	0.0045	0	0.006	0.002	0.03	0.007	0	0.0045	0
Portfolio 3	0.00640	0.0062	0.56	0	0	0.05	0.003	0.002	0.006	0.004	0	0
Portfolio 4	0.0520	0.0007	NAN	–	–	–	–	–	–	–		–
Portfolio 5	0.8988	0.8998	NAN	–	–	–	–	–	–	–	–	–

Table 6.37 Comparison with other NIA – 2020–21

Algorithm	Population size	$r_{\min}$	$r_{\max}$
LX-BBO	30	0.000221	0.00728
	50	0.00518	0.00728
	100	-9E-06	0.0072
SCA	30	0.000343	0.9298
	50	0.00032	0.333
	100	0.0000434	0.5656
PM-SCA	30	0.0000343	0.9298
	50	0.000032	0.333
	100	0.0000434	0.5656
R-SCA	30	0.00011	0.7777
	50	0.000343	0.323
	100	0.00011	0.7766
C-SCA	30	0.00011	0.7773
	50	0.00000343	0.323
	100	0.000088	0.7766
G-SCA	30	0.0000332	0.9998
	50	0.0011	0.4434
	100	0.00011	0.8988
Poly-SCA	30	0.000211	0.676
	50	0.00232	0.576
	100	0.0000656	0.576

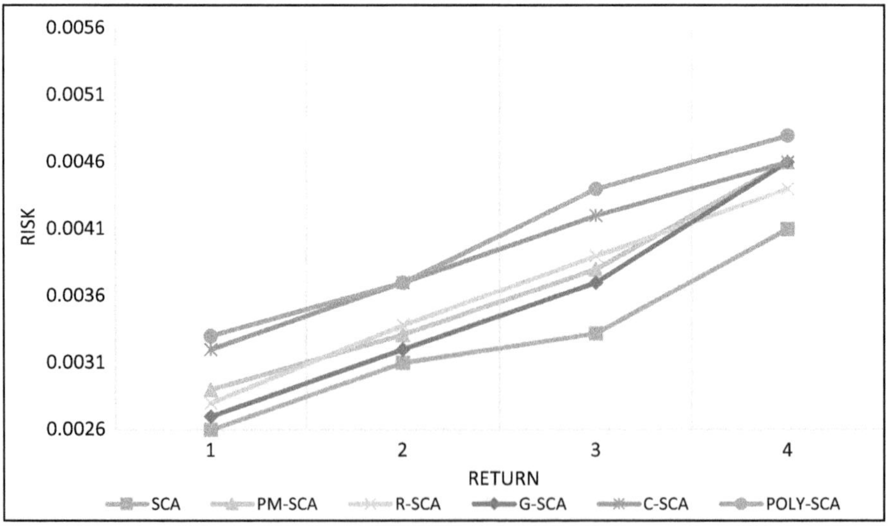

Fig. 6.4 Optimal portfolio for population size 30

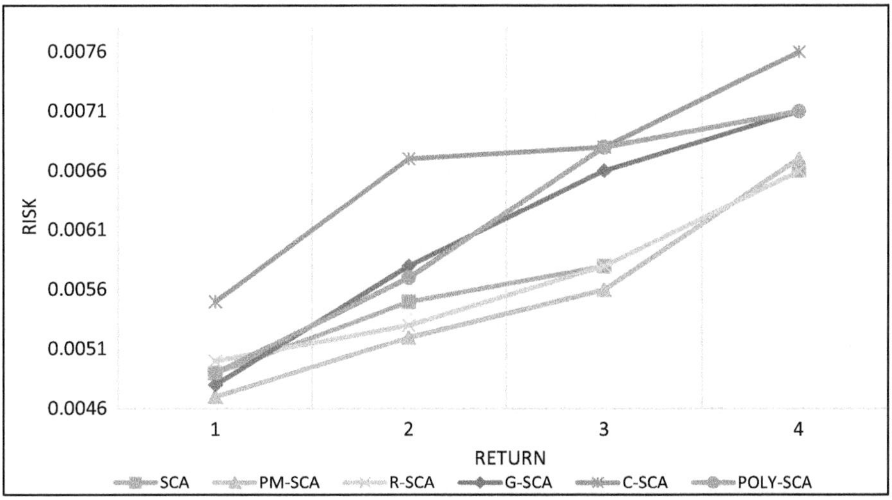

Fig. 6.5 Optimal portfolio for population size 50

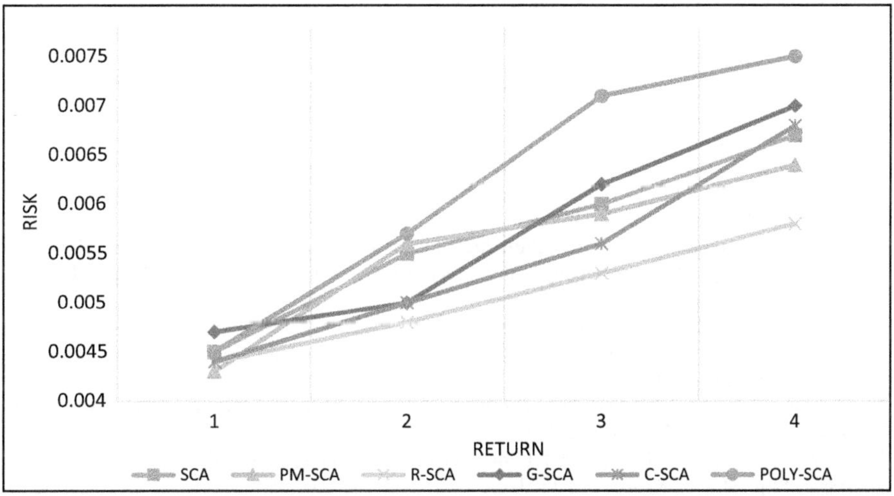

Fig. 6.6 Optimal portfolio for population size 100

diversify their portfolio by investing in a variety of securities. Portfolio's variance can be reduced by proper diversification for a given level of return. Diversification's benefits in terms of maintaining a portfolio's expected return (while reducing portfolio risk at the same time) can be seen when assets with low or even negative correlation are combined. The sensitivity analysis on five algorithms for different population sizes concludes that poly-SCA performed better than another variant of SCA for portfolio-based optimization.

References

1. Ahmadzade, H., Gao, R.: Covariance of uncertain random variables and its application to portfolio optimization. J. Ambient. Intell. Humaniz. Comput. **11**(4) (2019). https://doi.org/10.1007/s12652-019-01323-0
2. Ahmadzade, H., Gao, R., Dehghan, M.H., Ahmadi, R.: Partial triangular entropy of uncertain random variables and its application. J. Ambient. Intell. Humaniz. Comput. **9**, 1455–1464 (2018)
3. Aranha, C., Iba, H.: Modelling cost into a genetic algorithm-based portfolio optimization system by seeding and objective sharing. In: Proceedings of IEEE Congress on Evolutionary Computation, Singapore, pp. 196–203 (2007)
4. Banerjee, M., Garg, V. (communicated): Solving structural and reliability optimization problems by investing efficient mutation strategies embedded in Sine-Cosine Algorithm. Int. J. Syst. Assur. Eng. Manag. (2022)
5. Bonami, P., Lejeune, M.A.: An exact solution approach for portfolio optimization problems under stochastic and integer constraints. Oper. Res. **57**, 650–670 (2009)
6. Brandtner, M., Wolfgang, K., Rischau, R.: Entropic risk measures and their comparative statics in portfolio selection: coherence vs convexity. Eur. J. Oper. Res. **264**, 707–716 (2018)
7. Califore, G.C.: Multi-period portfolio optimization with linear control policies. Automatica. **44**(10), 2463–2473 (2008)
8. Daun,Y.C.,: A Multi-objective Approach to portfolio optimization. **8**, 1–12 (2007)
9. DeMiguel, V., Garlappi, L., Nogales, F.J., Uppal, R.: A generalized approach to portfolio optimization: improving performance by constraining portfolio norms. Manag. Sci. **55**, 798–812 (2009)
10. Ertenlice, O., Kalayci, C.B.: A survey of swarm intelligence for portfolio optimization: algorithms and applications. Swarm Evol. Comput. **39**, 36–52 (2018)
11. Fiacco, A., Cormick, M.C.G.: Nonlinear programming: sequential unconstrained minimization techniques. Comput. J. **12**, 207 (1968)
12. Garg, V., Deep, K.: Portfolio optimization using Laplacian biogeography-based optimization. Springer. **56**, 1117–1141 (2019)
13. Garg, V., Deep, K.: Efficient mutation strategies embedded in Laplacian-biogeography-based optimization algorithm for unconstrained function minimization. Int. J. Appl. Swarm Intell. **7**, 12–44 (2016a)
14. Garg, V., Deep, K.: Performance of Laplacian biogeography-based optimization algorithm on CEC 2014 continuous optimization benchmarks and camera calibration problem. Swarm Evol. Comput. **27**, 132–144 (2016b)
15. Garg, V., Deep, K.: A state-of-the-art review of biogeography-based optimization. Adv. Intell. Syst. Comput. **336**, 533–549 (2015)
16. Garg, V., Deep, K.: Constrained Laplacian biogeography-based optimization. Int. J. Syst. Assur. Eng. Manag. **8**, 867–885 (2016)
17. Gupta, P., Mehlawat, M.K., Inuiguchi, M., Chandra, S.: Fuzzy portfolio optimization. In: Studies in Fuzzy Items & Soft Computings, vol. 316. Springer, Berlin/Heidelberg (2014)
18. Huang, X., Jiang, G., Gupta, P., Mehlawat, M.K.: A risk index model for uncertain portfolio selection with background risk. Comput. Oper. Res. **132**, 1–15 (2021)
19. Hu, Y., Liu, K., Zhang, X., Su, L., Ngai, E.W.T., Liu, M.: Application of evolutionary computation for rule discovery in stock algorithmic trading: a literature review. Appl. Soft Comput. **36**, 534–551 (2015)
20. Karmarkar, N.A.: New polynomial-time algorithm for linear programming. Combinatorica. **4**, 373–395 (1984)
21. Konno, H., Yamazaki, H.: Mean-absolute deviation portfolio optimization model and its application to Tokyo stock market. Manag. Sci. **37**, 519–531 (1991)
22. Konno, H., Suzuki, K.: A mean-variance-skewness portfolio optimization model. J. Oper. Res. Soc. Jpn. **38**, 173–187 (1995)

23. Levy, N.K., Markowitz, M.H.: Portfolio optimization with factors, scenarios, and realistic short positions. Oper. Res. **53**, 586–559 (2005)
24. Ma, X., Gao, Y., Wang, B.: Portfolio optimization with cardinality constraints band on hybrid differential evolution. Comput. Intell. Bioinfo. (2012)
25. Markowitz, H.: Portfolio selection. J. Financ. **7**, 77–91 (1952)
26. Mansini, R., Seperanza, M.: Heuristic algorithm for the portfolio selection problem with minimum transaction lots. Eur. J. Oper. Res. **114**, 219–233 (2003)
27. Mahawat, M.K., Gupta, P., Khan, A.Z.: Portfolio optimization using higher moments in an uncertain random environment. Inf. Sci. **567**, 348–374 (2021)
28. Mehralizade, R., Mohammad, A., Gildeh, B.S., Ahmadzade, H.: Uncertain random portfolio selection based on risk curve. Soft. Comput. **25**, 9789–9810 (2020)
29. Orito, Y., Hanada, Y., Shibata, S., Yamamoto, H.: A new population initialization approach based on bordered hessian for portfolio optimization problems. In: Proceedings of IEEE International Conference on Systems, Man, and Cybernetics (SMC), Manchester, England, pp. 1341–1346 (2013)
30. Pinar, M.: Robust scenario optimization based on downside-risk measure for multi-period portfolio selection. OR Spectr. **29**, 295–309 (2007)
31. Rubio, A., Bermúdez, J.D., Vercher, E.: Forecasting portfolio returns using weighted fuzzy time series methods. Int. J. Approx. Reason. **75**, 1–12 (2016)
32. Sasaki, M., Laamrani, A., Yamashiro, M., Aiehegn, C.: Portfolio optimization by fuzzy interactive genetic algorithm journal of advanced. Manag. Sci. **6**, 125–131 (2018)
33. Sharpe, W.F.: A linear programming algorithm for mutual funds portfolio selection. Manag. Sci. **13**, 499–510 (1967)
34. Shiang-Tai-Liu: Solving portfolio optimization problem based on extension principle. In: Conference on Industrial Engineering and Other Application of Applied Intelligent System, pp. 164–174 (2010)
35. Singh, A., Dharmaraja, S.: A portfolio optimisation model for credit risky bonds with Markov model credit rating dynamics. Int. J. Financial Mark. Deriv. **6**, 102–119 (2017)
36. Takriti, S., Ahmed, S.: On robust optimization of two-stage systems. Math. Program. Ser. **99**, 109–126 (2004)
37. Zhang, W.G., Liu, Y.J.: Credibility mean-variance model for multi-period portfolio selection problem with risk control. OR Spectr. **36**, 113–132 (2015)
38. Zhongfeng, Q.: Mean-variance model for portfolio optimization problem in the simultaneous presence of random and uncertain return. Eur. J. Oper. Res. **245**, 480–488 (2015)
39. Zhai, J., Bai, M., Hao, J.: Uncertain random mean–variance–skewness models for the portfolio optimization problem. J. Math. Program. Oper. Res., 2–24 (2021)

Chapter 7
Detecting Group Shilling Profiles in Recommender Systems: A Hybrid Clustering and Grey Wolf Optimizer Technique

Saumya Bansal and Niyati Baliyan

1 Introduction

With the expansion and deluge of information available over the Web, it becomes tedious for users to process and make a sensible decision based on it. For instance, on a Friday night, to watch a movie on Netflix, users may have to watch trailers of a large number of movies before reaching a final decision, which takes a lot of time and energy, and they may still not end up with the right choice. Information overload is when a huge volume of information is available than can be processed by the user [23]. Collaborative filtering (CF) is one such recommendation technique that can solve the information overload problem by filtering out the information and providing recommendations, satisfying the user's interest based on his/her history [3, 7, 49]. Forty percent of apps installed from the Play Store and 60% of videos watched on YouTube are results of recommendations. Further, CF may display items that users might not have thought of searching.

However, CF is vulnerable to shilling attacks due to its open nature [24, 48] and reliance on user profiles to generate recommendations [4, 5, 50]. In these attacks, a large number of attack profiles, also known as shillers, are inserted into the dataset to introduce bias in recommendations [4, 5]. Depending upon the purpose of an attack, i.e., promotion or demotion of an item, the attack can be classified as a push or nuke attack, respectively. Different attack models [40] are used to generate shillers, which look identical to genuine user profiles, making it difficult to distinguish between the

S. Bansal (✉) · N. Baliyan
Department of Information Technology, Indira Gandhi Delhi Technical University for Women, Delhi, India
e-mail: saumya004phd18@igdtuw.ac.in; niyatibaliyan@igdtuw.ac.in

© The Author(s), under exclusive license to Springer Nature Switzerland AG 2022

D. Singh et al. (eds.), *Design and Applications of Nature Inspired Optimization*, Women in Engineering and Science, https://doi.org/10.1007/978-3-031-17929-7_7

two and thus are considered in a similar neighborhood set of target user while generating recommendations.

Several detection methods have been proposed in the past to filter attack profiles from the dataset. Some unsupervised machine learning techniques use traditional methods such as clustering; however, they require prior knowledge of the total number of attack profiles [30]. On the contrary, supervised techniques for shilling attack detection are mostly built on hand-designed features that are difficult to extract [33]. To the best of our knowledge, the fusion of k-means and swarm intelligence (SI) technique has not been explored by the researchers to detect fake profiles mounted in the dataset. Further, the proposed fusion method does not neglect group behavior that exists in shilling profiles nor require prerequisites such as hand-designed features or prior knowledge of attack profiles. Due to the ease of use and excellent results shown by the bioinspired SI technique, grey wolf optimizer (GWO), on various problems including parameter tuning, economy dispatch, classification, clustering, power engineering, to name a few [15, 20, 21, 37], we explored it from the perspective of detecting attack profiles mounted in the dataset.

In this chapter, we proposed a fusion method based on k-means clustering and GWO for the detection of shilling attacks, namely, Grey Wolf Optimization Technique for Detecting Shilling Profiles (GWODS) that works directly on the rating matrix and shows significant results when tested on datasets of different sizes. Firstly, k-means is used to find the suspicious cluster of users exploiting the collusive behavior of attack profiles. Then, GWO takes the suspicious cluster and finds attack profiles, taking inspiration from the social hierarchy and hunting behavior of grey wolves, i.e., to encircle the prey before attacking it. The involvement of minimal parameters, ease of implementation, derivation-free nature, use of fewer operators as opposed to the evolutionary algorithm (crossover, mutation), and excellent results make it more noticeable to be explored in the future by researchers.

The rest of the chapter is organized as follows: Related work and motivation is discussed in Sect. 2. Section 3 gives a brief overview of shilling attacks. The basic approach of GWO is discussed in Sect. 4. The proposed approach, GWODS, is detailed in Sect. 5. Section 6 throws light on experiments and results. Section 7 concludes the work and discusses future scope.

2 Related Work and Motivation

Attacking a system is a two-player (attacker and defender) game, with each player's motive being "to win." The attacker's win is in successfully exploiting the vulnerability of the system and manipulating the system's functionality. The designer's win is in reducing the system's vulnerability, making the attack expensive, curtailing the attacker's possibility of a return, and creating a robust system. From the perspective of shilling attacks, detection methods can be classified as supervised or unsupervised.

Supervised detection requires building a model based on selected attributes of attack profiles and labeling the training data. Mobasher et al. [33] introduced two attributes, namely, filler mean target difference and weighted degree agreement successful for detection of segment attack. C4.5, which is used to generate a decision tree, was used to build a binary profile classifier. However, it requires hand-designed features as a prerequisite, which are difficult to get. Authors in [45] extracted features from user profiles based on the statistical properties of attack models and then used a variant of boosting algorithm, i.e., rescale AdaBoost (RAdaBoost), as a classifier. A collaborative shilling detection model that decomposes user-item matrix and user-user co-occurrence matrix into latent factors is proposed [12]. These latent factors are then used to detect shillers using decision tree as a classifier. However, Yang et al. [45] and Dou et al. [12] show low detection rates for small filler and attack sizes. Supervised detection techniques having base in deep learning are presented in Zhou et al. [51] and Tong et al. [42]. The proposed algorithm learns about profiles directly from the user-item rating matrix instead of hand-designed features. Tong et al. [42] considered one convolution and pooling layer each, while two convolution and pooling layers each are considered in Zhou et al. [51]. The algorithms effectively detect fake profiles but are highly dependent on training samples, which incurs huge cost, especially for the training of large datasets. Hao et al. [18, 19] proposed detection methods based on multiple views, namely, ratings, item popularity, and user graph, using 17 artificial features and stacked denoising autoencoders (SDAe), followed by principal component analysis (PCA), respectively, for feature extraction. The detection efficiency of both approaches can further be improved. A detection method using four model-specific and six generic attributes using k-NN and support vector machine (SVM) as a classification approach is proposed in Batmez et al. [6]. An outlier degree detection algorithm based on feature selection and entropy to select metrics and calculate the user's outlier degree, dynamically, is proposed in Cao et al. [9]. Zhou et al. [50] proposed a two-phase SVM-TIA detection method using the borderline SMOTE method to balance the number of attack profiles in the training set to get rough detection results in phase 1. The target items are analyzed from attack profiles in phase 2. This approach has shown reasonable detection results in the case of average attack but shows poor detection precision in other attacks.

Unsupervised methods do not require labeled data [8]. However, a few works discussed in the literature require certain prior knowledge about attack profiles, which is difficult to get in the real world. The basis of many unsupervised detection methods is clustering with the purpose to detect a group of attack profiles instead of a single attack profile, thereby distinguishing shillers from genuine users [28–30]. Chirita et al. [10] introduced the rating deviation from mean agreement (RDMA), considering rating deviations between profiles. Another method proposed by Zhang et al. [46] combines PCA with data complexity overcoming PCA's drawback of knowing the number of shillers in advance, which is unreal to have. However, it requires cutoff k to be close to the attack size to achieve significant results. Another method on the same lines that combines PCA with perturbation is proposed in Deng et al. [11]. The purpose of adding perturbation is to protect profiles on the boundary from misclassification in contrast to the previous method. The authors [28–30] proposed an approach that also exploits the similarity structure that exists in shilling profiles to filter out a group of profiles using PCA and probabilistic latent semantic analysis (PLSA). Although it requires no training data which saves computation time, preliminary knowledge of fake profiles is a prerequisite and does not guarantee effective detection of low-quality shilling attacks. Liu et al. [25] came up with another unsupervised method exploiting time-based Kalman filter, while Zhang et al. [47] take into consideration user's suspicious degree based on past behavior using hidden Markov model and hierarchical clustering. However, the latter algorithm fails when the test set consists of purely genuine or fake profiles.

Shilling attack detection is a binary classification problem dividing user profiles into two categories: genuine or fake [43]. GWO is a SI technique that can be modified to be applied as a binary classification technique. Manikandan [27] proposed a diabetes prediction model to predict the disease at an early stage using GWO with fuzzy sets to prevent harmful effects that can occur at a later stage. It outperformed ant colony optimization with fuzzy sets. Elhariri et al. [13] used GWO for finding out the optimal feature set for the diagnosis of Parkinson's disease. A SVM-based technique using GWO for dimensionality reduction keeping accuracy high and outperforming SVM for dimensionality reduction is proposed in Elhariri et al. [13], taking benefits of multi-objective characteristics of GWO [14]. Different works have been carried out using GWO for feature reduction including – combining rough sets with GWO [44], hybridizing GWO with particle swarm optimization (PSO) [1], and optimal feature selection which outperformed GA and PSO [15]. Another area where GWO shows high accuracy, marking its success, is training multilayer perceptron [31].

The literature review highlighted several limitations of current work, such as preliminary knowledge of attack profiles, hand-designed features, and training cost involved in the case of labeled data. Further, GWO shows multi-objective characteristics on a binary classification problem by reducing dimensionality and maximizing classification accuracy at the same time. Detecting shilling attacks, being a binary classification problem, inspired us to develop a mathematical model based on the social and hunting behavior of wolves to find shilling profiles inserted in the dataset that manipulate the behavior of the recommender system (RS).

The following are the major contributions of the work:

- A novel approach, namely, GWODS, for the detection of shilling profiles is proposed.
- It does not require prior knowledge of attack profiles and works directly on the rating matrix.
- GWODS is simple, is easy to implement, uses fewer operators, and provides excellent results.
- An average precision of 99% is achieved using GWODS.

3 Shilling Attacks

The recommendations created by CF vary according to user profiles added. Thus, adding fake profiles can highly manipulate items being recommended to the user [17]. The goal of such attacks, known as "shilling attacks" or "profile injection attacks," is to push or nuke an item. The general form of the attack model [3] that is used to create attack profiles is shown in Fig. 7.1. However, depending on the attack type, the attack model differs slightly.

The symbols along with their description are provided in Table 7.1.

From the attacker's perspective, the best attack is one that requires a minimum amount of information about the dataset, demands minimum efforts, and maximizes the similarity between shilling and genuine profiles. The number of attack profiles inserted is another factor that affects the strength of a successful attack [8]. Different attack models are discussed below:

(i) Average Attack

The average attack is a powerful attack that proves to be successful even with a smaller filler size and can be used as a push or nuke attack [8, 34]. The average rating of each item is required by the attacker to mount such an attack. The attack model is shown in Fig. 7.2.

Where each rating assigned to I_F is the mean rating of that item across users.

(ii) Average Over Popular Items Attack (AoP Attack)

The AoP attack resembles the average attack model shown in Fig. 7.2 with an only change in the selection of filler items. In AoP attack, I_F are chosen from top $x\%$ of most popular items, where x is selected to ensure non-detection [40], while in the average attack, I_F are chosen randomly from the entire item set.

Fig. 7.1 Attack model

I_S	I_F	I_Φ	I_T

Table 7.1 Symbols with their description

Symbol	Description
I_S	Selected items playing major role in minimizing distinction among genuine and shilling profiles
I_F	Randomly chosen filler items to complete the attack profile
I_Φ	Items with no ratings
I_T	Target item

I_F	I_Φ	I_T

Fig. 7.2 Average attack model

(iii) Bandwagon Attack

It is almost as successful as an average attack but does not need information about the mean of each item and thus is more practical to mount. It is based on highly visible items or items that a significant number of users have rated. These items are termed as selected items (I_S) and are assigned maximum rating along with the target item. I_F are assigned ratings around the overall the l mean of rating matrix [8, 34, 40]. It follows the attack model as shown in Fig. 7.1.

(iv) Segment Attack

It is another low-knowledge attack that mounts the attack profiles by targeting a set of users that may be interested in the target item instead of the entire user's set, therefore, making it resource-saving and meaningful [8, 33]. The segment attack is similar to the bandwagon attack. I_S are given the maximum ratings, while I_F are the minimum ratings. Further, it can be used to push or nuke the target item.

(v) Power Item Attack (PIA)

In PIA, items with a high number of user ratings are the popular items [40]. These items make the set of selected items (I_S) and are given ratings around the item mean. I_F are set to null and I_T are given maximum/minimum rating, depending upon the type of attack. It follows the attack model shown in Fig. 7.1 to create attack profiles.

4 Grey Wolf Optimizer (GWO)

Motivation

GWO is a SI technique that is a class of meta-heuristic techniques. SI algorithms are designed on lines of social and hunting behavior of natural colonies, namely, swarms, herds, and flocks. GWO proposed by Mirjalili in the year 2014 [32] mimics the social and hunting behavior of grey wolves to catch prey with the motive to find more optimized solutions to existing problems. Some of the applications of GWO [2, 14, 21, 22, 32, 36, 41] are as follows: ease to operate, high convergence rate, and few operators unlike Genetic Algorithm (mutation, crossover, and so on). It saves information about all search states unlike other classes of the meta-heuristic algorithm such as an evolutionary algorithm. GWO maintains high classification accuracy while solving dimensionality reduction problem and thus taking benefits of its multi-objective characteristics. To avail the abovementioned advantages of GWO, a significant amount of efforts have been utilized on applying GWO to challenges in a variety of disciplines.

Description and Algorithm

Grey wolves are social animals who live in a pack with a clear hierarchy of power. The average group size is 5–12 wolves. Alpha is the head of a group that directs all other wolves for hunting, sleeping, and other activities. Beta and delta assist alpha in decision-making and other group activities. Omega wolves are at the bottom of the hierarchy and follow the orders of dominant ones. The fittest solution in the GWO mathematical model is alpha, followed by beta, and so on, as shown in Fig. 7.3.

The process of predation is mainly divided into three steps:

A. Encircling

Grey wolves are capable of recognizing the location of prey (may not be optimal) and encircling it. Equations (7.1) and (7.2) describe the mathematical equations used for encircling.

$$\vec{D} = \mid \vec{C}.\vec{X}_p(t) - \vec{X}(t) \mid \tag{7.1}$$

$$\vec{X}(t+1) = \vec{X}_p(t) - \vec{A}.\vec{D} \tag{7.2}$$

where t is the current iteration, $\vec{X}_p$ is the position vector of prey, and $\vec{X}$ indicates the position of the grey wolf. Vectors $\vec{A}$ and $\vec{C}$ are calculated using Eqs. (7.3) and (7.4).

$$\vec{A} = 2\vec{a}.\vec{r_1} - \vec{a} \tag{7.3}$$

$$\vec{C} = 2.\vec{r}_2 \tag{7.4}$$

where $\vec{r_1}$ and $\vec{r}_2$ are random vectors in the range [0,1]. $\vec{a}$ is linearly decreasing value from 2 to 0 guaranteeing exploration. Encircling is shown in Fig. 7.4.

B. Hunting

After encircling, alpha, beta, and delta take note of the three best solutions and oblige other wolves to update their positions [26]. The following equations are proposed for the same.

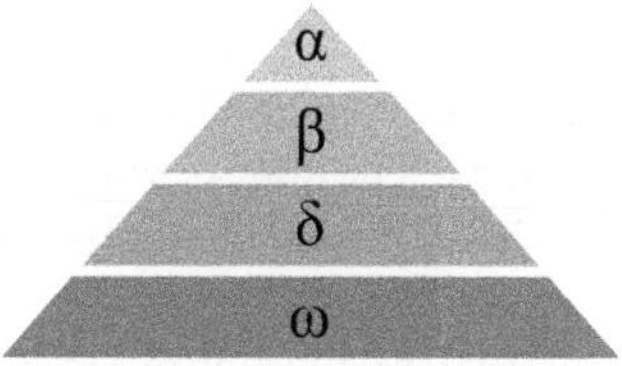

Fig. 7.3 Grey wolf hierarchy

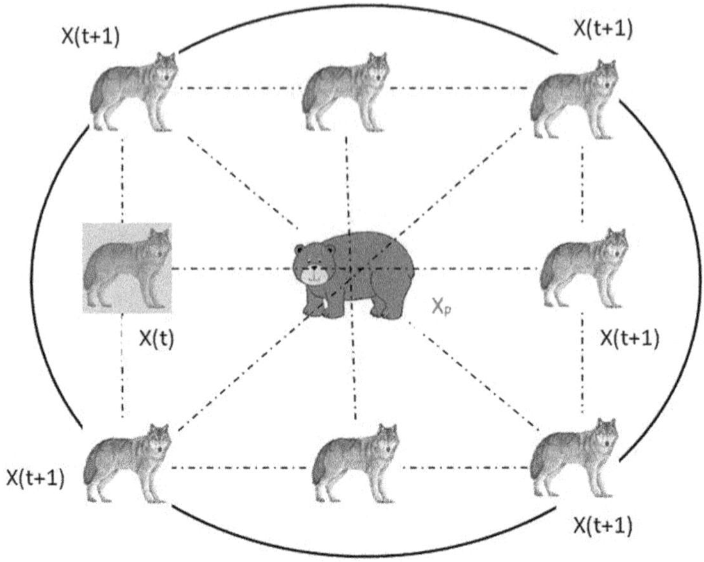

Fig. 7.4 Position of grey wolf around the prey *Xp*. Grey wolf can update position around the prey using Eqs. (7.1) and (7.2)

$$\overrightarrow{D_\alpha} = |\overrightarrow{C_1}.\overrightarrow{X_\alpha} - \vec{X}|, \overrightarrow{X_1} = \overrightarrow{X_\alpha} - \overrightarrow{A_1}.\left(\overrightarrow{D_\alpha}\right) \tag{7.5}$$

$$\overrightarrow{D_\beta} = |\overrightarrow{C_2}.\overrightarrow{X_\beta} - \vec{X}|, \overrightarrow{X_2} = \overrightarrow{X_\beta} - \overrightarrow{A_2}.\left(\overrightarrow{D_\beta}\right) \tag{7.6}$$

$$\overrightarrow{D_\delta} = |\overrightarrow{C_3}.\overrightarrow{X_\delta} - \vec{X}|, \overrightarrow{X_3} = \overrightarrow{X_\delta} - \overrightarrow{A_3}.\left(\overrightarrow{D_\delta}\right) \tag{7.7}$$

$$\vec{X}(t+1) = \frac{\overrightarrow{X_1} + \overrightarrow{X_2} + \overrightarrow{X_3}}{3} \tag{7.8}$$

where $\vec{X}(t+1)$ is the position of the grey wolf after updation at iteration $(t + 1)$.

C. Attacking

The hunt is finished by attacking the prey. This is achieved by a decrease in the value of $\vec{a}$. When $|A| < 1$, grey wolves pack is attracted/converges to prey and finishes the process.

To sum up, GWO starts with a population of wolves (search agents) with random positions. The fitness values of search agents are computed using the fitness function. With iterations, alpha, beta, and delta are assigned the best positions, and the positions of other search agents are changed accordingly. The parameter $\vec{a}$ plays a vital role in the entire process. The GWO marks the end of the hunt with the satisfaction of the termination condition. The algorithm is described below:

Algorithm 1: GWO
Input: Problem-dependent dataset
Initialize positions of search agents and $\vec{a}$
Calculate fitness of each search agent
$\overrightarrow{X_\propto}$, $\overrightarrow{X_\beta}$, $\overrightarrow{X_\delta} = 0$
Assign best, second best, and third best solution to $\overrightarrow{X_\propto}$, $\overrightarrow{X_\beta}$, $\overrightarrow{X_\delta}$, respectively,
while! max_iter
  Update position of all search agents using equation (5) – equation (8)
  Update $\vec{a}$
  Calculate fitness of all search agents
  Update $\overrightarrow{X_\propto}$, $\overrightarrow{X_\beta}$, $\overrightarrow{X_\delta}$
return $\overrightarrow{X_\propto}$

5 GWODS

Motivation

The importance of RS for continuity cannot be overstated. Malicious users may jeopardize the predictions by mounting shilling profiles in the dataset. Our goal is to eliminate or reduce the impact of such profiles on recommendations that are generated. Due to the same underlying methodology used to generate shillers, there exists a significant correlation among them [29]. As a result, detecting shillers can be viewed as a dimensionality reduction problem, i.e., lowering strongly correlated characteristics and thereby lowering dataset redundancy. K-means, which is an efficient clustering algorithm, is used to partition suspicious users into a cluster. Then, GWO classifies suspicious users into genuine and shilling profiles using the social and hunting behavior of grey wolves. GWO is the recent SI technique and has shown remarkable results in feature reduction in various domains of machine learning [13]. Furthermore, shilling profile identification is a binary classification problem, with 1 indicating a real profile and 0 indicating a false profile. In light of this, binary functions were used in the proposed method.

Proposed Approach

We have proposed an algorithm GWODS for detecting fake profiles mounted in the dataset following different attack models. Instead of single profile detection,

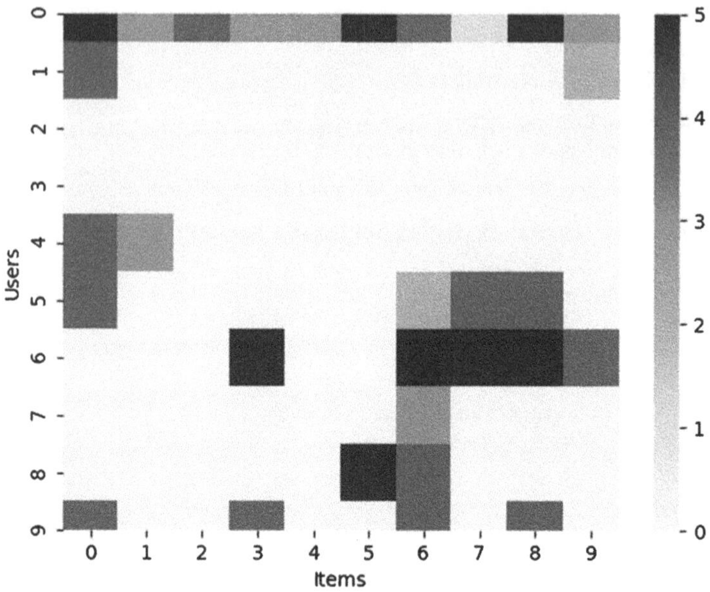

Fig. 7.5 Ratings given by users to items on the scale of 1–5

GWODS works on collusive behavior that exists in shilling profiles. The algorithm is presented stepwise below:

(i) Preprocessing Phase

The data is synthesized into a matrix of user-item rating matrix. The matrix of the first ten users and items is shown as a heat map in Fig. 7.5.

(ii) Clustering of Users

The idea behind this phase is to group suspicious people into a cluster, based on the assumption that shillers have a higher connection among them than authentic ones. Therefore, this step would return the cluster containing the most suspicious users. To find such a cluster, the Pearson correlation coefficient is computed among users, followed by clustering using K-means. The top-N strongly connected users are then found, followed by a cluster number including most of the top-N users. Finally, the cluster number is returned, which will be used in the later step.

(iii) Transpose of Matrix

In this step, we store the rating matrix as its transpose considering users as features.

(iv) Initialization Step

We initialize different variables and vectors in this step.

Table 7.2 Randomly initialized population of wolves consisting of four search agents and five users

Search agent	User1	User2	User3	User4	User5
1	0	1	0	1	1
2	1	1	1	0	0
3	0	0	1	0	0
4	0	1	0	1	1

(a) α_{pos}, β_{pos},and δ_{pos} are one-dimensional binary vectors of size $(1\times\ n\ \_\ users)$ initialized as zero vectors.

where α_{pos}, β_{pos},and δ_{pos} are the position vector of α, β, and δ, respectively, defining each user as fake or genuine. One (1) represents a genuine profile and 0 represents a fake profile.

(b) α_{score}, β_{score}, and δ_{score} are the fitness score of α, β, and δ, respectively, which are initialized to 0.
(c) Randomly initialize the population of wolves of size $(search\_agents \times n\_users)$ with value 1 or 0 as shown in Table 7.2. Here, 1 denotes the genuine profile, whereas 0 denotes a fake profile.

(v) Computation of the Feature's Importance

Features very similar to each other do not contribute much to the functionality of any system and are thus considered redundant. To know the importance of each feature and find redundancy in the dataset, we compute the importance of each feature using the *feature_importance* attribute of random forest regressor imported from *sklearn.ensemble*. A random forest is an ensemble technique that has proved to be effective in finding the importance of features [35], by combining the results of multiple decision trees instead of one, and thus overcomes the drawback of sensitivity to training data that exists in the decision tree. *feature_importance* returns the importance of each feature in determining the splits. The value of feature importance is between 0 and 1. The aggregation of the importance of all features is 1. Here, users are considered as features.

(vi) Mathematical Computation on Lines of GWO

(a) First, compute the fitness of each search agent using Eq. (7.9) and step v.

$$\mathrm{fit}(i) = (\alpha \times agg\_imp\_feature[i]) + \left(\beta \times \frac{selected\_features[i]}{total\_features}\right) \tag{7.9}$$

where

$\alpha, \beta = 0.5$ to mark the balance between two
$i\epsilon\ search\ \_\ agents$

$selected\_features[i]$ = number of 1's in the search agent's vector
$agg\_imp\_feature[i]$ = sum of feature's importance computed in step v.

Here, the importance of all features activated (i.e., 1) in the search agent, and not belonging to the selected cluster, is added, as well as the importance of all features deactivated (i.e., 0) in the search agent and belonging to the selected cluster, from step ii.

(b) Assign the position vector and score of the fittest (best) search agent to α, second fittest search agent to β, and third fittest search agent to δ.
(c) Update a [39]

$$a = 2 - l \times \frac{2}{\max\_iter} \tag{7.10}$$

where $l \in \max\_iter$

(d) Update the positions of each search agent using Eqs. (7.11), (7.12) and (7.13), drawing inspiration from the original procedure of GWO's encircling.

$$D_\alpha = |(C1 \times \alpha_{pos}[j]) - position[i][j]|; X1 = \alpha_{pos}[j] - (A1 \times D_\alpha) \tag{7.11}$$

$$D_\beta = |(C2 \times \beta_{pos}[j]) - position[i][j]|; X2 = \beta_{pos}[j] - (A2 \times D_\beta) \tag{7.12}$$

$$D_\delta = |(C3 \times \delta_{pos}[j]) - position[i][j]; X3 = \delta_{pos}[j] - (A3 \times D_\delta) \tag{7.13}$$

$$X = \frac{X1 + X2 + X3}{3} \tag{7.14}$$

where $A1$, $A2$, and $A3$ are calculated using Eq. (7.3); $C1$, $C2$, and $C3$ are calculated using Eq. (7.4); and $position[i][j]$ represents the positional value of search agent 'i' for feature 'j'.

Using the hunting step Eq. (7.8) as inspiration, find the sigmoid of X and update the position vector of a search agent.

(e) Repeat step vi until max_iter is achieved or the method converges, i.e., no improvement over the previous two iterations.

(vii) Use α_{pos} for detecting shilling profiles in the dataset.

Algorithm 2: GWODS

Input: MovieLens Dataset

Transform input into a matrix (R) of user-item ratings.
Cluster users using k-means based on correlation among them.
Find cluster number consisting of top- N highly correlated users.
$R = R^T$
Initialize α_{pos}, β_{pos} and δ_{pos}; α_{score}, β_{score} and δ_{score}
Randomly initialize population of grey wolf in position array
Compute importance of each feature using *feature _ importance*
Compute fitness of each search agent using equation (9)
for l in range(max _ *iter*):
    $fit1 = fitness\ of\ all\ search\ agents$
    for i in range(search_agents):
        $fitness = fit1[i]$
        if $fitness > \alpha_{score}$:
            $\alpha\_score = fitness$
            $\alpha\_pos = position[i]$
        if $fitness < \alpha_{score}$ and $fitness > \beta_{score}$:
            $\beta\_score = fitness$
            $\beta\_pos = position[i]$
        if $fitness < \alpha_{score}$ and $fitness < \beta_{score}$ and $fitness > \delta_{score}$:
            $\delta\_score = fitness$
            $\delta\_pos = position[i]$
    endfor
    $a = 2 - l \times \left(\frac{2}{\max\_iter}\right)$
    $rand = random.\ random()$
    for i in range ($search\ \_\ agents$):
      for j in range ($total\ \_features$):
          Compute X using equation (11) – equation (14)
          if $sigmoid(X) < rand$
            $position[i][j] = 0$
          else:
            $position[i][j] = 1$
      endfor
    endfor
endfor
return α_{pos}

6 Experiments and Results

In this section, dataset and experimental setup are discussed. Further, parameters used in GWODS and evaluation metrics are described. It is further extended by comparing the proposed approach on two binary functions, followed by convergence rate analysis, then followed by detailed analysis on the superior operator, and finally concluding by a comparative analysis of GWODS with all six state-of-the-art approaches.

Dataset and Experimental Setup

The three publicly available MovieLens (ML) datasets by the GroupLens [16] have been used for experimentation purposes as described in Table 7.3. Each user rates at least 20 items on a scale of 1–5, where 5 signifies the highest rating. These datasets are preprocessed to form the user-item rating matrix. All users corresponding to datasets are considered genuine profiles. The fake profiles/shillers are inserted into the datasets using different attack models.

The configuration of the system used for experimentation is as follows: Intel® Core™ i7 CPU@2.60GHz, 8GB RAM, Windows10, 64bit OS, Python 3.6. The libraries of python used for implementation are NumPy, Pandas, Sklearn, Random, Math, Time, Matplotlib, Seaborn, and Xlrd.

Parameter Setting

There are a few parameters that need to be initialized to implement GWO as shown in Table 7.4. Furthermore, just two hyperparameters (a and C) that aid the learning process must be adjusted to reap the benefits of GWO.

Table 7.3 Description of datasets

Dataset	Users	Items	Ratings	Sparsity (%)
ML 100K	1000	1700	100,000	93.7
ML 1M	6000	4000	1,000,000	95.8
ML 100K (latest)	600	9000	100,000	98.1

Table 7.4 Parameters and their values

Parameter	Value
Search agents	12
Max_iter	100
No of clusters	10
Alpha	0.5

Evaluation Metrics

Several common measures were utilized to assess the performance of the suggested strategy [1, 39, 50]. The average of M runs is computed for each evaluation metric, with M set to 10.

(a) Average Accuracy

It indicates the reliability of GWODS in classifying genuine and fake profiles.

$$AvgAcc = \frac{1}{M}\sum\nolimits_{i=1}^{M} \frac{X^i}{total\_features} \times 100 \tag{7.15}$$

where X^i indicates correctly identified labels at i^{th} iteration.

(b) Average Detection Rate

It defines the percentage of correctly identified fake profiles.

$$AvgDet = \frac{1}{M}\sum\nolimits_{i=1}^{M} \frac{Y^i}{total\_fake\_profiles} \times 100 \tag{7.16}$$

where Y^i indicates correctly classified fake profiles at i^{th} iteration.

(c) Average False Alarm Rate

It identifies the percentage of genuine profiles classified as fake over M runs.

$$AvgFAR = \frac{1}{M}\sum\nolimits_{i=1}^{M} \frac{FP^i}{genuine\_profiles} \times 100 \tag{7.17}$$

where FP^i represents genuine profiles misclassified as fake at i^{th} iteration.

(d) Average F-Measure

It is the harmonic mean of precision and recall. The number of accurately classified fake profiles divided by the number of classified fake profiles is known as precision (*P*). The number of fake profiles accurately identified, divided by the total number of fake profiles, is known as recall (*R*).

$$AvgFMeasure = \frac{1}{M}\sum\nolimits_{i=1}^{M} \frac{(2 \times P \times R)}{(P + R)} \tag{7.18}$$

It gives equal weightage to *P* and *R*, and thus the goal is to maximize it.

Experiments and Results

This section summarizes and discusses the findings of different experiments conducted from various perspectives.

Comparison of Binary Operators

Shilling profile detection is a binary classification problem as depicted in Fig. 7.6. Therefore, a function to convert GWO into a binary version should exist. The two binary functions that have been mentioned in the literature are *sigmoid* [1] and *tanh* [38].

To find a binary function that suits best for the proposed approach, we have computed and compared the average results of 10 runs on both functions. First, the convergence rate of GWODS is one criterion that needs to be analyzed. Experiments have been conducted on all three datasets. However, a convergence graph for only 100K has been shown, owing to the same underlying graphs on all three datasets. From Fig. 7.7, it can be noted that GWODS shows similar convergence behavior on both functions and converges at the 6–7th iteration.

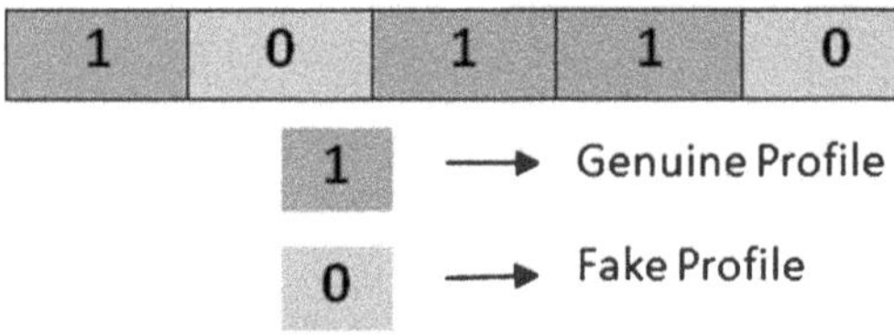

Fig. 7.6 Representation of solution in feature selection

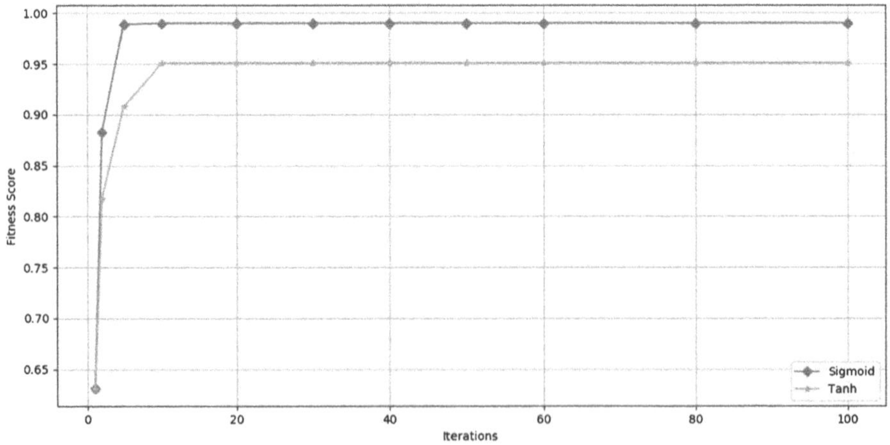

Fig. 7.7 Convergence graph

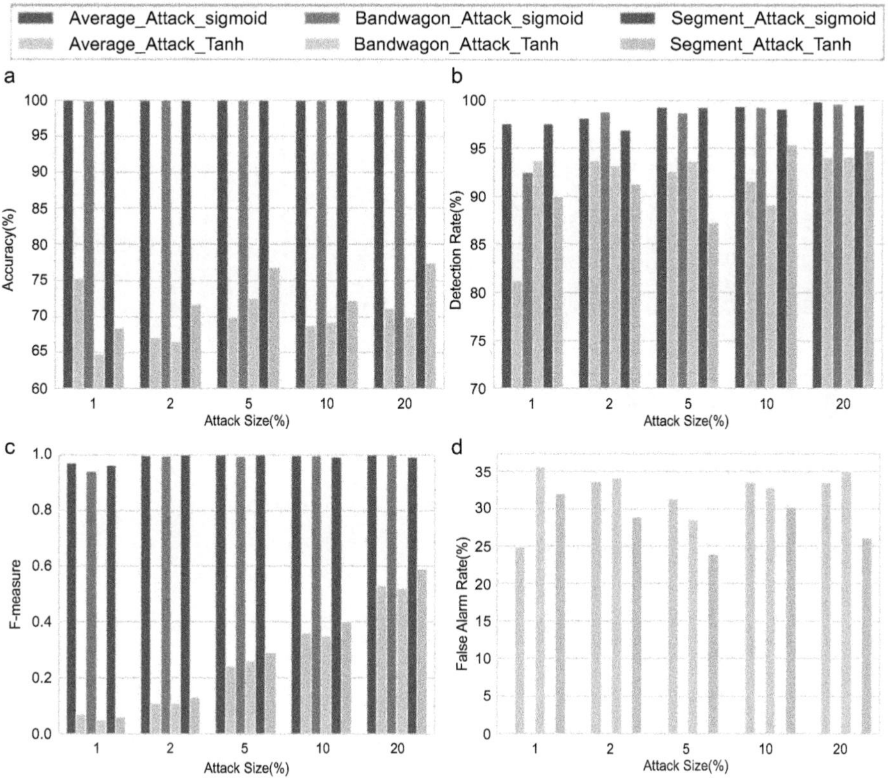

Fig. 7.8 Comparative results of GWODS on binary functions using ML 100K on filler size 3%

Further, *sigmoid* and *tanh* functions are compared on different metrics, namely, accuracy, detection rate, F-measure, and FAR on different attack models and attack sizes ranging from 1% to 20%. From Figs. 7.8, 7.9, and 7.10, it can be observed that sigmoid has outperformed *tanh* on all the three datasets considered. The accuracy, detection rate, and F-measure of GWODS using tan*h* are less in comparison to the sigmoid operator on all three attacks, namely, average, bandwagon, and sigmoid. The FAR of GWODS using sigmoid is approximate to 0, whereas using *tanh* operator, a high value has been observed, signifying misclassification of genuine profiles as shillers. The same pattern has been observed on all three datasets irrespective of the attack model considered. Seeking the excellent performance of sigmoid operator in detecting fake profiles, all further experiments and analysis are done using sigmoid.

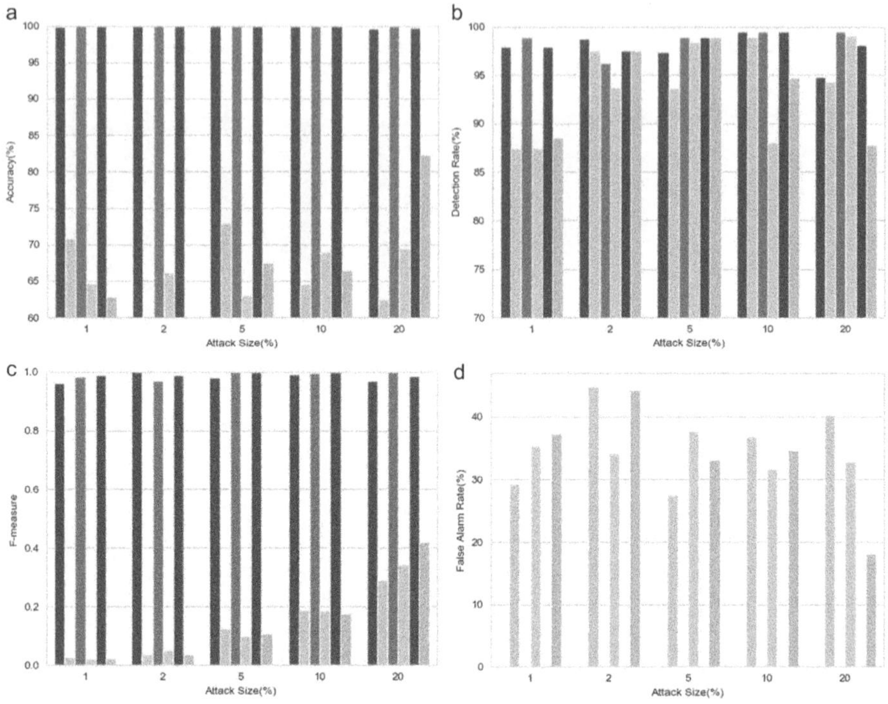

Fig. 7.9 Comparative results of GWODS on binary functions using ML 1M on filler size 3%

Result Analysis

The performance of GWODS has been analyzed by conducting experiments from various perspectives. The results have been shown in Tables 7.5, 7.6, 7.7, 7.8, 7.9, 7.10, 7.11, 7.12, 7.13, 7.14, 7.15, and 7.16. Filler size is kept small as higher the filler size, more information is required by an attacker to mount attack, which is difficult to get. Moreover, as most entries in a user's profile are null, filler size is kept low, i.e., 1%, 3%, and 5%, to resemble the genuine profiles. Keeping the filler size low increases the chances of winning from the attacker's viewpoint.

Different attacks are mounted considering different attack sizes. However, GWODS has shown a high detection rate in all cases considered. It is further important to note that the accuracy of GWODS on all three datasets considered is above 99% in almost all cases, depicting high accuracy on all three of the datasets considered. The detection rate is also above 95% in all cases considered of ML 100K and ML 1M, except at attack size 1% and filler size 3% for ML 100K.However, in such a case, 92.5% detection rate indicates that 9 out of 10 fake profiles are correctly classified. In the case of ML 100K (latest), 87.5% detection rate on an average in case of 1% attack size signifies the misclassification of 1 out of 6 attack profiles considered, number of fake users being 6. It is further worth noting that not more than 1 fake profile has been misclassified considering all cases.

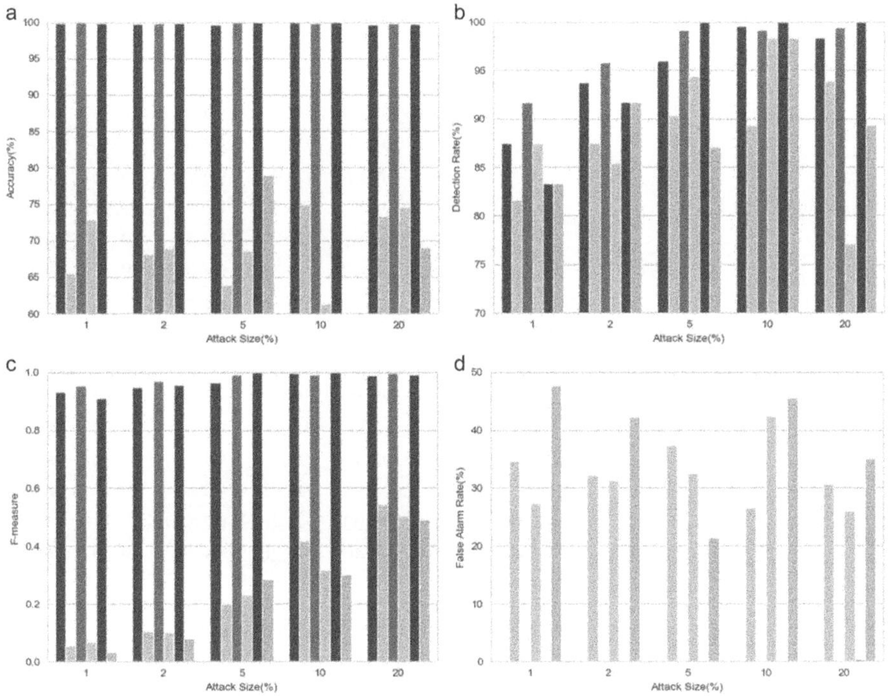

Fig. 7.10 Comparative results of GWODS on binary functions using ML 100K (latest) on filler size 3%

Table 7.5 Accuracy of shillers mounted utilizing various attack models on ML 100K

		Attack size (%)						
	Filler size	1	2	5	10	15	20	30
Average attack	1%	99.97	100	100	99.86	99.93	99.99	98.94
	3%	99.94	100	100	99.98	99.95	100	99.71
	5%	99.71	100	100	99.97	100	99.97	99.77
Bandwagon attack	1%	99.86	100	100	99.95	99.78	99.97	99.73
	3%	99.89	100	100	99.97	99.95	99.98	99.56
	5%	99.94	100	100	100	100	99.91	99.74
Segment attack	1%	99.92	99.98	100	100	99.8	99.78	99.75
	3%	99.92	100	100	99.98	100	99.92	99.57
	5%	99.92	100	99.92	99.93	99.94	99.93	99.47
AOP attack	1%	99.94	99.92	99.82	99.90	99.95	99.91	99.83
	3%	99.89	99.94	100	99.95	99.90	99.95	99.91
	5%	99.89	99.76	99.87	99.90	99.88	99.93	99.67
Power item attack	1%	99.84	99.92	99.94	99.80	99.95	99.88	99.87
	3%	99.92	100	99.87	99.80	99.97	99.93	99.56
	5%	99.89	99.92	99.89	99.92	99.90	99.80	99.89

Table 7.6 Detection rate of shillers mounted utilizing various attack models on ML 100K

		Attack size (%)						
	Filler size	1	2	5	10	15	20	30
Average attack	1%	97.50	97.50	98.93	98.27	99.55	99.53	97.60
	3%	97.75	98.12	99.20	99.33	98.93	99.80	99.02
	5%	97.75	97.50	99.46	99.33	99.73	99.40	99.02
Bandwagon attack	1%	97.50	96.87	98.67	99.20	98.75	99.53	98.93
	3%	92.50	98.75	98.67	99.20	99.20	99.53	98.62
	5%	95.00	96.25	98.40	99.33	99.64	99.13	98.89
Segment attack	1%	97.50	96.25	99.46	99.20	98.58	98.80	98.93
	3%	97.50	96.87	99.20	99.06	99.55	99.46	98.98
	5%	97.50	96.25	98.13	99.06	99.64	99.46	98.13
AoP attack	1%	95.00	97.36	96.80	9893	99.64	99.60	99.91
	3%	100	97.36	100	99.46	99.64	99.73	99.23
	5%	100	97.36	98.40	98.93	99.64	99.60	98.93
Power item attack	1%	95.00	97.36	98.93	98.93	99.64	99.47	99.45
	3%	92.50	100	98.93	98.40	99.82	99.73	98.82
	5%	97.50	96.05	98.40	99.20	99.46	99.20	99.20

Table 7.7 F-measure of shillers mounted utilizing various attack models on ML 100K

		Attack size (%)						
	Filler size	1	2	5	10	15	20	30
Average attack	1%	0.98	0.99	0.99	0.99	0.99	0.99	0.97
	3%	0.97	0.99	0.99	0.99	0.99	0.99	0.99
	5%	0.95	0.99	0.99	0.99	1	0.99	0.99
Bandwagon attack	1%	0.98	1	0.99	0.99	0.98	0.99	0.99
	3%	0.94	0.99	0.99	0.99	0.99	0.99	0.98
	5%	0.97	0.99	0.99	0.99	0.99	0.99	0.99
Segment attack	1%	0.96	0.99	0.99	0.99	0.99	0.99	0.99
	3%	0.96	1	1	0.99	0.99	0.99	0.98
	5%	0.96	0.99	0.98	0.99	0.99	0.99	0.98
AoP attack	1%	0.97	0.98	0.98	0.99	0.99	0.99	0.99
	3%	0.95	0.98	1	0.99	0.99	0.99	0.99
	5%	0.95	0.94	0.98	0.99	0.99	0.99	0.99
Power item attack	1%	0.93	0.98	0.99	0.98	0.99	0.99	0.99
	3%	0.96	1	0.98	0.98	0.99	0.99	0.98
	5%	0.95	0.97	0.98	0.99	0.99	0.99	0.97

The high F-measure, i.e., above 0.9%, and low FAR, i.e., below 0.1, in most of the cases have been noted on all three datasets. However, in the case of attack size 30%, FAR as high as 0.35 has been observed on ML 100K and as high as 0.13on the ML 1M dataset, denoting misclassification of one genuine profile approximately. The F-measure has also seen a drop in attack size 1%, where both ML 100K and ML

Table 7.8 FAR of shillers mounted utilizing various attack models on ML 100K

		Attack size (%)						
	Filler size	1	2	5	10	15	20	30
Average attack	1%	0	0.03	0.01	0.07	0.11	0.01	0.25
	3%	0.02	0.01	0	0.05	0	0.03	0.18
	5%	0.21	0	0.02	0.06	0	0.01	0.1
Bandwagon attack	1%	0	0	0.03	0.07	0.17	0.03	0.13
	3%	0.02	0.01	0.03	0.05	0.03	0.02	0.26
	5%	0	0.01	0.01	0.02	0.03	0.03	0.10
Segment attack	1%	0	0.03	0.06	0.02	0.11	0.11	0.1
	3%	0.05	0	0	0.02	0.02	0.09	0.35
	5%	0.05	0.01	0.09	0.07	0.11	0.07	0.22
AoP attack	1%	0	0.02	0.02	0	0	0.02	0.02
	3%	0.10	0	0	0	0.05	0	0
	5%	0.10	0.18	0.05	0	0.07	0	0.10
Power item attack	1%	0.10	0.02	0	0.10	0	0.02	0.02
	3%	0	0	0.07	0.05	0	0.02	0.02
	5%	0.07	0	0.02	0	0.02	0.07	0.02

Table 7.9 Accuracy of shillers mounted utilizing various attack models on ML 1M

		Attack size (%)						
	Filler size	1	2	5	10	15	20	30
Average attack	1%	99.96	99.96	100	100	99.97	99.98	99.78
	3%	99.80	100	99.95	100	100	99.62	99.96
	5%	99.76	100	100	100	99.99	100	99.99
Bandwagon attack	1%	99.90	99.73	100	100	100	100	99.97
	3%	99.96	99.96	100	100	99.94	100	99.99
	5%	99.95	99.96	100	100	100	99.98	99.87
Segment attack	1%	99.95	100	100	100	100	99.98	100
	3%	99.97	100	100	100	100	99.78	100
	5%	99.97	100	99.95	100	99.96	100	100
AoP attack	1%	99.79	99.96	99.95	99.96	100	99.98	100
	3%	99.93	99.97	99.93	100	99.82	99.64	99.62
	5%	99.91	99.96	99.91	99.85	99.67	99.76	99.49
Power item attack	1%	99.78	99.71	99.96	99.96	100	99.89	99.90
	3%	99.78	99.95	99.98	99.23	99.92	99.65	99.68
	5%	99.81	99.97	99.91	99.92	99.75	99.93	99.81

1M have seen a drop as low as 0.94. Finally, only one user profile has been misidentified, demonstrating the great effectiveness of GWODS in detecting fake profiles created through shilling attacks.

GWODS shows outstanding detection results in the case of strong attacks, such as average, bandwagon, and segment attacks. However, on weak attack, such as

Table 7.10 Detection rate of shillers mounted utilizing various attack models on ML 1M

		Attack size (%)						
	Filler size	1	2	5	10	15	20	30
Average attack	1%	96.87	97.50	98.93	99.73	99.11	99.33	98.31
	3%	97.91	98.75	97.34	99.46	99.64	94.81	99.55
	5%	95.83	97.50	98.93	99.46	99.29	99.60	99.73
Bandwagon attack	1%	100	98.43	98.4	99.46	100	99.86	99.73
	3%	98.95	96.25	98.93	99.46	98.58	99.46	99.55
	5%	97.91	96.25	98.40	99.20	99.29	99.60	99.64
Segment attack	1%	95.83	97.50	98.93	98.93	99.64	99.20	99.82
	3%	97.91	97.50	98.93	99.46	99.64	98.13	100
	5%	97.91	97.50	96.80	100	99.64	99.73	99.64
AoP attack	1%	98.34	98.43	99.15	99.57	100	99.20	99.82
	3%	97.91	98.95	99.15	100	98.64	98.33	98.92
	5%	96.87	98.95	98.31	98.36	91.66	99.97	98.08
Power item attack	1%	96.87	98.95	99.78	99.57	100	99.59	99.59
	3%	95.83	97.91	99.78	100	99.43	98.36	98.92
	5%	97.91	99.47	99.15	99.15	98.64	99.59	99.31

Table 7.11 F-measure of shillers mounted utilizing various attack models on ML 1M

		Attack size (%)						
	Filler size	1	2	5	10	15	20	30
Average attack	1%	0.98	0.97	0.99	0.99	0.99	0.99	0.98
	3%	0.96	1	0.98	0.99	0.99	0.97	0.99
	5%	0.94	0.98	0.99	0.99	0.99	0.99	0.99
Bandwagon attack	1%	0.95	0.94	0.99	1	1	0.99	0.99
	3%	0.98	0.96	1	0.99	0.99	0.99	0.99
	5%	0.97	0.97	0.99	0.99	0.99	0.99	0.99
Segment attack	1%	0.97	1	1	1	1	0.99	0.99
	3%	0.98	0.98	1	1	1	0.98	1
	5%	0.98	0.98	0.98	0.99	0.99	1	0.99
AoP attack	1%	0.94	0.99	0.99	0.99	1	0.99	0.99
	3%	0.97	0.99	0.99	1	0.99	0.98	0.99
	5%	0.95	0.99	0.99	0.99	0.91	0.99	0.98
Power item attack	1%	0.89	0.94	0.99	0.99	1	0.99	0.99
	3%	0.97	0.98	0.99	0.99	0.99	0.98	0.99
	5%	0.91	0.99	0.99	0.99	0.99	0.99	0.99

random attacks, shillers tend to be scattered over multiple clusters, making it difficult for GWODS to identify them. However, these attacks are weak and do not have much impact on the recommendations generated.

Table 7.12 FAR of shillers mounted utilizing various attack models on ML 1M

		Attack size (%)						
	Filler size	1	2	5	10	15	20	30
Average attack	1%	0	0.05	0.02	0.01	0.02	0.01	0.08
	3%	0.01	0	0.03	0.02	0.01	0.03	0.03
	5%	0.09	0.02	0.02	0	0.01	0	0.02
Bandwagon attack	1%	0.09	0.24	0.01	0	0	0	0.04
	3%	0.02	0.04	0	0.02	0.02	0	0
	5%	0.02	0.04	0	0.01	0	0.03	0.13
Segment attack	1%	0	0	0	0	0	0	0.02
	3%	0	0.02	0	0	0	0.12	0
	5%	0	0.02	0.02	0.04	0.06	0	0
AOP attack	1%	0.06	0	0	0	0	0	0.02
	3%	0.05	0.01	0	0	0.06	0.08	0.08
	5%	0.04	0	0.02	0	0	0.08	0.08
Power attack	1%	0.18	0.17	0.02	0	0	0.04	0
	3%	0.17	0	0	0.08	0	0.08	0.08
	5%	0.16	0.01	0.04	0	0.08	0	0.04

Table 7.13 Accuracy of shillers mounted utilizing various attack models on ML 100K (latest)

		Attack size (%)						
	Filler size	1	2	5	10	15	20	30
Average attack	1%	99.87	99.79	99.72	99.92	99.85	99.89	99.90
	3%	99.87	99.79	99.64	99.96	99.82	99.65	99.68
	5%	99.83	99.71	99.84	99.73	99.75	99.93	99.81
Bandwagon attack	1%	99.95	99.87	99.92	99.85	99.78	99.76	99.65
	3%	99.91	99.87	99.92	99.85	99.85	99.89	99.74
	5%	99.91	99.87	99.8	99.85	99.92	99.76	99.49
Segment attack	1%	100	100	99.53	100	99.57	99.86	98.88
	3%	99.83	99.83	100	100	99.85	99.72	99.49
	5%	100	100	99.84	99.85	100	99.86	95.34
AoP attack	1%	99.91	99.95	99.88	99.96	99.92	99.91	99.83
	3%	99.83	99.95	99.88	99.14	99.92	99.94	99.91
	5%	99.91	99.91	99.80	99.85	99.88	99.93	99.67
Power item attack	1%	99.95	99.79	99.88	99.85	99.93	99.86	99.84
	3%	99.91	99.87	99.96	99.40	99.84	99.96	99.94
	5%	99.91	99.95	99.87	99.95	99.92	99.82	99.88

Comparison of GWODS with State-of-the-Art Approaches

In this subsection, a comparison of GWODS with the following state-of-the-art approaches is illustrated. Table 7.17 describes various baseline methods considered for comparison.

Table 7.14 Detection rate of shillers mounted utilizing various attack models on ML 100K (latest)

		Attack size (%)						
	Filler size	1	2	5	10	15	20	30
Average attack	1%	87.50	95.83	96.77	99.18	99.18	99.59	99.59
	3%	87.50	93.75	95.96	99.59	98.64	98.36	98.90
	5%	87.50	91.66	98.38	98.77	98.64	99.59	99.31
Bandwagon attack	1%	100	95.83	99.19	98.77	98.64	98.77	98.77
	3%	91.66	95.83	99.19	99.18	98.91	99.38	99.04
	5%	91.66	95.83	95.96	98.77	99.45	99.97	98.08
Segment attack	1%	100	100	96.77	100	97.82	100	95.62
	3%	83.33	91.66	100	100	98.91	100	98.36
	5%	100	100	96.77	98.36	100	99.18	91.80
AoP attack	1%	91.66	97.91	97.58	99.59	99.45	99.62	99.91
	3%	92.50	97.91	97.58	95.90	99.65	99.76	99.26
	5%	95.00	95.83	98.38	98.36	99.65	99.63	98.93
Power item attack	1%	100	95.83	97.58	98.36	99.63	99.47	99.45
	3%	95.00	95.83	99.19	96.72	96.77	99.82	99.73
	5%	95.00	97.50	92.50	97.50	99.44	99.22	99.26

Table 7.15 F-measure of shillers mounted utilizing various attack models on ML 100K (latest)

		Attack size (%)						
	Filler size	1	2	5	10	15	20	30
Average attack	1%	0.93	0.94	0.97	0.99	0.99	0.99	0.99
	3%	0.93	0.94	0.96	0.99	0.99	0.98	0.99
	5%	0.91	0.92	0.98	0.98	0.99	0.99	0.99
Bandwagon attack	1%	0.98	0.96	0.99	0.99	0.99	0.99	0.99
	3%	0.95	0.96	0.99	0.99	0.99	0.99	0.99
	5%	0.95	0.96	0.97	0.99	0.99	0.99	0.98
Segment attack	1%	1	1	0.95	1	0.98	0.99	0.97
	3%	0.90	0.95	1	1	0.99	0.99	0.98
	5%	1	1	0.98	0.99	1	0.99	0.90
AoP attack	1%	0.95	0.98	0.98	0.99	0.99	0.99	0.99
	3%	0.94	0.98	0.98	0.95	0.99	0.99	0.99
	5%	0.97	0.97	0.98	0.99	0.99	0.99	0.99
Power item attack	1%	0.98	0.95	0.98	0.99	0.99	0.99	0.99
	3%	0.97	0.96	0.99	0.96	0.98	0.99	0.99
	5%	0.97	0.98	0.96	0.98	0.99	0.99	0.97

Table 7.18 shows the comparative analysis of six baseline approaches with GWODS in terms of precision under different filler and attack sizes on the ML dataset of size 100K.

As shown in Table 7.18, the precision of GWODS is higher than that of the baseline approaches under all three types of attacks considered. SVM-TIA and RAdaBoost show high precision in average attack; however, low precision is

Table 7.16 FAR of shillers mounted utilizing various attack models on ML 100K (latest)

		Attack size (%)						
	Filler size	1	2	5	10	15	20	30
Average attack	1%	0	0.12	0.12	0	0.04	0.04	0
	3%	0	0.08	0.16	0	0	0.08	0.08
	5%	0.04	0.12	0.08	0.16	0.08	0	0.04
Bandwagon attack	1%	0.04	0.04	0.04	0.04	0.04	0.04	0.08
	3%	0	0.04	0.04	0.08	0	0	0.04
	5%	0	0.04	0	0.04	0	0.08	0.08
Segment attack	1%	0	0	0.49	0	0.16	0.16	0.16
	3%	0	0	0	0	0	0.32	0.16
	5%	0	0	0	0	0	0	0.36
AoP attack	1%	0	0	0	0	0	0.02	0.02
	3%	0	0	0	0.05	0.05	0	0
	5%	0	0	0.12	0	0.07	0	0.10
Power item attack	1%	0.04	0.12	0	0	0	0.02	0.02
	3%	0	0.04	0	0.26	0	0	0.02
	5%	0	0	0	0	0.02	0.07	0.02

Table 7.17 Baseline approaches

Approach	Methodology	Limitation
RAdaBoost [45]	Extracted features from user profiles and used rescale AdaBoost as classifier	Efficiency needs to be improved
SVM-TIA [50]	Detection of attack profiles and target items are done in phase 1 and phase 2, respectively, along with borderline-SMOTE	Low detection precision except in average attack
CoDetector [12]	Proposed collaborative shilling detection using decision tree as classifier	Low detection accuracy in case of low filler and attack size
CNN-SAD [42]	1 convolution and 1 pooling layer is used for classification of profiles	Incurs huge cost for the training of large datasets
MV-EDM [18]	Proposed multiview ensemble method based on 17 artificial detection features	Based on human engineering features
SDAe-PCA [19]	Based on multiple views to get insight of user behavior. SDAe and PCA for feature extraction	Efficiency needs to be improved

observed in the case of PIA and AoP attack. These results depict poor adaptability of SVM-TIA and RAdaBoost under various attacks. CoDetector suffers from poor precision when attack and filler size is low. Compared with baseline approaches, GWODS works directly on the matrix of user-item ratings, does not need training time and preliminary knowledge of shillers, and is easy to implement and detect group profiles. Further, it outperforms other approaches in terms of precision values under different attack models with different filler and attack sizes.

Table 7.18 Detection precision of different algorithms with filler size 3%

Attack size	Technique	3%	5%	10%	12%
Average attack	RAdaBoost	0.651	0.732	0.799	0.823
	SVM-TIA	0.942	0.986	0.992	0.920
	CoDetector	0.396	0.623	0.836	0.910
	CNN-SAD	0.821	0.810	0.864	0.896
	MV-EDM	0.826	0.836	0.887	0.904
	SDAe-PCA	0.834	0.884	0.901	0.912
	GWODS	**0.991**	**1.000**	**0.994**	**0.962**
AoP attack	RAdaBoost	0.398	0.423	0.620	0.698
	SVM-TIA	0.676	0.694	0.760	0.733
	CoDetector	0.354	0.698	0.796	0.876
	CNN-SAD	0.740	0.736	0.746	0.894
	MV-EDM	0.794	0.808	0.856	0.902
	SDAe-PCA	0.801	0.823	0.886	0.903
	GWODS	**0.973**	**1.000**	**1.000**	**0.997**
Power item attack	RAdaBoost	0.278	0.298	0.402	0.424
	SVM-TIA	0.684	0.644	0.674	0.526
	CoDetector	0.358	0.514	0.696	0.698
	CNN-SAD	0.601	0.654	0.688	0.696
	MV-EDM	0.824	0.812	0.865	0.883
	SDAe-PCA	0.824	0.844	0.864	0.901
	GWODS	**0.991**	**0.984**	**0.994**	**0.995**

To summarize, GWODS is an unsupervised methodology that adapts a recently developed SI methodology called GWO. It is simple to set up and use, has a small number of parameters, and produces excellent results. This is another reason for a large volume of great works in a short time.

7 Conclusion and Future Work

Shilling attacks have the power of manipulating recommendations and thus are very harmful to the CF system. To minimize/nullify effects of shilling attacks on CF, we proposed a novel fusion method, namely, GWODS based on k-means algorithm and GWO for detection of shilling profiles mounted by attackers in the dataset. K-means clustering algorithm is used to get the most suspicious cluster, which is then worked upon by GWO using the introduced fitness function and mimicking hunting behavior of wolves to differentiate between fake and genuine profiles. Further, the proposed method works directly on the user-item rating matrix exploiting the collusive behavior that exists among shillers and does not require prerequisites, such as preliminary knowledge of shillers or hand-designed features.

Experiments on MovieLens datasets of varying sizes and sparsity demonstrate effective results in terms of detection rate, accuracy, false alarm rate, precision, recall, and F-measure. Further, it outperformed six state-of-the-art approaches considered, overcoming their drawbacks. Finally, GWODS prevents the generation of bias recommendations and thus can be employed as a preprocessing phase of any RS.

In the future, we will try to explore the viability of attacks, where shilling profiles have the same rating pattern as genuine profiles. The proposed method might fail in correctly classifying profiles in such a scenario. In this chapter, our focus is on push attack; however, a nuke attack can also be worked upon by minimum changes in the attack model.

Data Availability Statement The datasets generated during and/or analyzed during the current study are available in the GroupLens repository, https://grouplens.org/datasets/movielens

References

1. Al-Tashi, Q., Kadir, S.J.A., Rais, H.M., Mirjalili, S., Alhussian, H.: Binary optimization using hybrid grey wolf optimization for feature selection. IEEE Access. **7**, 39496–39508 (2019)
2. Al-Tashi, Q., Rais, H.M., Abdulkadir, S.J., Mirjalili, S., Alhussian, H.: A review of grey wolf optimizer-based feature selection methods for classification. In: Evolutionary Machine Learning Techniques, pp. 273–286. Springer, Singapore (2020)
3. Bansal, S., Baliyan, N.: A study of recent recommender system techniques. Int. J. Knowl. Syst. Sci. (IJKSS). **10**(2), 13–41 (2019)
4. Bansal, S., Baliyan, N.: Bi-MARS: a Bi-clustering based memetic algorithm for recommender systems. Appl. Soft Comput. **97**, 106785 (2020a)
5. Bansal, S., Baliyan, N.: A multi-criteria evaluation of evolutionary algorithms against segment based shilling attacks. In: 10th International Conference Soft Computing for Problem Solving (SocProS). IIT Indore – accepted (2020b)
6. Batmaz, Z., Yilmazel, B., Kaleli, C.: Shilling attack detection in binary data: a classification approach. J. Ambient. Intell. Humaniz. Comput. **11**(6), 2601–2611 (2020)
7. Bedi, P., Gautam, A., Bansal, S., Bhatia, D.: Weighted bipartite graph model for recommender system using entropy based similarity measure. In: The International Symposium on Intelligent Systems Technologies and Applications, pp. 163–173. Springer, Cham (2017)
8. Burke, R., O'Mahony, M.P., Hurley, N.J.: Robust collaborative recommendation. In: Recommender Systems Handbook, pp. 961–995. Springer, Boston (2015)
9. Cao, G., Zhang, H., Fan, Y., Kuang, L.: Finding shilling attack in recommender system based on dynamic feature selection. In: SEKE, pp. 50–55 (2018)
10. Chirita, P.A., Nejdl, W., Zamfir, C.: Preventing shilling attacks in online recommender systems. In: Proceedings of the 7th Annual ACM International Workshop on Web Information and Data Management, pp. 67–74 (2005)
11. Deng, Z.J., Zhang, F., Wang, S.P.: Shilling attack detection in collaborative filtering recommender system by PCA detection and perturbation. In: 2016 International Conference on Wavelet Analysis and Pattern Recognition (ICWAPR), pp. 213–218. IEEE (2016)
12. Dou, T., Yu, J., Xiong, Q., Gao, M., Song, Y., Fang, Q.: Collaborative shilling detection bridging factorization and user embedding. In: International Conference on Collaborative Computing: Networking, Applications and Worksharing, pp. 459–469. Springer, Cham (2017)

13. Elhariri, E., El-Bendary, N., Hassanien, A.E.: Bio-inspired optimization for feature set dimensionality reduction. In: 2016 3rd International Conference on Advances in Computational Tools for Engineering Applications (ACTEA), pp. 184–189. IEEE (2016)
14. Emary, E., Yamany, W., Hassanien, A.E., Snasel, V.: Multi-objective gray-wolf optimization for attribute reduction. Procedia Comput. Sci. **65**, 623–632 (2015)
15. Emary, E., Zawbaa, H.M., Hassanien, A.E.: Binary grey wolf optimization approaches for feature selection. Neurocomputing. **172**, 371–381 (2016)
16. Grouplens (2003). Movielens. Available: https://grouplens.org/datasets/movielens/
17. Gunes, I., Kaleli, C., Bilge, A., Polat, H.: Shilling attacks against recommender systems: a comprehensive survey. Artif. Intell. Rev. **42**(4), 767–799 (2014)
18. Hao, Y., Zhang, P., Zhang, F.: Multiview Ensemble Method for Detecting Shilling Attacks in Collaborative Recommender Systems. Security and Communication Networks (2018)
19. Hao, Y., Zhang, F., Wang, J., Zhao, Q., Cao, J.: Detecting Shilling Attacks with Automatic Features from Multiple Views. Security and Communication Networks (2019)
20. Hassan, H.A., Zellagui, M.: Application of grey wolf optimizer algorithm for optimal power flow of two-terminal HVDC transmission system. Adv. Electr. Electron. Eng. **15**(5), 701–712 (2018)
21. Hatta, N.M., Zain, A.M., Sallehuddin, R., Shayfull, Z., Yusoff, Y.: Recent studies on optimisation method of Grey Wolf Optimiser (GWO): a review (2014–2017). Artif. Intell. Rev. **52**(4), 2651–2683 (2019)
22. Faris, H., Aljarah, I., Al-Betar, M.A., Mirjalili, S.: Grey wolf optimizer: a review of recent variants and applications. Neural Comput. & Applic. **30**(2), 413–435 (2018)
23. Jannach, D., Zanker, M., Felfernig, A., Friedrich, G.: Recommender Systems: An Introduction. Cambridge University Press (2010)
24. Lam, S.K., Riedl, J.: Shilling recommender systems for fun and profit. In: Proceedings of the 13th International Conference on World Wide Web, pp. 393–402 (2004)
25. Liu, X., Xiao, Y., Jiao, X., Zheng, W., Ling, Z.: A novel Kalman Filter based shilling attack detection algorithm. arXiv preprint arXiv:1908.06968. (2019)
26. Lu, C., Gao, L., Li, X., Hu, C., Yan, X., Gong, W.: Chaotic-based grey wolf optimizer for numerical and engineering optimization problems. Memet. Comput. **12**(4), 371–398 (2020)
27. Manikandan, K.: Diagnosis of diabetes diseases using optimized fuzzy rule set by grey wolf optimization. Pattern Recogn. Lett. **125**, 432–438 (2019)
28. Mehta, B.: Unsupervised shilling detection for collaborative filtering. In: AAAI, pp. 1402–1407 (2007)
29. Mehta, B., Hofmann, T., Fankhauser, P.: Lies and propaganda: detecting spam users in collaborative filtering. In: Proceedings of the 12th International Conference on Intelligent User Interfaces, pp. 14–21 (2007)
30. Mehta, B., Nejdl, W.: Unsupervised strategies for shilling detection and robust collaborative filtering. User Model. User-Adap. Inter. **19**(1–2), 65–97 (2009)
31. Mirjalili, S.: How effective is the Grey Wolf optimizer in training multi-layer perceptrons. Appl. Intell. **43**(1), 150–161 (2015)
32. Mirjalili, S., Mirjalili, S.M., Lewis, A.: Grey wolf optimizer. Adv. Eng. Softw. **69**, 46–61 (2014)
33. Mobasher, B., Burke, R., Williams, C., Bhaumik, R.: Analysis and detection of segment-focused attacks against collaborative recommendation. In: International Workshop on Knowledge Discovery on the Web, pp. 96–118. Springer, Berlin/Heidelberg (2005)
34. Mobasher, B., Burke, R., Bhaumik, R., Williams, C.: Toward trustworthy recommender systems: an analysis of attack models and algorithm robustness. ACM Trans. Internet Technol. (TOIT). **7**(4), 23-es (2007)
35. Rosaria Silipo, M. W.: (2019). Available at https://thenewstack.io/3-new-techniques-for-data-dimensionality-reduction-in-machine-learning/
36. Niu, P., Niu, S., Chang, L.: The defect of the Grey Wolf optimization algorithm and its verification method. Knowl.-Based Syst. **171**, 37–43 (2019)

37. Pradhan, M., Roy, P.K., Pal, T.: Oppositional based grey wolf optimization algorithm for economic dispatch problem of power system. Ain Shams Eng. J. **9**(4), 2015–2025 (2018)
38. Sahoo, A., Chandra, S.: Multi-objective grey wolf optimizer for improved cervix lesion classification. Appl. Soft Comput. **52**, 64–80 (2017)
39. Sharma, P., Sundaram, S., Sharma, M., Sharma, A., Gupta, D.: Diagnosis of Parkinson's disease using modified grey wolf optimization. Cogn. Syst. Res. **54**, 100–115 (2019)
40. Si, M., Li, Q.: Shilling attacks against collaborative recommender systems: a review. Artif. Intell. Rev. **53**(1), 291–319 (2020)
41. Tawhid, M.A., Ali, A.F.: A hybrid grey wolf optimizer and genetic algorithm for minimizing potential energy function. Memet. Comput. **9**(4), 347–359 (2017)
42. Tong, C., Yin, X., Li, J., Zhu, T., Lv, R., Sun, L., Rodrigues, J.J.: A shilling attack detector based on convolutional neural network for collaborative recommender system in social aware network. Comput. J. **61**(7), 949–958 (2018)
43. Wang, Y., Zhang, L., Tao, H., Wu, Z., Cao, J.: A comparative study of shilling attack detectors for recommender systems. In: 2015 12th International Conference on Service Systems and Service Management (ICSSSM), pp. 1–6. IEEE (2015)
44. Yamany, W., Emary, E., Hassanien, A.E.: New rough set attribute reduction algorithm based on grey wolf optimization. In: The 1st International Conference on Advanced Intelligent System and Informatics (AISI2015), November 28–30, 2015, Beni Suef, Egypt, pp. 241–251. Springer, Cham (2016)
45. Yang, Z., Xu, L., Cai, Z., Xu, Z.: Re-scale AdaBoost for attack detection in collaborative filtering recommender systems. Knowl.-Based Syst. **100**, 74–88 (2016)
46. Zhang, F., Deng, Z.J., He, Z.M., Lin, X.C., Sun, L.L.: Detection of shilling attack in collaborative filtering recommender system by pca and data complexity. In: 2018 International Conference on Machine Learning and Cybernetics (ICMLC), vol. 2, pp. 673–678. IEEE (2018a)
47. Zhang, F., Zhang, Z., Zhang, P., Wang, S.: UD-HMM: an unsupervised method for shilling attack detection based on hidden Markov model and hierarchical clustering. Knowl.-Based Syst. **148**, 146–166 (2018b)
48. Zhang, S., Ouyang, Y., Ford, J., Makedon, F.: Analysis of a low-dimensional linear model under recommendation attacks. In: Proceedings of the 29th Annual International ACM SIGIR Conference on Research and Development in Information Retrieval, pp. 517–524 (2006)
49. Zhao, X., Ma, Z., Zhang, Z.: A novel recommendation system in location-based social networks using distributed ELM. Memet. Comput. **10**(3), 321–331 (2018)
50. Zhou, W., Wen, J., Xiong, Q., Gao, M., Zeng, J.: SVM-TIA a shilling attack detection method based on SVM and target item analysis in recommender systems. Neurocomputing. **210**, 197–205 (2016)
51. Zhou, Q., Wu, J., Duan, L.: Recommendation attack detection based on deep learning. J. Inf. Secur. Appl. **52**, 102493 (2020)

Chapter 8
Single Image Reflection Removal Using Deep Learning

Sushil Kumar, Peeyush Joshi, Vanita Garg, and Hira Zaheer

1 Introduction

It is often the case that the subject that we are trying to photograph is on the other side of the glass and we end up taking a photograph through a glass, as the glass in between is simply unavoidable or the hassle is not worth the efforts. Photographs, thus, taken contain undesirable reflections and degrade the visibility of the scene by blurring, obstructing or deforming the background scene and may result in failure or degradation of processing and analysing capabilities of computer-vision algorithms, such as object detection, event detection, object recognition, image segmentation, video tracking, etc. The problem of getting reflection-free images taken through glass is of great interest in the image processing and computer vision community and has practical demands.

$$\boldsymbol{I} = \boldsymbol{R} + \boldsymbol{B} \tag{8.1}$$

where
$\boldsymbol{I}$: n × m × 3 matrix which represents the reflection-contaminated image
$\boldsymbol{R}$: n × m × 3 matrix which represents the reflection layer
$\boldsymbol{B}$: n × m × 3 matrix which represents the background layer

S. Kumar (✉) · P. Joshi
Department of Computer Science & Engineering, National Institute of Technology Warangal, Hanamkonda, Telangana, India
e-mail: kumar.sushil@nitw.ac.in; pjoshi@student.nitw.ac.in

V. Garg · H. Zaheer
School of Basic and Applied Sciences, Galgotias University, Greater Noida, Uttar Pradesh, India

© The Author(s), under exclusive license to Springer Nature Switzerland AG 2022

D. Singh et al. (eds.), *Design and Applications of Nature Inspired Optimization*, Women in Engineering and Science, https://doi.org/10.1007/978-3-031-17929-7_8

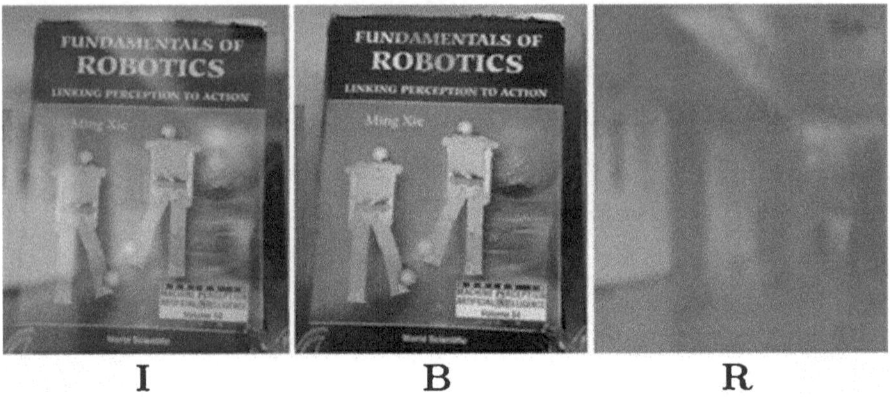

Fig. 8.1 Reflection-contaminated image "I", background layer "B" and reflection layer "R"

The goal of the work is to approximate the background layer ***B*** from the acquired image ***I***. Figure 8.1 illustrates the reflection-contaminated image as well as the ground truth for the background and the reflection layers.

The problem of removing reflection from a single image is ill-posed as, for a given reflection-contaminated image, there could be infinite possible decompositions into the background layer and the reflection layer; the same is illustrated with the help of an example image in Fig. 8.2. Also, lack of sufficient labelled data for training and reflection and background layers containing data from natural scenes adds to the ill-posedness of the problem.

Most of the existing methods to remove reflection use specialized hardware or multiple images to make the problem less ill-posed and produce. Recently, some research works used deep learning methods, which outperform the existing methods, but, still, they use very complex architectures and blur out or degrade the quality of the images and fail in cases when the background and the reflection layers are very similar in terms of brightness and structural appearance.

Our contributions to address the above-mentioned issues are as follows:

- We have trained a relatively simpler architecture end-to-end neural network to estimate the background layer.
- We have created a loss function based on SSIM score, which is better suited when comparing the similarities between images.
- We have created a larger labelled training dataset using data from multiple sources.

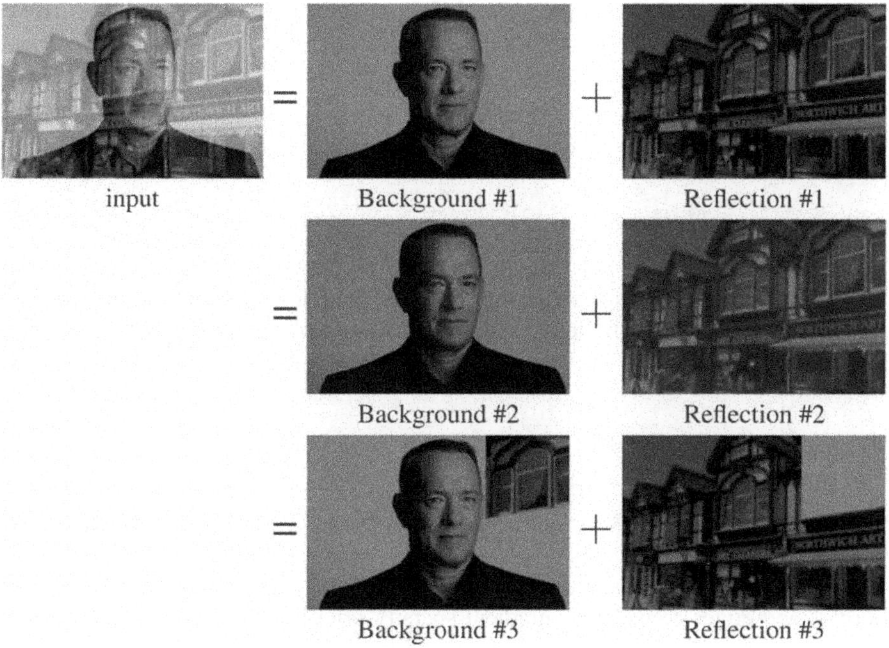

Fig. 8.2 Three possible separations of a reflection-contaminated image into the background and the reflection layers

2 Literature Survey

The problem of how to remove reflection artefacts from an image has been widely researched in the image processing and computer vision community. Existing work can be classified into two categories based on the number of inputs required to produce a single reflection-free image. The first category includes methods requiring multiple inputs (such as multiple images or the use of specialized hardware to capture the image), and the second category includes methods requiring single image as the input. Single image methods can be further classified based on the approach they use to solve the problem, conventional mathematical approaches or learning-based approaches.

Multi-image Methods

Multiple related images can be used to make the problem of reflection removal less ill-posed and easier to solve but make the process of capturing images difficult. Guo et al. [1] and Y. Li and M. S. Brown [2] use images taken from slightly different angles or video sequence. Agrawal et al. [3] use image pairs taken with and without firing flash. Schechner et al. [4] use polarizer to obtain multiple polarized images. Kong et al. [5] use image pairs with the subject in and out of focus. These methods produce state-of-the-art results but are highly limited in practicability due to the complex process of capturing the images.

Single Input Methods

When compared with multi-image approaches, trying to suppress or remove reflection artefacts from a single image is difficult because of the constrained data.

Traditional Approaches

The following approaches use conventional mathematical approaches to remove the reflection.

Levin et al. [6] proposed an oversimplified approach based on local features of corners and edges considering gradient sparsity prior. Authors proposed a method that decomposes the reflection-contaminated image into two images such that the total number of corners and edges is minimized. However, this method performs poorly as the complexity in the images texture rises. Levin et al. [7] rely on user assistance to simplify the problem. Although this method successfully manages to separate the reflections from a single image to a certain degree, manually marking the image for the presence of reflection is difficult and is only practical for a small number of images. Shih et al. [8] reduce the ill-posedness by the use of ghosting cues and exploit the Gaussian mixture model (GMM) to learn image priors. Ghosting cues are the double reflections shifted by some distance, arising due to light being reflected at both the surfaces of a glass pane. Ghosting cues arise mostly in case of double pane glass or if the glass is quite thick, so this method works only on a small subset of images containing reflection. Wan et al. [9] assume prior that the background layer contains sharp and well-defined edges and the reflection layer is relatively smoother and use this relative difference in the smoothness as a cue to create a depth of field (DoF) confidence map, which then is used to classify edges as part of either the background layer or the reflection layer. This method cannot remove reflection from images with tiny textures or small reflection artefacts.

Learning-Based Approaches

Recent works have leveraged deep learning capabilities to solve the reflection removal problem.

Fan et al. [10] follow the same prior assumption as [9], i.e. reflection layer is off-focus and blurry. They created a synthetic dataset that mimics the assumed prior and proposed a two-stage cascaded network. The first stage predicts the edges of the background layer, and the predicted edges are used by the second layer to guide the background layer recovery. Wan et al. [11] improved [10] two stages into a single end-to-end concurrent network to predict the edges and separate the layers. Zhang et al. [12] combined three losses (feature loss, adversarial loss and exclusion loss) to train the proposed end-to-end network. The network and the losses are tuned to exploit both low-level and high-level information; still, this method performs poorly on images with high exposure. Recently GAN (Generative Adversarial Networks)-based methods [13, 14] have yielded good results, but still have issues handling images with extreme exposures, and [13] produces fails to produce images with natural colours as the colour tone is altered when the parts of reflection appear in the background. Also, the problem inherent with GANs is their complexity, both in terms of network architecture and the time and parameter tuning required to train the network. Some other related articles [15–20], and proposed deep learning-based IoT methods to solve different problems.

3 Proposed Method

Training Dataset

All the existing learning-based single image reflection removal methods fail to fully take advantage of their respective proposed models due to the lack of labelled training data. Lack of labelled training data is a common problem in computer vision community and though there are some workarounds even they are limited in cases in which they can be applied. The most common workaround is creating a synthetic dataset. The problem with creating a synthetic dataset is that they usually fail to truly mimic the wide range and variety of classes present in natural datasets, which in turn limits the capabilities of the method to deal with naturally occurring images. Another workaround is assuming priors and proposing a method considering the priors. Priors usually restrict the scope of the approach by setting some bounds on the input and thereby making the approach more tailored towards dealing with inputs from the smaller range. Such methods may or may not perform equivalently for inputs outside this range.

We have followed the first approach, i.e. to expand the dataset using synthetic images. We have used data from multiple sources to accomplish this and merged it with images from already available datasets to train a reflection removal model.

PASCAL Visual Object Classes (VOC) dataset [15] is used to create synthetic images with reflection artefacts. To synthesize one image, two images are selected from the dataset and cropped into 256 × 256-sized patches. Then, one patch is selected as the background, and the other one as the reflection. Both the images are merged using the following equation:

Fig. 8.3 Image triplet (B, R, I) from the training dataset

$$\boldsymbol{I} = \boldsymbol{\alpha} * \boldsymbol{B} + \boldsymbol{\beta} * (\boldsymbol{G} \otimes \mathbf{R}) \tag{8.2}$$

where

I*, *B and ***R*** are n × m × 3 matrices representing the resulting synthetic image, the background patch, and the reflection patch, respectively

$\boldsymbol{\alpha}$**:** blending weight for the background patch

$\boldsymbol{\beta}$**:** blending weight for the reflection patch and $\boldsymbol{\beta} = (\mathbf{1} - \boldsymbol{\alpha})$

***G*:** represents the Gaussian blur operation applied on reflection patch

Reflection patch is blurred out using Gaussian blur, and then blending weight $\alpha \in [0.6, 0.8]$ is used to combine both the images. The generated dataset contains 50,000 synthetic images. An image triplet (containing the background, the reflection and the final blended result) from the training dataset can be seen in Fig. 8.3.

Model Description (Table 8.1)

Loss Function

Loss value is a measure of how off the predictions are from true values. Loss function reflects the performance of the model and provides a quantitative measure of accuracy. The loss function is a key aspect in determining how good a solution the trained model is as the objective function being realized while in training phase is to minimize the loss. Therefore, the loss function must be chosen in a way that minimization of the loss value results in the model predicting value close to the true values, and for this to happen the loss function must be tailored to the problem being solved. As images are at the centre of reflection removal problem, we will first

Table 8.1 Model architecture

Layer (type)	Connected to	# Filters	Kernel size	Activation	Output shape
conv2d_1(Conv2D)	conv2d[0][0]	64	9 × 9	ReLU	256 × 256 × 64
conv2d_2 (Conv2D)	conv2d_1[0][0]	64	5 × 5	ReLU	256 × 256 × 64
conv2d_3 (Conv2D)	conv2d_2[0][0]	64	5 × 5	ReLU	256 × 256 × 64
conv2d_4 (Conv2D)	conv2d_3[0][0]	64	5 × 5	ReLU	256 × 256 × 64
conv2d_5 (Conv2D)	conv2d_4[0][0]	64	5 × 5	ReLU	256 × 256 × 64
conv2d_6 (Conv2D)	conv2d_5[0][0]	64	5 × 5	ReLU	256 × 256 × 64
conv2d_7 (Conv2D)	conv2d_6[0][0]	64	5 × 5	ReLU	256 × 256 × 64
conv2d_8 (Conv2D)	conv2d_7[0][0]	64	5 × 5	ReLU	256 × 256 × 64
conv2d_9 (Conv2D)	conv2d_8[0][0]	64	5 × 5	ReLU	256 × 256 × 64
conv2d_10 (Conv2D)	conv2d_9[0][0]	64	5 × 5	ReLU	256 × 256 × 64
conv2d_11 (Conv2D)	conv2d_10[0][0]	64	5 × 5	ReLU	256 × 256 × 64
conv2d_12 (Conv2D)	conv2d_11[0][0]	64	5 × 5	ReLU	256 × 256 × 64
conv2d_13 (Conv2D)	conv2d_12[0][0]	64	5 × 5	ReLU	256 × 256 × 64
tf_op_layer_add (TensorFlowOpLayer)	conv2d_9[0][0], conv2d_13[0][0]	–	–	ReLU	256 × 256 × 64
conv2d_14 (Conv2D)	tf_op_layer_add [0][0]	64	5 × 5	ReLU	256 × 256 × 64
conv2d_15 (Conv2D)	conv2d_14[0][0]	64	5 × 5	ReLU	256 × 256 × 64
tf_op_layer_add_1 (TensorFlowOpLayer)	conv2d_7[0][0], conv2d_15[0][0]	–	–	ReLU	256 × 256 × 64
conv2d_16 (Conv2D)	tf_op_layer_add_1 [0][0]	64	5 × 5	ReLU	256 × 256 × 64
conv2d_17 (Conv2D)	conv2d_16[0][0]	64	5 × 5	ReLU	256 × 256 × 64
tf_op_layer_sub (TensorFlowOpLayer)	conv2d_5[0][0], conv2d_17[0][0]	–	–	ReLU	256 × 256 × 64
conv2d_18 (Conv2D)	tf_op_layer_sub[0] [0]	64	5 × 5	ReLU	256 × 256 × 64
conv2d_19 (Conv2D)	conv2d_18[0][0]	64	5 × 5	ReLU	256 × 256 × 64
conv2d_20 (Conv2D)	conv2d_19[0][0]	64	5 × 5	ReLU	256 × 256 × 64
conv2d_21 (Conv2D)	conv2d_20[0][0]	64	5 × 5	ReLU	256 × 256 × 64
conv2d_22 (Conv2D)	conv2d_21[0][0]	64	9 × 9	ReLU	256 × 256 × 64
conv2d_23 (Conv2D)	conv2d_22[0][0]	3	9 × 9	ReLU	256 × 256 × 3

Padding = "same"
Strides = (1,1)
Total params: 2,744,131
Trainable params: 2,744,131
Non-trainable params: 0

take a metric that can precisely measure the similarities between two images and use it inside the loss function to calculate the loss value.

Structural similarity (SSIM) index provides the quantitative measure of structural similarity between images and is formulated on a similar basis using which the human visual system assess the similarity between two scenes. Our visual system has

Fig. 8.4 Original image, increased contrast, blurred image

evolved to extract structural information from the scene; therefore, calculating the structural resemblance between two images can provide a decent approximation of actual similarity between them.

SSIM provides better similarity estimation than other measures for images as every pixel is weighted equally in case of peak signal-to-noise ratio (PSNR) and mean squared error (MSE), irrespective of the fact that any change in its value will be noticeable to the human observer or not. This could lead high variations in MSE and PSNR scores for the image pairs when the contrast or brightness changes in one of the image, even though these modifications don't have a significant effect on human observer assessing image similarity as can be seen in Fig. 3.2. Therefore, structural similarity index is more likely to find such image pairs more similar, as the structural information in the image pair would resemble closely, as the SSIM index is calculated on various windows of an image (Fig. 8.4).

SSIM index ranges from 0 to 1, 0 meaning that the images share no structural similarity and 1 meaning perfect structural similarity between images, which is only possible for identical images. Three components, namely, luminance, contrast and structure, are used in the process of calculating SSIM index for two perfectly aligned images of same size $\boldsymbol{x}$ and $\boldsymbol{y}$.

Luminance comparison $\boldsymbol{l}(\boldsymbol{x}, \boldsymbol{y})$ is given by:

$$l(x, y) = \frac{2\mu_x\mu_y + C_1}{\mu_x^2 + \mu_y^2 + C_1} \tag{8.3}$$

Contrast comparison $\boldsymbol{c}(\boldsymbol{x}, \boldsymbol{y})$ is given by:

$$c(x, y) = \frac{2\sigma_x\sigma_y + C_2}{\sigma_x^2 + \sigma_y^2 + C_2} \tag{8.4}$$

Structure comparison $\boldsymbol{s}(\boldsymbol{x}, \boldsymbol{y})$ is given by:

$$s(x, y) = \frac{\sigma_{xy} + C_3}{\sigma_x\sigma_y + C_3} \tag{8.5}$$

where

$\boldsymbol{\mu_x}$ is the average of intensities of $\boldsymbol{x}$, $\boldsymbol{\mu_y}$ is the average of intensities of $\boldsymbol{y}$,

$\boldsymbol{\sigma_x}^2$ is the variance of intensities of $\boldsymbol{x}$, $\boldsymbol{\sigma_y}^2$ is the variance of intensities of $\boldsymbol{y}$,
$\boldsymbol{\sigma_{xy}}$ is the covariance of intensities of $\boldsymbol{x}$ and $\boldsymbol{y}$, and
$\boldsymbol{C_1}$, $\boldsymbol{C_2}$ and $\boldsymbol{C_3}$ are used to avoid instability when denominators are close to zero.
$C_1 = (K_1 L)^2$, $C_2 = (K_2 L)^2$, $C_3 = C_2/2$,
$K_1 << 1$ and $K_2 << 1$, and L is the dynamic range.

Using the above-mentioned three components, SSIM index is calculated as follows:

$$\mathbf{SSIM}(\boldsymbol{x}, \boldsymbol{y}) = \boldsymbol{l}(\boldsymbol{x}, \boldsymbol{y}) \cdot \boldsymbol{c}(\boldsymbol{x}, \boldsymbol{y}) \cdot \boldsymbol{s}(\boldsymbol{x}, \boldsymbol{y}) \tag{8.6}$$

Substituting the values of $l(x,y)$, $c(x,y)$ and $s(x,y)$ in the above equation, we get

$$\mathbf{SSIM}(\boldsymbol{x}, \boldsymbol{y}) = \frac{(2\mu_x\mu_y + C_1)(2\sigma_{xy} + C_2)}{\left(\mu_x^2 + \mu_y^2 + C_1\right)\left(\sigma_x^2 + \sigma_y^2 + C_2\right)} \tag{8.7}$$

This can be converted into loss function to calculate the loss between the estimated background layer and the actual background layer as follows:

$$\mathbf{loss_{SSIM}}\left(y_{true}, y_{pred}\right) = \mathbf{1} - \mathbf{SSIM}\left(y_{true}, y_{pred}\right) \tag{8.8}$$

4 Experiment and Results

In this section, we present the details of the experiments performed and their evaluation. Detailed discussion on the impact of various parameters of the proposed approach on the overall performance is also included.

Training Details

Trained the network with the following parameters:

Number of epochs: 65
Batch size: 32
Validation split: 0.2
Shuffle: True
Optimizer: Adam ($\alpha = 0.0001$, $\beta 1 = 0.9$, $\beta 2 = 0.999$)
Loss function: MSE, loss_SSIM

A combination of MSE and our custom loss function based on SSIM index has been used during training. The process of training was carried out in two phases: in

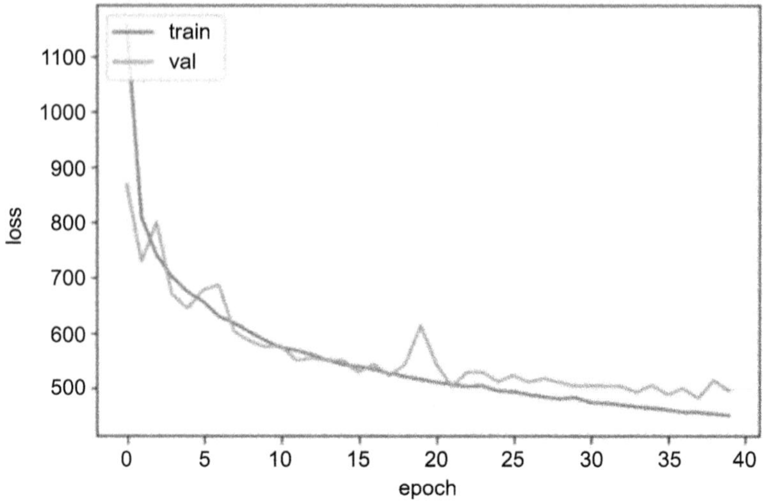

Fig. 8.5 Training and validation loss vs epoch graph – Phase I

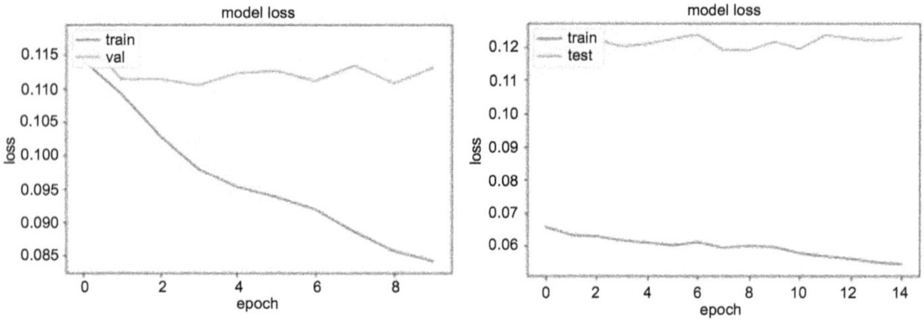

Fig. 8.6 Training and validation loss vs epoch graph – Phase II

the first phase, we have used the entire training dataset with MSE as the loss function and trained the network for 40 epochs, and, in the second phase, the network was trained for a total of 25 epochs on smaller subsets of the training dataset with SSIM-based loss function (Figs. 8.5 and 8.6).

Experimental Set-Up

Experiments were carried out on the system with the following configurations:

CPU: Intel Xeon Silver 4114
Memory: 64 GB DDR4
GPU: NVIDIA Quadro P5000

GPU Memory: 16 GB GDDR5X
Storage: 4 TB
Operating system: Ubuntu 18.04.4 LTS (Bionic Beaver)

Deep learning libraries used: Keras with TensorFlow backend, TensorFlow 2.1.0, CUDA 10.1, cuDNN 7.6.

Programming language and major libraries used: Python 3.6, NumPy, OpenCV, Matplotlib.

Performance Evaluation Metrics

For performance evaluation, the most common metrics in comparing two images are PSNR value and SSIM score (refer to Sect. 3.3 for a detailed description of SSIM index). Peak signal-to-noise ratio (PSNR) is the ratio between a signal's maximum power and the power of corrupting noise that affects the quality of images and videos. Generally, PSNR is conveyed on a logarithmic decibel scale. The formula for PSNR between the original image and the noisy image is given in the following equation:

$$\mathrm{PSNR} = 20 * \log_{10} \frac{max_f}{\sqrt{\mathrm{MSE}}} \tag{8.9}$$

where
max_f – maximum signal value present in the original image

Mean squared error (MSE) is

$$\mathrm{MSE} = \frac{1}{mn} \sum_{0}^{m-1} \sum_{0}^{n-1} \| \mathrm{f}(i,j) - \mathrm{g}(i,j) \|^2 \tag{8.10}$$

where
f – original image in matrix form
g – predicted image in matrix form
m – number of rows in input images
n – number of columns in input images
i, j – co-ordinates of a current pixel location in input images

Testing Dataset

Benchmarking SIR2 dataset [16] with images containing real scenes is used to assess the performance and capabilities of the trained network. SIR2 dataset is released by

Table 8.2 Comparison of average SSIM scores for proposed and competing methods

Method	SSIM
LB14 [2]	0.793
AY07 [7]	0.834
SK15 [8]	0.785
WS16 [9]	0.862
FAN17 [10]	0.854
XR18 [12]	0.823
Proposed (*after Phase I*)	0.7855682
Proposed (*after Phase II*)	0.81121135

Table 8.3 Comparison of average PSNR values for proposed and competing methods

Method	PSNR
LB14 [2]	21.735
AY07 [7]	21.436
XR18 [12]	20.28
Proposed (after Phase I)	15.966344
Proposed (after Phase II)	16.880268

Rapid-Rich Object Search (ROSE) Lab, NTU, Singapore. It has a large number of diverse images containing a reflection, along with the corresponding ground truth of their reflection and background layers. It contains both indoor (controlled) scenes and outdoor (wild) scenes. Indoor scenes include postcards and solid objects used in day-to-day life, such as fruits, toys, mugs, etc. Outdoor scenes contain real-world entities, such as trees, gardens, cars, buildings, etc. with varying illuminations, scales and distances. SIR2 dataset contains a total of 500 image triplets with 200 triplets each for postcard dataset and solid object dataset and 100 triplets for wild scene dataset (Table 8.2 and 8.3 and Fig. 8.7).

5 Conclusion and Future Work

In this dissertation, we have studied the single image reflection removal problem and proposed a method to suppress the reflection and recover the background layer. Our approach focuses mainly on using simple network architecture along with a loss function tailored to the demands of the problem. To address the issue of lack of labelled training data, we have created and used synthetic dataset for training our network.

Experimental results validate the efficacy and efficiency of our approach. A similar approach can be used in solving the problems, such as super resolution, where the current approaches use complex network architectures, including autoencoders and generative adversarial networks.

Fig. 8.7 Reflection removal results on test images by the proposed model

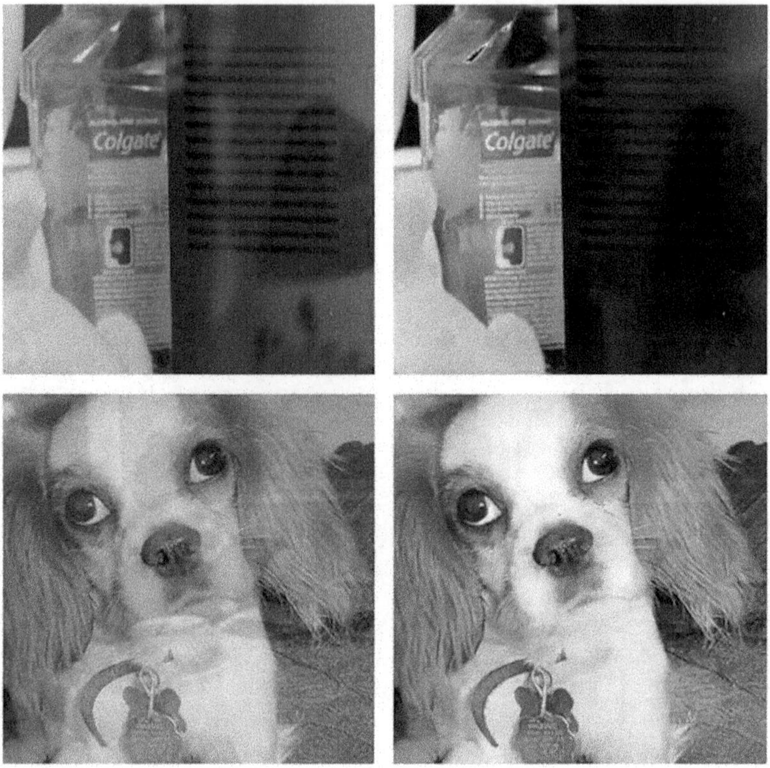

Fig. 8.7 (continued)

Our method has produced decent results but still fails to outperform the state-of-the-art method. Future works can focus on using the ground truth of the reflection layer in addition to the ground truth of the background layer to further improve the effectiveness of the approach.

References

1. Wei, K., Yang, J., Fu, Y., Wipf, D., Huang, H.: Single image reflection removal exploiting misaligned training data and network enhancements. In: 2019 IEEE/CVF Conference on Computer Vision and Pattern Recognition (CVPR), pp. 8170–8179 (2019). https://doi.org/10.1109/CVPR.2019.00837
2. Abiko, R., Ikehara, M.: Single image reflection removal based on gan with gradient constraint. IEEE Access **7**, 148790–148799 (2019). https://doi.org/10.1109/ACCESS.2019.2947266. Author, F., Author, S.: Title of a proceedings paper. In: Editor, F., Editor, S. (eds.) CONFERENCE 2016, LNCS, vol. 9999, pp. 1–13. Springer, Heidelberg (2016)
3. Veringham, M., Van Gool, L., Williams, C.K.I., Winn, J., Zisserman, A.: The pascal visual object classes (VOC) challenge. Int. J. Comput. Vis. **88**(2), 303–338 (2010)

4. Wan, R., Shi, B., Duan, L.-Y., Tan, A.-H., Kot, A.C.: Benchmarking single-image reflection removal algorithms. In: 2017 IEEE International Conference on Computer Vision (ICCV), pp. 3942–3950 (2017). https://doi.org/10.1109/ICCV.2017.423
5. Gopikrishnan, S., Priakanth, P., Srivastava, G.: DEDC: sustainable data communication for cognitive radio sensors in the internet of things. Sustain. Comput. Inf. Syst. **29**, 100471 (2021). https://doi.org/10.1016/j.suscom.2020.100471
6. Vallathan, G., John, A., Thirumalai, C., Mohan, S., Srivastava, G., Lin, J.C.-W.: Suspicious activity detection using deep learning in secure assisted living IoT environments. J. Supercomput. **77**(4), 3242–3260 (2021). https://doi.org/10.1007/s11227-020-03387-8
7. Guo, T., Yu, K., Srivastava, G., Wei, W., Guo, L., Xiong, N.N.: Latent discriminative low-rank projection for visual dimension reduction in green internet of things. IEEE Trans. Green Commun. Netw. **5**(2), 737–749 (2021). https://doi.org/10.1109/TGCN.2021.3062972
8. Zhu, D., Sun, Y., Du, H., Cao, N., Baker, T., Srivastava, G.: HUNA: a method of hierarchical unsupervised network alignment for iot. IEEE Internet Things J. **8**(5), 3201–3210 (2021). https://doi.org/10.1109/JIOT.2020.3020951
9. Guo, X., Cao, X., Ma, Y.: Robust separation of reflection from multiple images. In: 2014 IEEE Conference on Computer Vision and Pattern Recognition, pp. 2195–2202 (2014). https://doi.org/10.1109/CVPR.2014.281
10. Li, Y., Brown, M.S.: Single image layer separation using relative smoothness. In: 2014 IEEE Conference on Computer Vision and Pattern Recognition, pp. 2752–2759 (2014). https://doi.org/10.1109/CVPR.2014.346
11. Agrawal, A., Raskar, R., Nayar, S., Li, Y.: Removing photography artifacts using gradient projection and flash-exposure sampling. ACM Trans. Graph. **24**, 828–835 (2005). https://doi.org/10.1145/1186822.1073269
12. Schechner, Y.Y., Shamir, J., Kiryati, N.: Polarization and statistical analysis of scenes containing a semireflector. J. Optic. Soc. Am. A. **17**(2), 276–284 (2000). https://doi.org/10.1364/JOSAA.17.000276
13. Kong, N., Tai, Y.-W., Shin, J.S.: A physically-based approach to reflection separation: from physical modeling to constrained optimization. IEEE Trans. Pattern Anal. Mach. Intell. **36**(2), 209–221 (2014). https://doi.org/10.1109/TPAMI.2013.45
14. Levin, A., Zomet, A., Weiss, Y.: Separating reflections from a single image using local features. In: Proceedings of the 2004 IEEE Computer Society Conference on Computer Vision and Pattern Recognition, 2004. CVPR 2004, vol. 1 (2004). https://doi.org/10.1109/CVPR.2004.1315047
15. Levin, A., Weiss, Y.: User assisted separation of reflections from a single image using a sparsity prior. In: Pajdla, T., Matas, J. (eds.) Computer Vision – ECCV 2004, pp. 602–613. Springer, Berlin/Heidelberg (2004)
16. Shih, Y., Krishnan, D., Durand, F., Freeman, W.T.: Reflection removal using ghosting cues. In: 2015 IEEE Conference on Computer Vision and Pattern Recognition (CVPR), pp. 3193–3201 (2015). https://doi.org/10.1109/CVPR.2015.7298939
17. Wan, R., Shi, B., Hwee, T.A., Kot, A.C.: Depth of field guided reflection removal. In: 2016 IEEE International Conference on Image Processing (ICIP), pp. 21–25 (2016). https://doi.org/10.1109/ICIP.2016.7532311
18. Fan, Q., Yang, J., Hua, G., Chen, B., Wipf, D.: A generic deep architecture for single image reflection removal and image smoothing. In: 2017 IEEE International Conference on Computer Vision (ICCV), pp. 3258–3267 (2017). https://doi.org/10.1109/ICCV.2017.351
19. Wan, R., Shi, B., Duan, L.-Y., Tan, A.-H., Kot, A.C.: CRRN: multi-scale guided concurrent reflection removal network. In: 2018 IEEE/CVF Conference on Computer Vision and Pattern Recognition, pp. 4777–4785 (2018). https://doi.org/10.1109/CVPR.2018.00502
20. Zhang, X., Ng, R., Chen, Q.: Single image reflection separation with perceptual losses. In: 2018 IEEE/CVF Conference on Computer Vision and Pattern Recognition, pp. 4786–4794 (2018). https://doi.org/10.1109/CVPR.2018.00503

Chapter 9
Social Media Analysis: A Tool for Popularity Prediction Using Machine Learning Classifiers

Sachin Goel, Monica, Harshita Khurana, and Parita Jain

1 Introduction

Our project targets at opinion mining for the popularity prediction using machine learning classifiers. Natural language processing (NLP) is used for data analysis, i.e., to find the emotions and tone behind the text in the comment section. This is often a way for an individual to categorize and determine the opinions about the famous personalities. We have used the concepts of data processing, data mining, and machine learning for mining the text for sentiment analysis and for further prediction of popularity. Our project plays an important role both academically and economically as it helps in product reviewing, sarcasm identification, building management systems, identifying the effectiveness of an educational institute by collecting student's inputs, etc. In this, we have also used Python libraries to filter out the collected data from social media platforms, such as Twitter, and fetch out features from it for analyses. Analysis is done using some concepts of machine learning for predicting the amount of negative and positive comments. The project also focuses on political opinion mining for the popularity prediction. The project can be made in Python using pandas, NumPy, and NLTK library and concepts of machine learning. In this we have provided the data, analyzed it, and predicted the popularity of a person [1].

Considering a text about the opinions of the people, initially, we can count how many people know about that person, what they're talking about, and then we can

S. Goel (✉) · Monica
Department of IT, ABES Engineering College, Ghaziabad, India

H. Khurana
Department of CSE (Data Science), ABES Engineering College, Ghaziabad, India

P. Jain
Department of CSE, KIET Group of Institution, Ghaziabad, India

© The Author(s), under exclusive license to Springer Nature Switzerland AG 2022

D. Singh et al. (eds.), *Design and Applications of Nature Inspired Optimization*, Women in Engineering and Science, https://doi.org/10.1007/978-3-031-17929-7_9

classify that he/she is popular or not. This can be done using natural language processing in machine learning. The opinion mining helps in extracting the polarity, i.e., the amount of positive and negative words or sentences in the comments. Further, we can use classifiers for predictions of popularity. Our agenda here is to search for data and to retrieve it from social media platform, such as Twitter. In this we will extract the information from the comment section of Twitter, which consists of words, sentences, paragraphs, punctuations, conjunctions, and special characters. Hence, unwanted data is removed. The NLP (natural language processing) and NLTK toolkit in Python are employed here to analyze the large amount of natural language data. Extracting features from filtered data with the assistance of Python libraries, such as pandas and NumPy, it will create a dataset of fetched data and features. Use of CountVectorizer is to have an idea of machine learning for creating the vocabulary of the known words for features. We have fetched earlier using Python libraries [2]. Using machine learning classifier, such as naive Bayes classifier, for predicting the output. The filtered-out data will help us to predict the output on the premise of negative and positive features of the words within the comments. Testing the accuracy by taking the test on different personalities so matching actual popularity with prediction get within the output [3].

2 Related Works

Neri [4] suggests that there is a huge virtual space called social media where the people can express their opinion on everybody. They can give their reviews or provide ratings to anything and anyone. According to them, first, we need to consider and perform various analyses, such as syntactic, semantic, pragmatic, and discourse integration, and then we need to start the actual execution part. In his project he has performed unsupervised learning algorithm, i.e., clustering. The conclusion provided by their study is they have used 1000 Facebook posts to check on the sentiments of the people for various agencies, companies, etc. We can use this study in our project for how to clean and use the huge amount of data.

Mathapati et al. [5] have said that opinions about the people on social media help to take decisions. Every website is containing a large amount of text that are opinionated. So, any prediction for example, popularity predictions, is a tedious task because of the huge data. They say that this problem can be solved by sentiment analysis. They have used various sentiment analysis classifiers, which include reviews, summarizing reviews, etc. They have applied different types of filtering, such as content-based filtering, policy-based personalization, and text representation. Various data expansion techniques are also discussed by the author. The main aim of this project is to provide a friendly concept of information filtering, which gives the user a choice.

Sarlan and Basri [6] focus on the attention that is given to the social media. The authors focused on computationally measuring the perception of the customer. They use the people's various emotions and opinions, disclose about their lives, and use the dataset of various tweets at providing and taking out useful information. Results classify tweets into positives and negatives. Using pie chart and HTML page, a web application is developed. Django is used for making Web applications that is made to run on Linux server. Prototyping used by the authors is in development.

Dharmarajan and Abirami [7] have used the social media platforms such as Twitter, to investigate the content and the relations among the actors of the network. They have used the tools, such as sentiment analysis. It can also be defined as the branch of opinion mining. According to the authors, the major aim of opinion mining is to listen and process the data that users post on social media. This paper describes various results the authors have obtained from the social network and sentiment analysis of the Twitter channel, related to a pop music event.

Huang et al. [8] stated that sentiment analysis and topic classification are frequently used in customer care marketing. They have proposed a method to solve these issues. They have used social media services for user-generated content, some common subjects, and a topic classification method. Issues with the previous system are: (1) conventional solutions and (2) each post to be assigned has only one sentiment label. Addressing all the issues, they have used multitask multi-label (MTML) system and have trained multiple models with multiple labels so that it can be used to solve and address class ambiguity.

Dhiman and Kumar [40, 41] have majorly worked upon algorithms that are bioinspired algorithms, such as spotted hyena optimizer and emperor penguin optimizer, to solve real-life issues. The work finds its use in various engineering applications.

Dhiman and Kaur [43] suggested an algorithm that is based on the migration and attacking behaviors of seabird sooty terns in nature. These two steps are used to exploit and explore the search space in each way. The analysis of the proposed algorithm's convergence behavior and its computational complexity have been examined. The algorithm is good at competing against other optimization algorithms.

Kaur et al. [42] worked on a metaheuristic optimization algorithm and further implemented the work on six constrained and one unconstrained engineering design problems to further verify its robustness. The proposed algorithm is very effective at solving problems that are difficult to solve with traditional optimization techniques.

Chatterjee's work [45] is more inclined toward artificial intelligence. The importance of patent grant nowadays and the consequences of its failure have also been discussed. The misconception of protecting the computer programs and algorithms through copyright is also clarified.

Vaishnav et al. [47] had performed the analysis of Covid-19 updates, such as the total cases, recoveries, and deaths, using ML algorithms. The data has been collected from various Indian states and WHO official platform. Random forest and decision tree regression models are used to get the required results.

3 Proposed Methodology

Problem Identification

Opinion mining analysis- From large and unstructured database volumes, we traced public views and emotions for a particular thing and provided valuable insights. Positive, negative and neutral sentiments are represented by three classes of polarity i.e. positive, negative and zero respectively. Each comment is assigned a value between 0 and 1. Value nearest to 1 represents a subjective value and an objective value for counter value.

We have used the framework through which we have explained the head away from collections, opinion mining for popularity prediction, and Twitter classification. We have classified the opinions from various social media platforms where users have expressed their opinions about politics and people related to it. We have applied various ML classifiers to build our classification model. We have stored the retrieved information in CSV files. And then we filtered the data out. The model was tested and accuracy was found. We gather belief-supported collected hashtags associated with views about famous personalities. Retrieved tweets are saved in Excel sheets under subsequent fields. We have a huge amount of data in the database with us. We need to take useful information out of it. This is the process of data filtering. It is the process to purify our data so that we can get the useful part and remove the redundant and unnecessary part. It is the first and most important step. If it is not done correctly, our whole process may be a failure.

A good and accurate dataset will help in increasing the overall efficiency and accuracy of the whole process. After we have filtered the data and taken out the features, the next step is to create a dataset. A dataset is nothing but basically an n*m matrix, where n is the total number of features and m is the total number of data points. After the creation of the dataset, we use the various ML classifiers. These classifiers are used to predict the outcomes or the target that we want to achieve [9]. The methodology proposed by us is to initially clean the data, using data mining approach, take out the useful information, and make the dataset ready. Then, after the dataset prepared for the classifier will be fed into the classifier, we'll fit the classifier accordingly. Finally, we will be using the cleaned testing data to get the desired outcome [10].

Data Gathering

We gather belief-supported collected hashtags associated with views about famous personalities. Tweets that were being retrieved from social media platforms, such as Twitter accounts, are saved in Excel sheets under subsequent fields. The tweets that are being gathered is around 90,000–100,000 [11]. We select hashtags that are more of being political nature and that of trending on Twitter that represent each view of everyone.

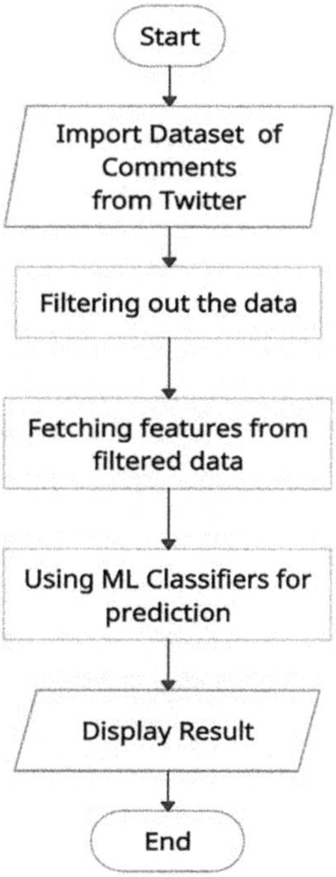

Fig. 9.1 Proposed methodology

Data Filtering

We have a huge amount of data in the database with us. We need to take useful information out of it. This is the process of data filtering. It is the subset of the entire data you have. In our case, we have a huge amount of data, names of the people who are commenting, the stop words and punctuations in our data, etc (Fig. 9.1).

These things are not useful in predicting the popularity of a person. It is mere sideline information that is available to us. Thus, we can leave behind these data and choose more meaningful information, such as review of the person [12].

It is the process to purify our data so that we can get the useful part and remove the redundant and unnecessary part. It is the first and most important step. If it is not done correctly, our whole process may be a failure. A good and accurate dataset will help in increasing the overall efficiency and accuracy of the whole process [13]. Thus, we can conclude that data filtering is the most important step and should be done in an effective manner.

Fetching Features

Vital step in fetching features is to determine essential data. Feature fetching is basically to extract the most common and useful information to label them as features so that the data can be trained on it. For example, in Twitter sentiment analysis, we have used the most common words occurring frequently to form features. We use a CountVectorizer for the same. We can also plot graphs to check the occurrence of the words that are occurring more frequently. Feature fetching is an important step for dataset creation. And if the proper dataset is not created, it can't be fed up with the classifier for training [14, 15].

Classification Using ML Classifier

After we have filtered the data and taken out the features, the next step is to create a dataset. A dataset is nothing but basically an n*m matrix, where n is the total number of features and m is the total number of data points. After the creation of the dataset, we use the various ML classifiers. These classifiers are used to predict the outcomes or the target that we want to achieve. There are various machine learning classifiers, such as SVM, naive Bayes, KNN, logistic regression, etc. Any of these classifiers can be used based on what we want to predict. Or how is our dataset?

These classifiers are used to train our model algorithm for learning. They are mathematical algorithms used to predict the outcomes. To make a model based on popularity prediction, we will use the NLP model [16, 17]. In machine learning, an algorithm is used for mapping the input set of data in the form of specific category of classes. It is started by predicting the class of the given set of data, which we retrieved from the social media platform (Fig. 9.2).

It helps in classifying the new data by checking in which category of class it falls. It is a supervised learning concept, which helps in classifying the set of data. It works based on the training data for defining the class category of the datasets [18]. The types of classifiers in machine learning are the following:

- Naive Bayes
- Decision tree
- K-nearest neighbor (KNN)
- Logistic regression
- Support vector machine
- Random forest

(i) *Naive Bayes*

Naive Bayes is an algorithm used for classification of the input datasets. It is a supervised learning algorithm and used the Bayes' theorem for problems of classification. It is termed as naive as it assumes each feature to be independent of other features whenever they occur, e.g., the different features of a car, such as shape, color, and model, help to identify the car. Therefore, every feature contributes to classify the class of the given data. It is termed as Bayes as it uses the Bayes' theorem principle. It predicts the probability of an object, which depends on the conditional probability. Naive Bayes classifier works by first converting the given input set of data, into tables of frequency. Then, it generates a table of likelihood from the

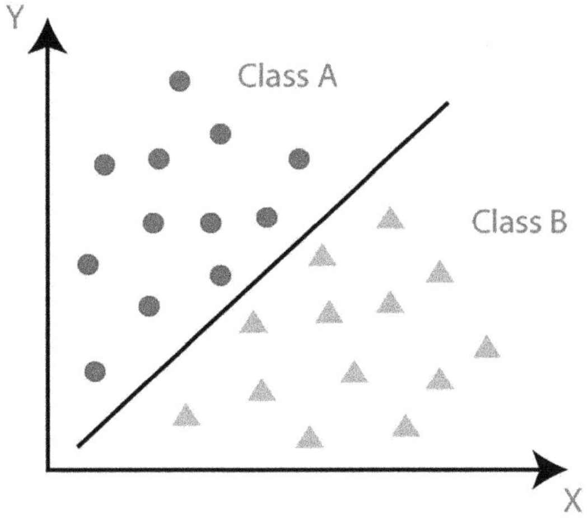

Fig. 9.2 Classification of set of data by classifier [18]

probabilities that it found from the given features of the datasets. Lastly, it uses the Bayes' theorem for calculating the posterior probability [19, 20].

(ii) *Decision Tree*

Decision tree is also a supervised learning algorithm in machine learning. It is used for classification problems as well as for regression problem. It uses the representation of the tree for solving the classification problem. It uses the two nodes: decision node and leaf node. The decision nodes have more than one branches and used to give the decision. The leaf nodes do not have any branches as they are the outputs of the decisions that are made by the decision nodes. It is also a test that is done on the features of the sets of data given.

It gives the graphical solution for all possible solutions by making decision on the condition given. It is like a tree as it starts from a root node and followed by the branches and forms a structure of a tree. It uses a strategy of questioning and answering, as it asks the questions first and, based on the answer, it expands its branches [21, 22].

(iii) *K-Nearest Neighbor*

It is the simplest algorithm of classification based on supervised learning. It compares the new set of data with the available data. If the new set of data matches with the available data, then it classifies it into a particular category [46].

It is used for classification problems as well as for regression problem. But it is used mostly for the problems of classification.

- It stores the data that is available to the KNN algorithm. Then, it classifies the given new set of data by matching the similarities between them.
- It does not make predictions or assumptions on the data; that is why it is also known as nonparametric algorithm.

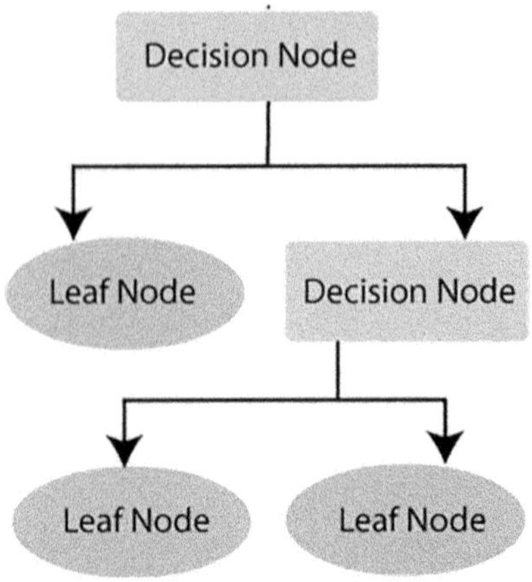

Fig. 9.3 Decision tree diagram for classification [23]

- It is termed as the lazy learning algorithm as it does not learn immediately from the datasets of the training. It first stored the provided sets of data and do actions on it during the time of classification. After getting the new sets of data, it classifies it by checking the similarity with the stored data [23] (Fig. 9.3).

  The KNN works through following steps:

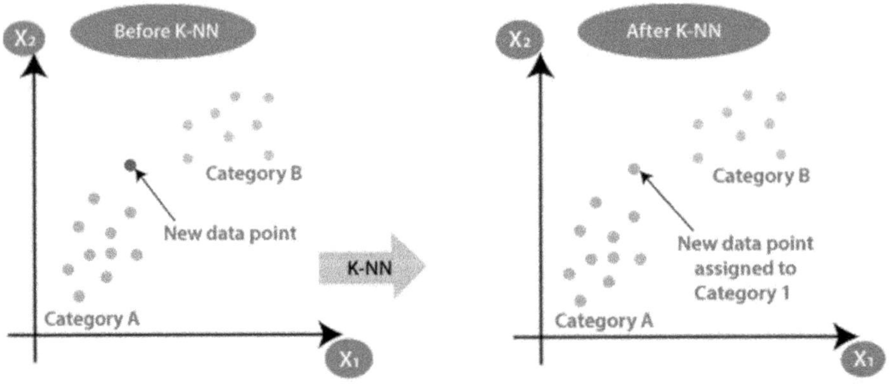

- First, select the neighbor with the K number.
- Then, find the distance of the K number of neighbors by Euclidean method.
- Select the K-nearest neighbors, which are calculated by the Euclidean method to calculate the distance.
- Now, count the data points from the K neighbor of every category.
- The maximum number of neighbors will be assigned the new points of data [24, 25].

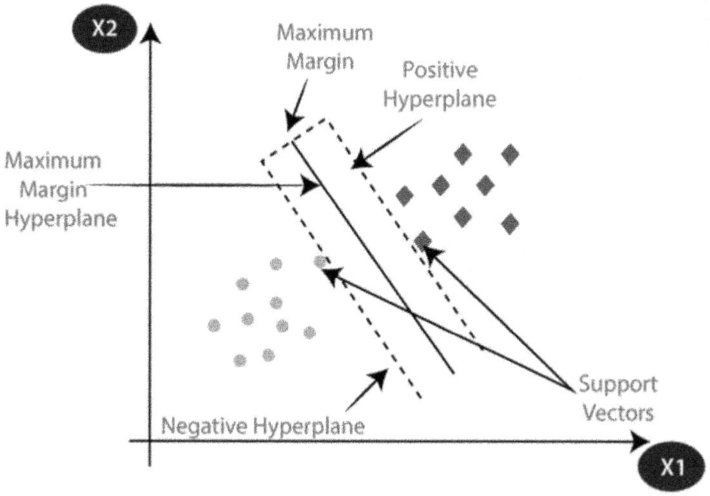

Fig. 9.4 Graph showing the SVM classification [27]

(iv) *Support Vector Machine*

It is an algorithm of classification based on supervised learning. It helps to find the hyperplane, which classifies the data points. It gives the best boundary of decision, hence, segregating it into classes of the n-dimensional space so that in the future the new points of data can be categorized easily. It is used for classification problems as well as for regression problem. But it is used mostly for the problems of classification (Fig. 9.4).

SVM creates a hyperplane by selecting the extreme vector points, which are known as support vectors. It is generally used for the purpose of classification of images, face detection, categorization of texts, etc. [26] There are two types of support vector machine:

Linear SVM – the datasets, when classified into two classes with the help of a single straight line, are said to be linearly separable data for this linear SVM is used. Linear SVM helps in finding the points that are closest to the lines from both classes and known as support vectors. There is a hyperplane that is made from a boundary. The distance between the support vector and hyperplane is termed as margin. When the hyperplane has a maximum margin, it is termed as optimal hyperplane.

Nonlinear SVM – if the data cannot be separable or classified with the help of a straight line, it is said to be nonlinear data. Nonlinear SVM is used for this data. SVM is very effective when there are cases of high dimensions. It uses the subsets for decision functions from the training points, therefore very memory efficient [27].

(v) *Random Forest*

Random forest is also a supervised learning algorithm of machine learning. It is used for classification problems as well as for regression problem. It uses the concept of combining the multiple classifiers for solving the problem with complexities and improves the model performance ensemble learning. This concept is termed as ensemble learning.

It is a classifier that has numbers of decision trees, which take average of the accuracy predicted on various sets of the given data. It does not rely on one single decision tree. It takes the prediction from every tree. It gives the final output of prediction from the prediction with major number of points. If there are a greater number of decision trees in the forest, then the accuracy becomes higher and the solution for the problem of overfitting prevented [28].

The working of the random forest has the following processes:

- First, select the K data points randomly from the training sets.
- Now, construct the decision trees with the help of selected points of subsets of data.
- Select the N number for decision trees, which you want to construct.
- Now, repeat steps 1 and 2.
- Now, from every decision tree, find the prediction for new data points.

Then, assign the new data points to majority predictions [29].

(vi) *Stochastic Gradient Descent*

It is used for classification based on probability. It is linked with a random probability. In this, randomly, we take few samples from datasets instead of the whole. The batch of each dataset is iterated from the sample of the sets of data for calculating the gradient. It is very helpful when there are big datasets. It uses one sample at one iteration for easy calculation to find out the probability. The sample of datasets first is shuffled randomly, and the iteration is performed on it. It gives an optimizing solution in a very computational problem by providing faster iterations [30].

Comparative Study of Different Models

1. Figure 9.5.

2. Figure 9.6.

Implementing Tools

To make a model based on popularity prediction, we will use the NLP model.

Fig. 9.5 Accuracy matrix for different classifiers and dataset

Dataset	Size of Dataset	KNN	Naïve Bayes	Decision Tree
Weather Nominal	Small (14 instances)	100%	92.857%	100%
Segment Challenge	Medium (1500 instances)	100%	81.667%	99%
Supermarket	Large (4627 instances)	89.842%	63.713%	63.713%

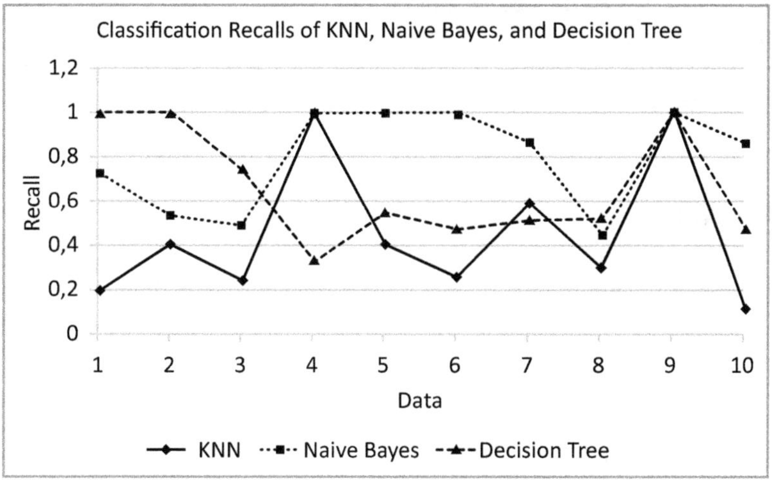

Fig. 9.6 Comparative study graph

Various modules for language processing are:

NLTK library
BERT
ALBERT
XLNet
StructBert
T-5

We are going to use the NLTK library here for our popularity prediction. Here, the work is divided into several parts:

- Clean_review () method – to clean the dataset
- Get_post_tag() method – to get the POS tag for cleaning the dataset
- Remove_stopwords() method – to remove stopwords
- Remove_punc () method – to remove punctuation
- Make_feature () method – using CountVectorizer to get the number of features and prepare the dataset
- Train() method – a method that contains classifiers to train the model
- Predict() method – to predict the data

We are trying to make a system that takes the details of a person and predicts her popularity [31].

Python

Machine learning can be implemented using R and Python. For our work, we have used Python. It can be defined as a branch of computer science in which we train machines to learn by themselves without the need of explicit programming.

We will import inbuilt libraries from Python, such as NLTK and SKLearn, for the use of ML classifiers.

Jupyter Notebook

It is an open-source application used for implementation of Python programs. It provides a very clear scheme and helps in easy sharing, editing, and documentation of the code.

Statistical NLP, Machine Learning, and Deep Learning

NLP applications are based on machine learning and deep learning concepts. The endless data streaming, which also involves voice and text data elements, is classified and labeled statistically to infer them proper meanings [32].

Deep Learning Models are generally dependent on Convolution Neural Networks (CNN) and Recurrent Neural Networks (RNN). NLP system learns regularly as it works on huge, raw, unstructured and unlabeled dataset [33] (Fig. 9.7).

Application of NLP

Natural Language Processing precedes the machine intelligence in modern days. Here are few examples:

Spam detection – today, NLP is used in spam detection technologies, which has proved itself better in this time. Text classifications uses email scanning for languages used in phishing or spams.

These indicators often use financial terms, bad grammar, and threatening languages. Spam detection is also one of the most useful problems of NLP that is particularly considered expert in solving [34].

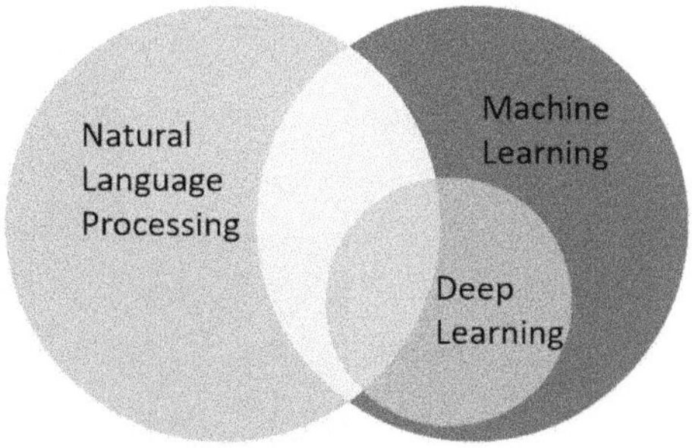

Fig. 9.7 Relation among NLP, Machine Learning and Deep Learning

Machine translation – it is most widely used in NLP technology at work nowadays. Google translate is also an example of these type translations. Effective translations are used to take the meaning and its language's tone quality and translate the language into similar meaning with the output language having meaningful impact.

Tools of machine translation are creating a very huge progress in accuracy terms and limit. The best method to test any of the machine tool is by translating the textual form from one language to the original one again.

Virtual agents and chatbots, such as Siri by Apple and Alexa by Amazon, use speech recognition, which is used for recognizing the patterns in the commands of the voice, and here natural language is used to reply with the specific actions and the useful additional comments. Chatbots are those types of machines that perform the same magic that is used in typed text entries [35, 36].

Social media sentiment analysis – this has nowadays became an important business tool for showing hidden data feed through channels of social media.

It can even analyze responses, posts, and social media reviews. It also extract emotions from replies to the promotion products, and event organizing informations regarding to the companies [37, 38].

Text summarization – It uses NLP techniques to evaluate and absorb large dataset. It then summarizes and adds synopsis to do indexing for the readers who cannot read full text. The best way to summarize applications is through reasoning, often used in semantic and NLG, to add meaningful texts. [39].

4 Result and Discussion

The result is displayed in the form of prediction output, i.e., confusion matrix and classification report, which we get from the machine learning classifier. We have used machine learning classifier, such as SVM classifier, for the predicted output, and we get the output as shown in Fig. 9.8.

Here, based on support vector classifier prediction of the output, we get the confusion matrix of 3 × 3 matrix, which consists of the negative, neutral, and positive data performance of classification. It is labeled as true and predicted label.

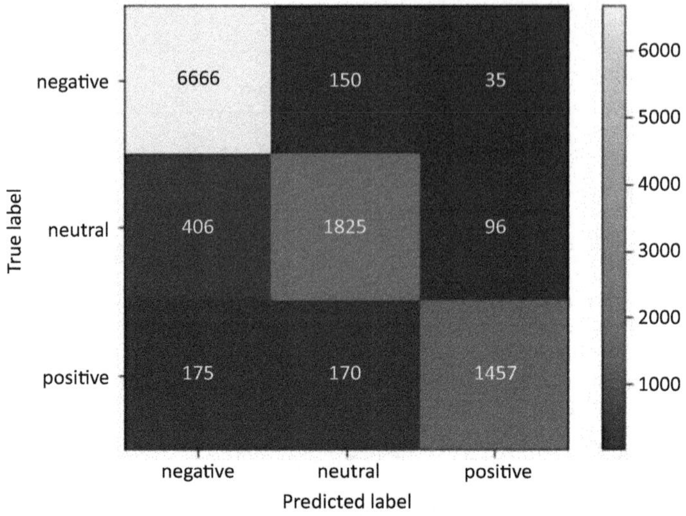

Fig. 9.8 The output of confusion matrix of SVM classifier

Table 9.1 The output of the classification report

	Precision	Recall	F1-score
Negative	0.92	0.97	0.95
Neutral	0.85	0.78	0.82
Positive	0.92	0.81	0.86
Accuracy			**0.91**

This matrix has compared the actual target values with those predicted by the machine learning model. In the confusion matrix also, we can see that negative is predicted more rightly. Others are also predicted well by the classifier.

After the confusion matrix, we get the classification report. It consists of the precision, recall, F1-score, and support column of negative, neutral, positive, and accuracy, macro avg., and weighted avg., respectively. The classification report we get is (Table 9.1):

The classification report elaborates on the precision, recall, F1-score, and support of our classifier and how well it is trained. The following is the output of the classification report:

Precision – It reveals the proportion of correctly predicted cases that actually resulted in a favorable outcome.

Here, we can see it is 92%, 85%, and 92% for negative, neutral, and positive data, respectively.

Recall – it shows the classifier ability to give the actual positive cases, which can predict correctly with the classification model. Here, it is 97%, 78%, and 81% for negative, neutral, and positive data, respectively.

F1-score – it is the harmonic mean of precision and recall. It gives the combination of ideas about these two metrics. If the precision and recall is equal, then the F1-score will be maximum. So, it is giving us the harmonic mean of both precision and recall.

Support – it has provided here the number of actual occurrences of the class in the specified dataset, which we have filtered out from the Twitter datasets of comments.

According to the report, both precision and recall are approx. 0.9 or reaching to it and our classifier has high accuracy. The negative values are predicted the best.

Therefore, performing more testing with the dataset will train the system, and we get the confusion matrix and classification report with more accurate predicted value.

Real-Time Applications

The work finds its applications academically as well as economically. It helps in reviewing products, sarcasm identification, building management systems, and identifying the effectiveness of educational institutes by collecting students' inputs.

Sentimental analysis and opinion mining help analysts and companies extricate bits of knowledge from user-generated social media and Web content.

Experimental Validation and Accuracy

With the help of various computational methods and doing investigation, when one comes up with a scientific binding that is not dependent much on computational resources, it is called experimental validation.

(a)

a)

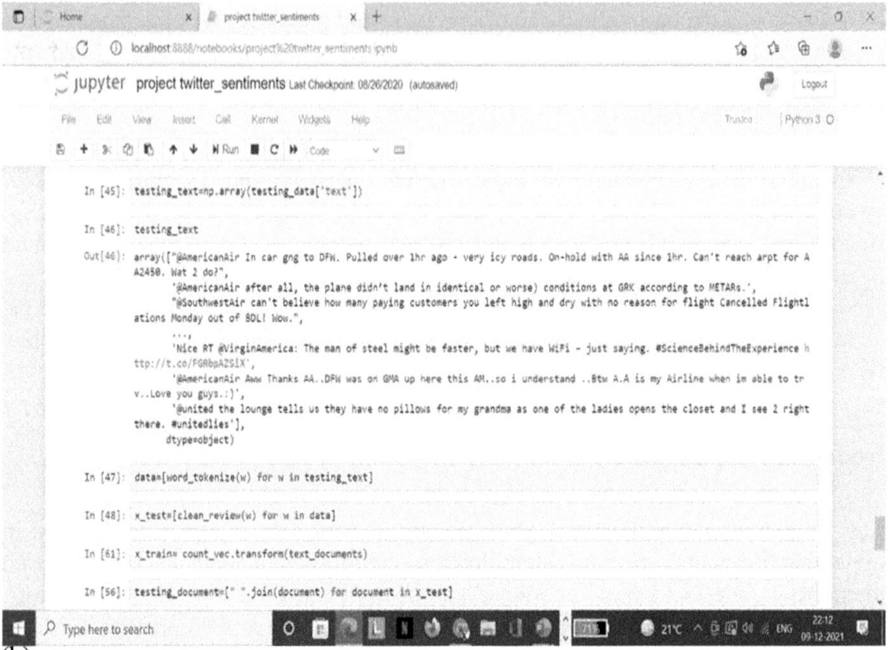
Home
project twitter_sentiments
localhost:8888/notebooks/project%20twitter_sentiments.ipynb
jupyter project twitter_sentiments Last Checkpoint: 08/26/2020 (autosaved)
Logout
File Edit View Insert Cell Kernel Widgets Help
Trusted
Python 3
Run
Code
In [45]: testing_text=np.array(testing_data['text'])
In [46]: testing_text
Out[46]: array(["@AmericanAir In car gng to DFW. Pulled over 1hr ago - very icy roads. On-hold with AA since 1hr. Can't reach arpt for AA2450. Wat 2 do?",
'@AmericanAir after all, the plane didn't land in identical or worse) conditions at GRK according to METARs.',
"@SouthwestAir can't believe how many paying customers you left high and dry with no reason for flight Cancelled Flightlations Monday out of BDL! Wow.",
...,
'Nice RT @VirginAmerica: The man of steel might be faster, but we have WiFi - just saying. #ScienceBehindTheExperience http://t.co/FGRbpAZSiX',
'@AmericanAir Aww Thanks AA..DFW was on GMA up here this AM..so i understand ..Btw A.A is my Airline when im able to trv..Love you guys.:)',
'@united the lounge tells us they have no pillows for my grandma as one of the ladies opens the closet and I see 2 right there. #unitedlies'],
dtype=object)
In [47]: data=[word_tokenize(w) for w in testing_text]
In [48]: x_test=[clean_review(w) for w in data]
In [61]: x_train= count_vec.transform(text_documents)
In [56]: testing_document=[" ".join(document) for document in x_test]
Type here to search
21°C
ENG
22:12
09-12-2021

(b)

b)

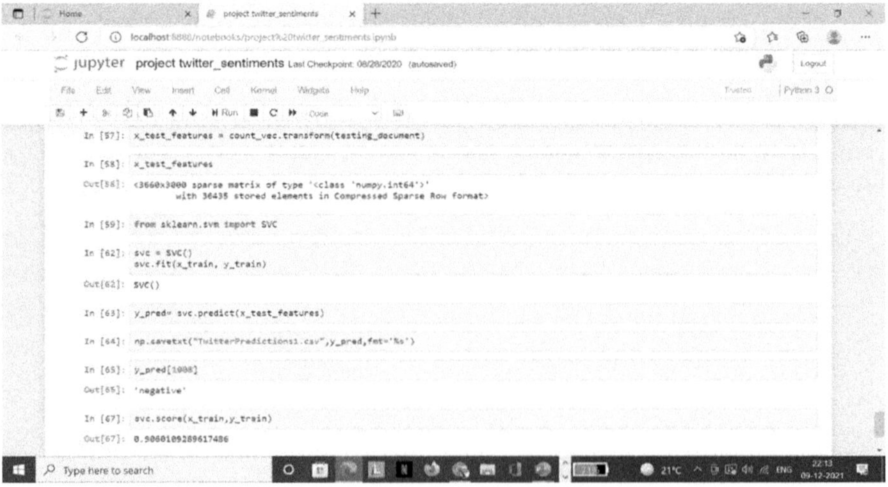
Home
project twitter_sentiments
localhost:8888/notebooks/project%20twitter_sentiments.ipynb
jupyter project twitter_sentiments Last Checkpoint: 08/26/2020 (autosaved)
Logout
File Edit View Insert Cell Kernel Widgets Help
Trusted
Python 3
Run
Code
In [57]: x_test_features = count_vec.transform(testing_document)
In [58]: x_test_features
Out[58]: <3660x3000 sparse matrix of type '<class 'numpy.int64'>'
with 36435 stored elements in Compressed Sparse Row format>
In [59]: from sklearn.svm import SVC
In [62]: svc = SVC()
svc.fit(x_train, y_train)
Out[62]: SVC()
In [63]: y_pred= svc.predict(x_test_features)
In [64]: np.savetxt("TwitterPredictions1.csv",y_pred,fmt='%s')
In [65]: y_pred[1000]
Out[65]: 'negative'
In [67]: svc.score(x_train,y_train)
Out[67]: 0.9060109289617486
Type here to search
21°C
ENG
22:13
09-12-2021

5 Conclusion and Future Scope

This paper allows us to predict the popularity of a person using various concepts of machine learning. The people can check the popularity and opinions about any personality from the popularity prediction. The paper is of great help for anyone to check how popular he/she is on social media platform. Accuracy will become better and better if we perform the predictions on more and more datasets.

6 Challenges and Limitations

There may be a faster and more efficient method available. The challenges faced during the opinion mining typically come when training models are not well trained. The comments or texts containing neutral sentiments, which do not have positive or negative sentiments in it, tend to pose a problem to the system and do not perform the task properly.

The challenge also comes when there are emojis, special characters, and irrelevant data in the text. So, in our project, we are not considering the emojis, but there are special characters and unnecessary data in the text. Ironical and sarcastic comments are not understood by the the system.

There are also positive and negative comments in the same sentence, which will be considered as one sentence. Such contradictory comments are manageable through opinion mining [44]. The system needs to train more and more as there are so many chances when the same sentence consists of more than one negative and positive comments.

References

1. Zhou, X., Etal.: Sentiment analysis on tweets for social events. In: Proceedings of the 2013 IEEE 17th International Conference on Computer Supported Cooperative Work in Design (CSCWD). IEEE (2013)
2. Agarwal, A., Xie, B., Vovsha, I., Rambow, O., Passonneau, R.: Sentiment analysis of twitter data. In: Annual International Conferences. Columbia University, New York (2012)
3. Boyd, D.M., Ellison, N.B.: Social network sites: definition, history, and scholarship. J. Comput.-Mediat. Commun. **13**(1), 210–230 (2007)
4. Neri, F., Aliprandi, C., Capeci, F., Cuadros, M., Tomas: Sentiment analysis on social media. In: IEEE/ACM International Conference on Advances in Social Networks Analysis and Mining (2012)
5. Mathapati, S., Manjula, S.H., Venugopal of University Visvesvaraya College of Engineering: Sentiment analysis and opinion mining from social media: a review. K R Glob. J. Comput. Sci. Technol.: C Softw. Data Eng. **16**(5), Version 1.0 (2016)

6. Sarlan, A., Nadam, C., Shuib Basri of Computer Information Science Universiti Teknologi PETRONAS Perak, Malaysia: Twitter sentiment analysis. In: International Conference on Information Technology and Multimedia (ICIMU), Putrajaya, Malaysia on November 18–20, 2014 (2014)
7. Dharmarajan, K., Abirami, K., Abuthaheer, F.: Sentiment analysis on social media. JETIR1903I34 J. Emerg. Technol. Innov. Res. (JETIR). **6**, 3 (2019) (ISSN-2349-5162)
8. Huang, S., Peng, W., Li, J., Lee, D.: Sentiment and topic analysis on social media: a multi-task multi-label classification approach. In: WebSci'13, Paris, France on 1–5 May, 2013 (2013)
9. Medhat, W., Hassan, A., Korashy, H.: Sentiment analysis algorithms and applications: a survey. Ain Shams Eng. J. **5**, 1093–1113 (2014)
10. Wang, M., Shi, H.: Research on sentiment analysis technology and polarity computation of sentiment words. In: Proceedings of the 2010 IEEE International Conference on Progress in Informatics and Computing, Shanghai, China, 10–12 December 2010, pp. 331–334 (2010)
11. Prabowo, R., Thelwall, M.: Sentiment analysis: a combined approach. J. Informeter. **3**, 143–157 (2009)
12. Agarwal, A., Xie, B., Vovsha, I., Rambow, O., Passonneau, R.: Sentiment analysis twitter data. In: Workshop on Languages in Social Media, pp. 30–38 (2011)
13. Airoldi, E.M., Blei, D.M., Fienberg, S.E., Xing, E.P.: Advances in neural information processing systems. In: Mixed Membership Stochastic Blockmodels, pp. 33–40 (2009)
14. Alelyani, S., Liu, H., Wang, L.: The effect of the characteristics of the dataset on the selection stability. In: Tools with Artificial Intelligence (ICTAI), 2011 23rd IEEE. International Conference on, pp. 970–977. IEEE (2011)
15. Nishida, K., Hoshide, T., Fujimura, K.: Improving tweet stream classification by detecting changes in word probability. In: ACM SIGIR (2012)
16. Rao, V., Sachdev, J.: A machine learning approach to classify news articles based on location. In: 2017 International Conference on Intelligent Sustainable Systems (ICISS), pp. 863–867 (2017)
17. Kumar, V., Minz, S.: Poem classification using machine learning approach. In: Proceedings of the Second International Conference on Soft Computing for Problem Solving (SocProS 2012), December 28–30, 2012, pp. 675–682 (2012)
18. Khairnar, J., Kinikar, M.: Machine learning algorithm for opinion mining and sentiment classification. Int. J. Sci. Res. Publ. **3**(6) (2013)
19. Rish, I., Hellerstein, J., Jayram, T.: An Analysis of Data Characteristics That Affect Naive Bayes Performance Technical Report RC21993. IBM T.J. Watson Research Center (2001)
20. Hellerstein, J., Thathachar, J., Rish, I.: Recognizing end-user transactions in the performance management. In: Proceedings of AAAI-2000, pp. 596–602. Austin (2000)
21. Bhargava, N., Sharma, G., Bhargava, R., Mathuria, M.: Decision tree analysis on j48 algorithm for data mining. Proc. Int. J. Adv. Res. Comput. Sci. Softw. Eng. **3**(6) (2013)
22. Beel, J., Langer, S., Genzmehr, M., Nürnberger, A.: Introducing Docear's research paper recommender system. In: Proceedings of the 13th ACM/IEEECS Joint Conference on Digital Libraries, Jully 22, 2013, pp. 459–460 (2013)
23. Kubat, M., Voting Jr., M.: Nearest neighbour subclassifiers. In: The Proceedings of the 17th International Conference on Machine Learning, ICML-2000, June 29–July 2, 2000, pp. 503–510. Stanford (2000)
24. Alpaydin, E.: Voting over multiple condensed nearest neighbors. Artif. Intell. Rev. **11**, 115–132 (1997) Kluwer Academic Publishers
25. Wilson, D.R., Martinez, T.R.: Reduction techniques for exemplar based learning algorithms. Mach. Learn. **38**(3), 257–286 (2000)
26. Zhang, Y., Zhu, Y., Lin, S., Liu, X.: Application of least squares support vector machine in fault diagnosis. In: ICICA 2011, Part II. CCIS, vol. 244, pp. 192–200. Springer, Heidelberg (2011)
27. Hu, Y., Zhuang, S., Peng, X., Xie, J., Chen, Y.: Products serial numbers recognition based on support vector machine. Mach. Elect. (2) (2012)

28. Ardekani, B.A., Bermudez, E., Mubeen, A.M., Bachman, A.H.: Alzheimer's disease neuroimaging and prediction of incipient Alzheimer's disease dementia in patients with mild cognitive impairment. J. Alzheimers Dis. **55**, 269–281. https://doi.org/10.3233/JAD160594
29. Borza, T., Engedal, K., Bergh, S., Benth, J., Selbaek, G.: The course of depression in late life as measured by the montgomery and asberg depression rating scale in an observational study of hospitalized patients. BMC Psychiatry. **15**, 191. https://doi.org/10.1186/s12888-015-0577-8
30. Dean, J., Corrado, G.S., Monga, R., Chen, K., Devin, M., Le, Q.V., Mao, M.Z., Ranzato, M.A., Senior, A., Tucker, P., Yang, K., Ng, A.Y.: Large scale distributed deep networks. In: Neural Information Processing Systems, pp. 1–11 (2012)
31. Pereira, F.C.N., Warren, D.H.D.: Definite clause grammars for language analysis – a survey of the formalism and a comparison with augmented transition grammars. Artif. Intell. **13**, 231–278
32. Loper, E., Bird, S.: NLTK: the natural language toolkit. In: Proceedings of the ACL Workshop on Effective Tools and Methodologies for Teaching Natural Language Processing and Computational Linguistics, pp. 62–69. Association for Computational Linguistics, Somerset. http://arXiv.org/abs/cs/0205028
33. Rao, D., Ravichandran, D.: Semi supervised polarity lexicon induction. In: Proceedings of the 12th Conference of the European Chapter of the Association for Computational Linguistics, pp. 675–682 (2009)
34. Mukherjee, A., Liu, B., Glance, N.: Spotting fake reviewer groups in consumer reviews. In: Proceedings of the 21st International Conference on World Wide Web, pp. 191–200. ACM, Lyon
35. Tripathi, S., Sarjgek, J.K.: Approaches to machine translation. Ann. Libr. Inf. Stud. **57**, 388–393 (2010)
36. Prasad, T.V., Muthukumaran, G.M.: Telugu to English translation using direct machine translation approach. Int. J. Sci. Eng. Investig. **2**(2), 25–35 (2013)
37. Tan, C., Lee, L., Tang, J., Jiang, L., Zhou, M., Li, P.: User-level sentiment analysis incorporating social networks. In: ACM KDD, pp. 1397–1405 (2011)
38. Jha, V., Savitha, R., Hebbar, S., Shenoy, P.D., Venugopal, K.R.: HMDSAD: Hindi multi-domain sentiment aware dictionary. In: Proceedings of the International Conference on Computing and Network Communications (CoCoNet), pp. 241–247. IEEE (2015)
39. Abbasighalehtaki, R., Khotanlou, H., Esmaeilpour, M.: Fuzzy evolutionary cellular learning automata model for text summarization Swarm. Evol. Comput. **30**, 1–16 (2016)
40. Dhiman, G., Kumar, V.: Spotted hyena optimizer: a novel bio-inspired based metaheuristic technique for engineering applications. Adv. Eng. Softw. **114**, 48–70 (2017)
41. Dhiman, G., Kumar, V.: Emperor penguin optimizer: a bio-inspired algorithm for engineering problems. Knowl.-Based Syst. **159**, 20–50 (2018)
42. Kaur, S., Awasthi, L.K., Sangal, A.L., Dhiman, G.: Tunicate Swarm Algorithm: a new bio-inspired based metaheuristic paradigm for global optimization. Eng. Appl. Artif. Intell. **90**, 103541 (2020)
43. Dhiman, G., Kaur, A.: STOA: a bio-inspired based optimization algorithm for industrial engineering problems. Eng. Appl. Artif. Intell. **82**, 148–174 (2019)
44. Kumar, R., Dhiman, G.: A comparative study of fuzzy optimization through fuzzy number. Int. J. Mod. Res. **1**, 1–14 (2021)
45. Chatterjee, I.: Artificial intelligence and patentability: review and discussions. Int. J. Mod. Res. **1**, 15–21 (2021)
46. Goel, S., Oberoi, S., Vats, A.: Construction cost estimator: an effective approach to estimate the cost of construction in metropolitan areas. In: 2021 3rd International Conference on Advances in Computing, Communication Control and Networking (ICAC3N), pp. 122–127 (2021). https://doi.org/10.1109/ICAC3N53548.2021.9725740
47. Vaishnav, P.K., Sharma, S., Sharma, P.: Analytical review analysis for screening COVID-19. Int. J. Mod. Res. **1**, 22–29 (2021) Spotted hyena optimizer: a novel bio-inspired based metaheuristic technique for engineering applications

Appendix

Benchmark Problems [1–4]

Fun	Test function	Properties	Bound	Global value
F_1	$\sum_{i=1}^{D} x_i^2$	Unimodal, Separable, Scalable	$[-100, 100]^D$	0
$F2$	$\sum_{i=1}^{D} \lvert x_i \rvert + \prod_{i=1}^{D} \lvert x_i \rvert$	Unimodal, Separable, Scalable	$[-10, 10]^D$	0
$F3$	$\sum_{i=1}^{D} \left(\sum_{j=1}^{i} x_j \right)^2$	Unimodal, Non-seperable, Scalable	$[-100, 100]^D$	0
$F4$	$\max_i \{\lvert x_i \rvert\}$	Unimodal, Non-seperable, Scalable	$[-100, 100]^D$	0
$F5$	$\sum_{i=1}^{D-1} \left[100\left(x_{i+1} - x_i^2\right)^2 + (x_i - 1)^2 \right]$	Multimodal, Non-seperable, Scalable, narrow velly from local to global optimum	$[-30, 30]^D$	0
F_6	$\sum_{i=1}^{D} \lfloor x_i + 0.5 \rfloor^2$	Unimodal, Seperable, Scalable	$[-100, 100]^D$	0
F_7	$\sum_{i=1}^{D} i x_i^4 + \mathrm{rand}(0\ \ 1)$	Unimodal, Seperable, Scalable	$[-1.28, 1.28]^D$	0
F_8	$\sum_{i=1}^{D} -x_i \sin \sqrt{\lvert x_i \rvert} + 418.982887D$	Multimodal, Seperable, Scalable, many local minima	$[-500, 500]^D$	0

(continued)

© The Editor(s) (if applicable) and The Author(s), under exclusive license to Springer Nature Switzerland AG 2022

D. Singh et al. (eds.), *Design and Applications of Nature Inspired Optimization*, Women in Engineering and Science, https://doi.org/10.1007/978-3-031-17929-7

(continued)

Fun	Test function	Properties	Bound	Global value
F_9	$10D + \sum_{i=1}^{D} \left(x_i^2 - 10\cos(2\pi x_i)\right)$	Multimodal, Seperable, Scalable, many local minima	$[-5.12, 5.12]^D$	0
F_{10}	$-20\exp\left(-0.2\sqrt{1/D\sum_{i=0}^{D} x_i^2}\right) - \exp\left(\sqrt{1/D}\sum_{i=0}^{D}\cos(2\pi x_i)\right) + 20 + e$	Multimodal, Seperable, Scalable, many local minima	$[-32, 32]^D$	0
F_{11}	$\frac{1}{4000}\sum_{i=1}^{D} x_i^2 - \prod_{i=1}^{D}\cos\left(\frac{x_i}{\sqrt{i}}\right) + 1$	Multimodal, Seperable, Scalable, many local minima	$[-600, 600]^D$	0
F_{12}	$\frac{\pi}{D}\left\{\begin{matrix} 10\sin^2(\pi y_1) + \sum_{i=1}^{D-1}(y_i - 1)^2 \\ \left[1 + 10\sin^2(\pi y_{i+1})\right] + (y_D - 1)^2 \end{matrix}\right\} + \sum_{i=1}^{D} u(x_i, 10, 100, 4)$ where $y_i = 1 + \frac{1}{4}(x_i + 1)$ and $u(x_i, a, k, m) = \begin{cases} k(x_i - a)^m & \text{if } x_i > a \\ 0 & \text{if } -a \le x_i \le a \\ k(-x_i - a)^m & \text{if } x_i < -a \end{cases}$	Multimodal, Seperable, Scalable, many local minima	$[-50, 50]^D$	0
F_{13}	$0.1\left\{\begin{matrix} \sin^2(3\pi x_1) \\ +\sum_{i=1}^{D-1}(x_i - 1)^2\left[1 + \sin^2(3\pi x_{i+1})\right] \\ +(x_D - 1)^2\left[1 + \sin^2(2\pi x_D)\right] \end{matrix}\right\} + \sum_{i=1}^{D} u(x_i, 5, 100, 4)$	Multimodal, Seperable, Scalable, many local minima	$[-50, 50]^D$	0
F_{14}	$-\exp\left(-0.5\sum_{i=1}^{D} x_i^2\right) + 1$	Convex, Unimodal, Seperable	$[-1, 1]^D$	0
F_{15}	$\sum_{i=1}^{D} x_i^2 + \left(\sum_{i=1}^{D} 0.5ix_i^2\right)^2 + \left(\sum_{i=1}^{D} 0.5ix_i^2\right)^4$	Unimodal, Non scalable, non Separable	$[-5, 10]^D$	0

Real-Life Applications [5, 6]

The following three real-life applications have been taken from the various literatures

RF₁: Parameter Estimation for Frequency-Modulated (FM) Sound Waves [3, 7]

Frequency-modulated (FM) sound wave fusion has a significant part in many modern music systems. In this application, we have to obtain a six-dimensional vector $P = (\alpha_1, \omega_1, \alpha_2, \omega_2, \alpha_3, \omega_3)$ by minimizing the sum of squared error between the estimated sound $\rho(s)$ and target sound $\rho_0(s)$ as defined in Eq. 1.

$$\text{Minimize } F(P) = \sum_{s=0}^{100} (\rho(s) - \rho_0(s))^2 \tag{1}$$

where

$$\begin{aligned} \rho(s) &= \alpha_1 \ \sin(\omega_1 s\phi + \alpha_2 \sin(\omega_2 s\phi + \alpha_3 \ \sin(\omega_3 s\phi))) \\ \rho_0(s) &= 1.0 \ \sin(5.0s\phi - 1.5^* \sin(4.8s\phi + 2.0 \ \sin(4.9s\phi))) \end{aligned} \tag{2}$$

$\phi = 2\pi/100$ such that all parameters are defined in the range [−6.4, 6.35].

RF2: Optimal Thermohydraulic Performance of an Artificially Roughened Air Heater [7]

The mathematical formulation of this simple maximized problem is defined as below:

$$\begin{aligned} &\text{Max } F = 2.51^*\text{Ine}^+ + 5.5 - 0.1R_M - G_H \\ &\text{where } R_M = 0.95p_2^{0.53}, G_H = 4.5(e^+)^{0.28}(0.7)^{0.57}, \\ &e^+ = p_1 p_3 (\bar{f}/2)^{1/2}, \\ &\bar{f} = (f_s + f_r)/2, \\ &f_s = 0.079p_3^{-0.25} \ \& \ f_r = 2\left(0.95p_2^{0.53} + 2.51 * In(1/2p_1)^2 - 3.75\right)^{-2} \\ &\text{Bounds are :} \\ &0.02 \le p_1 \le 0.8, \ 10 \le p_2 \le 40, \ 3000 \le p_3 \le 20000 \end{aligned} \tag{3}$$

RF₃: Spread-Spectrum Radar Polyphase Code Design [3, 7]

It is a well-known problem of optimal design in the field of spread-spectrum radar polyphase codes. This is a min-max nonlinear, non-convex optimization problem of continuous variable with multiple local optima and defined as below:

$$\begin{aligned} &\mathrm{Min}\, F(P) = Max\{\varphi_1(P), \varphi_2(P), \cdots \varphi_{2m}(P)\} \\ &P = (p_1, p_2, \cdots p_d) \in R^d | 0 \le p_j \le 2\pi, j = 1, \cdots, d \end{aligned} \tag{4}$$

where $m = 2d - 1$, and

$$\varphi_{2\mathrm{i}-1}(P) = \sum_{j=1}^{d} \cos\left[\sum_{k=|2i-j|+1}^{j} p_k\right], i = 1, \cdots, d$$

$$\varphi_{2\mathrm{i}}(P) = 0.5 + \sum_{j=i+1}^{d} \cos\left[\sum_{k=|2i-j|+1}^{j} p_k\right], i = 1, \cdots, d-1$$

$$\varphi_{m+i}(P) = -\varphi_i(P), i = 1, \cdots, m$$

References

1. Rahnamayan, S., Tizhoosh, H., Salama, M.: Opposition based differential evolution. IEEE Trans. Evol. Comput. **12**(1), 64–79 (2008)
2. Qin, A.K., Huang, V.L., Suganthan, P.N.: Differential evolution algorithm with strategy adaptation for global numerical optimization. IEEE Trans. Evol. Comput. **13**(2), 398–417 (2009)
3. Zhang, J., Sanderson, A.: JADE: adaptive differential evolution with optional external archive. IEEE Trans. Evol. Comput. **13**(5), 945–958 (2009)
4. Cai, Y., Wang, J., Yin, J.: Learning enhanced differential evolution for numerical optimization. Soft Comput. (2011). https://doi.org/10.1007/s00500-011-0744-x
5. Kumar, S., Kumar, P., Sharma, T.K., Pant, M.: Bi-level thresholding using PSO, Artificial Bee Colony and MRLDE embedded with Otsu method. Memetic Comput. **5**(4), 323–334 (2013)
6. Dor, A.E., Clerc, M., Siarry, P.: Hybridization of differential evolution and particle swarm optimization in a new algorithm: DEPSO-2S. In: Proceeding of SIDE 2012 and EC 2012, LNCS 7269, pp. 57–65. Springer, Berlin/Heidelberg (2012)
7. Singh, P., Chaturvedi, P., Kumar, P.: Control parameters and mutation based variants of differential evolution algorithm. J. Comput. Method Sci. Eng. **15**(4), 783–800 (2015)

Index

© The Editor(s) (if applicable) and The Author(s), under exclusive license to Springer Nature Switzerland AG 2022
D. Singh et al. (eds.), *Design and Applications of Nature Inspired Optimization*, Women in Engineering and Science, https://doi.org/10.1007/978-3-031-17929-7

GPSR Compliance
The European Union's (EU) General Product Safety Regulation (GPSR) is a set of rules that requires consumer products to be safe and our obligations to ensure this.

If you have any concerns about our products, you can contact us on

ProductSafety@springernature.com

In case Publisher is established outside the EU, the EU authorized representative is:

Springer Nature Customer Service Center GmbH
Europaplatz 3
69115 Heidelberg, Germany

www.ingramcontent.com/pod-product-compliance
Ingram Content Group UK Ltd.
Pitfield, Milton Keynes, MK11 3LW, UK
UKHW020636051126
16351UKWH00010B/47
* 9 7 8 3 0 3 1 1 7 9 3 0 3 *